Mortmere & Environs

Edward Upward
Art and Life

Peter Stansky

Edward Upward
Art and Life

ENITHARMON PRESS

First published in 2016
by Enitharmon Press
10 Bury Place
London WC1A 2JL

www.enitharmon.co.uk

Distributed in the UK by
Central Books
99 Wallis Road
London E9 5LN

Distributed in the USA and Canada
by Independent Publishers Group
814 North Franklin Street
Chicago, IL 60610
USA
www.ipgbooks.com

Text © Peter Stansky 2016

ISBN: 978-1-910392-84-3

Enitharmon Press gratefully acknowledges the financial support of
Arts Council England, through Grants for the Arts.

British Library Cataloguing-in-Publication Data.
A catalogue record for this book is available
from the British Library.

Designed in Albertina by Libanus Press
and printed in Wales by
Gomer Press

In memory of Susan Bell

Contents

Preface		9
Illustrations		12
1	*Family and Childhood*	15
2	*Repton*	37
3	*Cambridge*	70
4	*Out in the World*	102
5	*Schoolmaster at Alleyn's, 1932–1961*	148
6	*Being a Communist and a Writer*	172
7	*The Years Between*	233
8	*Free at Last*	282
Notes		327
Index		346
Acknowledgements		367
Photograph Credits		368

Preface

THE FIRST LINE of the prologue of *Journey to the Frontier,* the study that William Abrahams and I wrote of John Cornford and Julian Bell, two young Englishmen who had been killed in the Spanish Civil War, read: 'For our title, *Journey to the Frontier*, we have fused the titles of two characteristic works of the 1930s, *On the Frontier*, a play by W. H. Auden and Christopher Isherwood, and *Journey to the Border*, a novel by Edward Upward'. The study was published in 1966; I have thus been aware of Edward Upward for many years. Even earlier, perhaps the first paper I wrote on the British young writers of the 1930s while still an undergraduate was on Christopher Isherwood, although I doubt that I was aware then of his close friendship with Upward. Years later Upward's stalwart publisher, Stephen Stuart-Smith, knowing of my interest in this group of writers, kindly suggested that I might visit Edward on the Isle of Wight. To my great regret I wasn't able to make that visit, but Stephen did have him inscribe a copy of *The Mortmere Stories* by him and Isherwood to me. And then it was some years later, after Edward had died at the age of 105, that Stephen suggested that I try to write the biography of Edward himself. These pages are the result of that suggestion.

The book could not have been written without the help of many. The virtues of a book belong to those who have been so helpful in the making of a text; the faults are one's own. And one of the pleasures of working on a study such as this is getting to know others involved with the subject. Most important, of course, are the members of Edward's family, his daughter Katherine Allinson, her husband Jeff and her son David Allinson, who maintains a website devoted to his grandfather. Janet Upward, the widow of his son Christopher, was also immensely helpful. One of my best research experiences ever was spent reading Edward's letters to his son while much enjoying Janet's hospitality. Although this is in no sense an authorized biography, the family granted me permission to quote from Upward's writings; they read the manuscript carefully, making suggestions and saving me from many errors. Dave Allinson provided a plethora of photographs for the book. I am extremely fortunate in becoming a friend, through this project, of the leading Upward scholar, Benjamin Kohlmann, who was kind enough to read the manuscript. The editor of a collection of relevant essays, *Edward Upward and Left-Wing Literary Culture in Britain* (2013), his comments on the manuscript were invaluable. I am also deeply grateful to Katherine Bucknell. Edward Mendelson, the world's leading Auden scholar, was also kind enough to read the manuscript. Brian Hinton graciously gave me a tour of the Isle of Wight. Stephen Stuart-Smith, who knew Upward well and was so important in the revival of interest in him and his writings that took place in the late years of his long life, much improved my text through his close reading and his many suggestions, and of course he and his colleagues have performed with great skill the crucial task of transforming a text into a book. I am also very grateful for the meticulous copyediting of Jeff Wyneken. And to Dave Daly for dealing with those inevitable computer frustrations. Quotations from Christopher Isherwood and photographs taken by him are copyright 2016

PREFACE

by Don Bachardy, used by permission of the Wylie Agency, LLC. I thank Richard Bell for photographing Upward's MI5 file in the National Archives for me and for checking some of my quotations from Upward's manuscripts in the British Library, where Helen Melody was wonderfully helpful in facilitating my access to them before they were catalogued.

I am deeply grateful for the assistance of the librarians and archivists at his educational institutions: Repton School; Corpus Christi College, Cambridge; and Alleyn's School, Dulwich. As usual the hospitality and support of my sister, Marina Vaizey, in London were crucial in helping this project go forward. (Her son Edward may have played a role in securing the release of the MI5 file and I thank him for that.) My research was facilitated by the grant of an Emeritus Fellowship by the Andrew W. Mellon Foundation, and the book was written during a wonderful year spent at the Center for Advanced Study in the Behavioral Sciences, where a spirit of serendipity, as found among its Fellows, was immensely stimulating. And the services of its librarians and other members of its fine staff were very helpful. I am also grateful for the assistance of the staffs of the Stanford University Library, particularly Benjamin Stone, and of the History Department at Stanford, as well as the help provided by the Huntington Library, San Marino, and the Brotherton Library at the University of Leeds.

I had meant to surprise my dear friend Susan Bell by presenting her with a finished copy of this book and her discovering that it was dedicated to her. Alas, the pages that follow are now dedicated to her memory, with love.

PETER STANSKY

Illustrations

Frontispiece: Edward Upward c. 1928, photographer unknown, reproduced from the Edward Upward Archive (Add MS 72688, folio 254) by kind permission of the British Library.

Endpapers: The endpapers, reproduced from the Edward Upward Archive by kind permission of the British Library, show Christopher Isherwood's manuscript of the characters in Mortmere (Add MS 72691, folio 39) and Edward Upward's hand-drawn map of Mortmere (Add MS 72691, folio 36).

CHAPTER 1
Harold Upward's car and chauffeur, 21
Edfu, the Upwards' house in Romford, Essex, 23
Edward and Mervyn with their mother Isa Upward, 24
Harold Arthur Upward, 25
'Eddie', 'Mer', Laurence, July 1912, 26
The Upward family, 20 July 1912, 27
Allen Upward (1863–1926) receiving the degree of Bard from the Archdruid at the Welsh National Eisteddfod, August 1891, 29

CHAPTER 2
Repton School, 43
Geoffrey Fisher in 1922 when Headmaster of Repton, 49
Edward in the sixth form at Repton, 59
The Reptonian, June 1921, 62
Edward photographed in Rouen, 66
Christopher Isherwood's *Lions and Shadows*, 1938, 68

CHAPTER 3
'Eddie on the Cam! 11.08.23', 75
Edward in Christopher Isherwood's room at Cambridge, 1923, 78
Corpus Christi College, Cambridge, 85

ILLUSTRATIONS

Degree day at Cambridge, 23 June 1925, 92
Upward and Isherwood: a rare photograph of them together, early 1920s, 101

CHAPTER 4
Edward Upward, 1926, 103
Isherwood and Upward in the mirror, Marine Villa, Freshwater, 105
Christopher Isherwood holding *All the Conspirators*, May 1928, 107
Edward at Freshwater, May 1928, 108
The house near Lockerbie where Edward was a tutor in 1928, 109
Auden and Isherwood in 1928, 129
Upward with Barbara Wootton and the delegation to Russia, 1932, 138
Isherwood and Upward in Berlin, April 1932, 141
Stephen Spender, photographed by his brother Humphrey Spender, 1930s, 142
W. H. Auden, Christopher Isherwood and Cecil Day Lewis, 1937, 145

CHAPTER 5
Alleyn's School, Dulwich, 149
The Upwards' house, 154 Turney Road, Dulwich, 155
Hilda Upward, April 1937, 156
Edward at Sandown, September 1938, 156
Edward at Rossall School, Lancashire, 158
Hilda Upward holding her daughter Katherine, Cleveleys, 158
Edward with his children Christopher and Katherine, 159
Edward and Hilda, early 1940s, 161
Edward as a teacher at Alleyn's, 169

CHAPTER 6
Kathy, Hilda and Edward, walking in the country, 179
Front cover of *The Mind in Chains*, 1937, 200
Journey to the Border, Hogarth Press 1938, 207

ILLUSTRATIONS

John Lehmann in the 1930s, 209
Kathy, Edward and Hilda Upward, Jean Ross and daughter Sarah, Scotland, 1951, 217

CHAPTER 7
Cover of *In the Thirties*, 248
Edward in the garden of 3 Hill Street, September 1962, 253
The wedding of Christopher Upward and Janet Hutcheon, 1963, 254
Cover of *The Rotten Elements*, 255
Cover of *No Home but the Struggle*, 258
Edward, November 1969, 261

CHAPTER 8
Hilda and Edward, late 1983, 286
CND social, Tudor Rose Restaurant, Shanklin, 1984, 287
Edward at word-processor, 1993, 298
Mer and Edward at 3 Hill Street, Sandown, 1993, 299
Sir Stephen Spender in 1992, 304
Edward, 1995, 309
With Stephen Stuart-Smith at Freshwater, 4 September 1999, 313
Revisiting Marine Villa, Freshwater, 4 September 1999, 314
Cartoon by Nicola Jennings, *Guardian*, 8 April 2000, 316
Signing the sheets of *A Renegade in Springtime*, 2003, 317
With Sir Frank Kermode and Dannie Abse, 1 May 2003, 318
Edward on his 100th birthday, 9 September 2003, 319
Edward's 100th birthday, 320
Edward at 3 Hill Street, 2004, 321
Presentation of the Benson Medal, August 2005, 322
Signing the register of the Royal Society of Literature, 323

Chapter 1: Family and Childhood

EDWARD UPWARD PLAYS an intriguing role in the history and literature of England in the twentieth century. He almost exactly spanned the century, being born in 1903 and dying in 2009. All those interested in the literature of the period in England, particularly that of the Auden circle, may well know of Upward as an influence upon Auden as well as Christopher Isherwood's oldest and closest friend and early collaborator, who was memorably depicted as Allen Chalmers in Isherwood's compelling memoir *Lions and Shadows*. Upward felt however that he was an 'unmentionable man', largely forgotten; that his writings were ignored. He thought that a major reason for his marginalization was his deep commitment to Communism; he was an active party member from 1934 to 1948. Even after he left the party he still saw himself as a Marxist Leninist. Yet he managed to publish twelve books, which over the years received a fair amount of attention. He had obituaries in the major English papers at the time of his death. Over his lifetime he had two periods of rediscovery: first, at the time of the publication of his trilogy *The Spiral Ascent* (1962, 1969, 1977), and then the appearance from 1994 onwards of new and old work through the devotion and enterprise of Stephen Stuart-Smith, director of Enitharmon Press. Throughout his long life he agonized over his writing, as evidenced by the seventy-six volumes of notebooks that he kept from 1924 to 2002. In them he continually considered the eternal dilemma

CHAPTER 1: FAMILY AND CHILDHOOD

between art and life. Which was the greater and more important commitment: to devote oneself to the life of art and creation or to devote oneself to doing what one could to make the world a better place? Or to put it another way, as he frequently did, would one achieve a greater work of art through working first for a better society, or was it the other way around, that a better work of art would help bring about a better society?

These were considerations that might be found in many societies. But the story of his life is also an English one. Edward Upward, for better or worse, was a member of the middle class, the son of a doctor, with the standard education of one of his class: prep school, an English public school and then one of its ancient universities, in his case Cambridge. With that precision that the English are capable of he defined himself as a member of the 'middle-middle class'.[1] With both its advantages and disadvantages, Communist as he might have been, he was also an English gentleman. He was a man of great charm but also beset by terrible anxieties. It is that story that I am attempting to tell in these pages. I hope that it will be of interest in and of itself as the story of an important literary figure. Christopher Hitchens, not an admirer of Upward's politics, nevertheless wrote about him with some respect: 'Our knowledge of the literary and ideological generation of the '30s is radically incomplete without some awareness of its founding father, or perhaps better say founding brother'.[2] Telling the story of his life may also illuminate the English world in which he lived virtually throughout the twentieth century.

With the somewhat Cheshire cat smile of his youth and of his old age, Upward hovers over English literature, particularly that of the 1930s. In a piece about him entitled 'Dimmed by Dialectics', Samuel Hynes summed up his importance for that decade. 'Among the literary legends of the 1930s, Edward Upward is surely the most legendary figure . . . Among many gifted young men, he was thought to be the most gifted, as he was the most remote . . . He had a vision of existence as a realistic nightmare – a kind of allegory, but an hallucinatory one . . . It was not his work that was influential: rather, it seems, it was his vision of the ordinary world seen as hallucination that had genius, and engaged the attention of his friends . . . Everything is clear but nothing is intelligible'.[3] His ultimate aim, as Hynes later remarked, was to be a Marxist Proust.[4]

Edward Falaise Upward was born on 9 September 1903 at 1 Kingston Road, Romford, Essex, where his father, Harold, was a doctor. He was given the first name of his grandfather back four generations, his great-great-great-grandfather Edward Upward, who was born on the Isle of Wight in 1751. It was also the name of his grandfather's eldest son. His middle name, French for 'cliff', is coincidentally the name of a now demolished house in Ventnor, near Sandown, where Edward's father grew up. According to Edward, it was given to him at his grandmother's request and was based on the motto *Je fais fort et je falaise* (I make myself strong and I stand as firm as a cliff).[5] His father's family was quite well off, having done well in trade. They could trace themselves back to one John Upward on the Isle of Wight in the seventeenth century. Edward's grandfather, Edward Jackson Upward, had established on Pyle Street in Newport, the main town on the Isle of Wight, what is said to be the first wholesale grocery-importing business in England. A plaque on the modern buildings at the location of the original place of

CHAPTER 1: FAMILY AND CHILDHOOD

business states that on the site candles were made in 1650 and that a member of the Upward family was known to have sold them there in 1703. The legend on the plaque goes on to record, but without providing a beginning date, 'Then for over a century Upward & Rich Wholesale Grocers, Provision Merchants and Confectioners traded here until 1974'. Edward's grandfather was born in 1830 and died in 1913. His was a typical English success story. He first lived above the shop and then moved to a separate house in Newport. That house was called St Aubins. When a railway established itself around 1870 on the island, he moved to a more beautiful part on its south-east coast, in the town of Sandown, and commuted to work. There he acquired a newly built house, a second St Aubins; the name is still faintly visible on its gatepost. It may have been Edward who officially eliminated the name when he retired to the same house in 1961, as being perhaps pretentious, or more likely because the house was divided into two, 3 Hill Street as his retirement home and 3A as the retirement home for his brother Mer.[6]

As in residences so too in religion did the family follow a not unfamiliar path. Edward's grandfather was a Congregationalist. Edward's father, who probably didn't have much religion, officially became an Anglican under the influence of his wife. In his library Edward preserved her Book of Common Prayer, signed by her and acquired in December 1902. Contrary to her wishes, Harold Upward didn't enforce his wife's desire that the children assiduously attend Church of England services. Yet Edward might well have been influenced by the family's earlier nonconformity in view of his great admiration of John Bunyan and the moral, indeed religious nature of his commitment to Communism. Bunyan's *Pilgrim's Progress* was the first book he read on his own. In any case Edward refused to be confirmed in the Church of England at his public school, but presumably his official religious designation was the Church of England. His grandfather had two marriages, the first in 1855 to Caroline Finnimore, the daughter of a rich tomato grower from Jersey; their elopement caused her to be disinherited. After her early death in 1870, her father relented and left money to his grandson, Edward Finnimore Upward, born in 1856. He went to St John's College, Cambridge, unusual at the time for a nonconformist, and ventured into business unsuccessfully in Romford as a saddler, having enough private income, presumably from his maternal grandfather, to live on in Hampstead without working until his death in 1932. He would visit Edward's family, bringing presents much to the children's joy, Edward shouting out, 'What have you got for me?' Edward Jackson Upward was married secondly in 1873 to Eliza Ridgely of Huntingdon. It may have been at this time that he acquired the house on Hill Street where Edward's parents would spend their vacations. Edward's father retired there at the comparatively early age of fifty-eight. He had inherited the house; when he died Edward succeeded him. At first Edward and his wife Hilda decided to sell it as too big for them. A builder came to see it and pointed out that it could easily be converted into two houses, which indeed happened. Retiring in 1961, Edward lived there for more than forty years.

By his second marriage Edward's grandfather had two sons, Harold and George, and a daughter Bessie, who died at the age of six. The second son, George, born in 1875, was supposed to take over the business but didn't wish to, although he remained in its employ for all his working life. He was a pacifist and a socialist and disap-

CHAPTER 1: FAMILY AND CHILDHOOD

proved of business, oddly indicating that by refusing to be anything more than an employee. He never married. Harold, born in 1874, had an excellent education at a prep school in nearby Ventnor run by the eminent historian J. Holland Rose; then at a nonconformist boarding school, Amersham Hall in Buckinghamshire, where he was a contemporary and friend of John Neville Keynes, the father of John Maynard Keynes and himself in later life an eminent Cambridge figure as an economist, logician and university administrator. Harold then went to Christ's College, Cambridge, where he read medicine. He was good at sports, and there is a memorable 1892 photograph of the college's football team. (His father disapproved of his playing cards there but was less disapproving when Harold informed him that he generally won money in the pursuit!) One of the other football players and fellow medics was George Auden, later the father of W. H. Auden. It was Auden who noticed a photograph of the players when visiting Edward in Romford, pointing out that his father was in the group. There is the further nice coincidence that Auden's son was named Wystan after St Wystan, the ninth-century martyr, who gave his name to the church in the town of Repton. George Auden attended the school there. Repton was to play a crucial role in the life of the subject of this book.

Edward's grandfather, in accordance with a common English aspiration, pressed his son to move away from trade and into the professions. Harold felt forced into medicine. Although he was not totally happy with that choice, he had a quite successful career. Nevertheless Harold in later life may have wanted his second son, Mer, to be a doctor rather than the schoolmaster he became, embracing that career with far more enthusiasm than his older brother, Edward.

CHAPTER 1: FAMILY AND CHILDHOOD

Medicine was still something of a halfway house in terms of class, as George Eliot had so memorably pointed out some years before in *Middlemarch*. For instance, George Auden was listed as a figure of commerce rather than as a private resident in York and his wife was told by a relative that no one would call on her if she married a doctor. Edward quite early on learned the complicated class distinctions characteristic of English life, beginning in his earliest days with the differentiations in even a modest household between the status of ordinary servants, nursemaids and governesses. This was a period when the middle class still could afford quite a few live-in staff. Harold much enjoyed visits to London bookshops, his favourite authors being rather incongruously Kipling and T. S. Eliot, although Eliot was an admirer of Kipling. Edward felt his father would have preferred to have been a writer rather than a doctor. He was in later

Harold Upward's car and chauffeur

years very supportive of Edward's wish to pursue that career, reading and criticizing his work.

On 12 February 1902 Harold married Louisa Jones, known as Isa, at St Mary the Virgin in Wanstead. She was six years older than him. Her family, as the name suggests, was Welsh and her father was a publican, first owning a pub in Aberystwyth. He then moved to the London area, opening a pub, the Eagle, on Hollybush Hill in Wanstead, where it still is. He also acquired property in the neighbourhood and was very well off. But Isa was somewhat ashamed of her origins and was socially ambitious. In any case by the time she married, her parents had died. She lived quite close to her surviving relatives but saw comparatively little of them. Edward remembered his uncle Jack who had a strong Cockney accent. Isa was quite independent and had trained as an actress and as a nurse. The latter was useful as she managed her husband's practice. Before marriage she had spent quite a bit of time travelling around the world on her own – fairly unusual for a single woman at the time, other than a few intrepid Victorian women explorers. (Edward himself was never much of a traveller though he spent some months in France between Repton and Cambridge, and again some years later, and made a trip to Russia and two to Berlin in the early 1930s.) Isa had been to Sweden, Italy and Turkey among other places and told Edward stories about her trips. She brought back from Palestine a flask of Jordan water to be used for christening her children. Apparently Harold on the way to Edward's christening spilled some of it and topped it up with tap water. She and Harold met at the temple of Edfu in 1901 while he and his father were on a vacation in Egypt. This had lasting consequences for the family, not only bringing it into existence but providing 'Edfu' as an important term for the Upwards; it was the name of the second and third houses they had in Romford and also, as virtually Edward's initials, served as a pseudonym for some of the poems, stories and essays written early on by him and his brother. Harold set up his practice in Romford, perhaps rather arbitrarily chosen, although it was an area known by his half-brother and perhaps by his wife's family. He antagonized the local doctors by not following the common procedure of buying into an established practice. Rather he started out on his own, in effect as a rival to the doctors already in the town, depending upon word of mouth to bring him patients. Which it did.

Edward was born in their first Romford house. They then moved to a second, the one that they called Edfu, and finally built a

Edfu, the Upwards' house in Romford, Essex

CHAPTER 1: FAMILY AND CHILDHOOD

Right: Harold Arthur Upward

Opposite: Edward and Mervyn with their mother Isa Upward

third, also called Edfu, designed to serve as the previous ones had done as both home and office. The dining room was the waiting room for patients and was also where they had their main meal at midday, having breakfast and supper in the morning room overlooking the garden. (At the location of that house in Romford there is now a nondescript, small two-storey block of flats known as Upward Court, named in Edward's honour. He was invited to its dedication in May 1996.) Harold and his family lived there until he retired to the Isle of Wight. He was away during the First World War in the Royal Army Medical Corps in Norfolk, having volunteered to serve when the war broke out, and also abroad in Greece and Italy. It was in Romford that the five children were born: Edward in

CHAPTER 1: FAMILY AND CHILDHOOD

'Eddie', 'Mer' and Laurence, July 1912

1903 and his brother, John Mervyn, known as Mer in the family and John otherwise, in 1905.

Mer, unlike Edward, was on much better terms with his mother. He never married. After taking his B.A. at Sidney Sussex College, Cambridge, in 1928, having first read English and then archaeology and anthropology, he appears to have returned to live at home in Romford until 1933 when he took a job teaching at Radley College. The next year he became a very successful headmaster of the Port Regis Preparatory School in Broadstairs, Kent, remaining there for the rest of his career and travelling with the school when it moved to Motcombe Park near Shaftesbury in Dorset.[7] He retired in 1970 and took up permanent residence in the divided house on Hill Street. Another brother, Harold, was born in 1907 and died as an infant.

CHAPTER 1: FAMILY AND CHILDHOOD

The Upward family, 20 July 1912. Left to right: Isa with baby Yolande, Mer, Gladys (standing), Edward J. Upward, Laurence, Edward Falaise, Grandma Ridgely

Laurence was born in 1909. Suffering from schizophrenia starting in 1927, he was institutionalized at quite a young age, dying in his sixties. His ashes are buried at the foot of his mother's grave in Shanklin next to Sandown. The youngest child, a daughter named Yolande, was born in 1911. She went to one of the best-known and recently established girls' public schools in England, Benenden, which she disliked, finishing there in 1928. Despite not being too happy at the school, she nevertheless taught there briefly in 1933, replacing an ill mistress. After leaving Benenden, she spent time in Paris and Switzerland, then attended the London School of Speech and Drama and adopted the stage name of Yolande Vaughan. She acted at the repertory theatre in Northampton where she was a

CHAPTER 1: FAMILY AND CHILDHOOD

contemporary of Errol Flynn, who told her he was going to bluff his way to fame. She also performed with the Festival Theatre in Cambridge. During the war she worked as a Red Cross nurse at Osborne House, the former royal residence on the Isle of Wight, as well as with the Women's Naval Service for a period. After the war she was the secretary at her brother Mer's prep school. She married a master at the school, Norman Odell, and had two sons. Neither she nor Mer agreed with Edward politically, but they were nevertheless all through their lives on very good terms with their brother.[8]

In the case of Edward's father the family moved from trade to the professions. The next generation were schoolmasters, the two brothers and Yolande, the wife of one. Was that a step up, down or sideways? For Edward schoolmastering was frequently a chore, the necessary means to provide a living. The profession – is it a profession? – he wished for was to be a writer. Where does that fit in terms of class? Auden's father was a doctor, Cecil Day Lewis's a clergyman, Stephen Spender's a journalist, Christopher Isherwood's a member of the gentry. There was no literary tradition in Upward's family with one striking exception, the rather flamboyant Allen Upward, Edward's first cousin once removed. He was referred to by Edward as Uncle Allen, which would suggest he was close to the family, but I have not been able to discover evidence of their seeing much of one another. I believe he was the son of Edward's great-uncle George, and hence in a sense somewhat parallel in terms of family relationship to Edward's two paternal uncles. In the biographical material available about him he is described as Welsh rather than English, born in Worcester in 1863 into a family of Plymouth Brethren. Yet Ezra Pound in 1913 wrote about a visit to Allen Upward at what he

CHAPTER 1: FAMILY AND CHILDHOOD

Allen Upward (1863–1926) receiving the degree of Bard from the Archdruid at the Welsh National Eisteddfod, August 1891

called his family home on the Isle of Wight and was very taken with his unconventional views on religion and culture. He wrote about Upward's book *The Divine Mystery* of 1913, 'He has derived the word God from the word Goad ... He has related prophecy to astrology ... Modern marriage is, apparently ... derived from the laws of slave concubinage ... The lovely belief in a durable hot hell dates back to the Parsee who squatted over a naptha [sic] volcano'. In 1914 Pound may have derived the concept of the Vortex from Allen Upward's *The New Word*. Upward was a major influence in interesting Pound in Chinese literature. He was educated at Great Yarmouth Grammar School and the Royal (Catholic) University of Ireland. In his day he was fairly well known, now largely forgotten but of interest particularly to Ezra Pound scholars.

In what has been written about him he emerges as an Imagist poet and as a precursor of modernism. He led an extraordinarily

CHAPTER 1: FAMILY AND CHILDHOOD

varied life. He had strong political opinions on behalf of nationalism, supporting Irish Home Rule, and was not opposed to violence on its behalf. As well, he was in favour of nationalist activities in Greece and Wales. He stood unsuccessfully for Parliament in 1917 in Cardiff as a Lib-Lab candidate, sponsored by both the Liberal and Labour parties. He was a member of the bar and became a well-known radical lawyer; he fought in the Greco-Turkish War in 1897 and was a proconsul in Nigeria in 1901. He wrote on the occult for *The New Age* as well as having Imagist poems published in *Poetry*. They so impressed Pound that he included nine in his first anthology of the Imagist poets. Unlike Edward, Allen was a prolific writer, turning out fiction dealing with public events such as the Dreyfus affair and the Kaiser's telegram to the Boer Paul Kruger backing him against the British. In order to support himself he published quite a few spy and ghost tales as well. He wrote a volume of autobiography, *Some Personalities* (1921). He killed himself in 1926. One reason for his suicide was his sense that his philosophical writings such as *The New Word* (1910) and *The Divine Mystery* (1913) were unfairly neglected. *The New Word* was designed as a 'letter' to the Nobel Prize committee for literature. Pound meanly joked that Upward had killed himself because he felt in 1925 that he, rather than George Bernard Shaw, should have received the Nobel Prize.[9]

Allen Upward was a figure of interest and some fascination to Edward and may have provided the origin for the first name of Allen Chalmers, Edward's pseudonym in Isherwood's *All the Conspirators* and *Lions and Shadows*. Like Edward he was in the forefront of the writings of his time: Allen an Imagist associated with Ezra Pound and an influence upon him, and Edward as part of the new and most characteristic writing in Britain in the 1930s. He figures in Edward's novel *No Home but the Struggle* as 'Uncle Edmund' although the reader is told that he was a cousin with the honorary title of uncle. 'He was a small man with a pointed beard and he used to come roaring up the stairs on all fours pretending to be a lion'. In the novel he records a conversation with this 'writer of books': 'When I was sixteen and had begun to write poetry he advised me to take warning from his own experience and never want to earn my living by writing: he himself had made money out of it to start with, had sailed his own yacht on the Solent and had bought his suits from the very best tailors, but he had had to give too much of his energy to producing sensational novels instead of poems and philosophical books which could bring him no money though they alone gave him any real satisfaction to write'.[10] In 2001 Edward was working on a story, 'The Order of Genius', presumably never finished, about 'Uncle Allen' which he had started in 1990. He noted on 3 April: 'He had the courage to shoot himself ... Perhaps he was after his time and I am before mine'. Then on 11 April he wrote: 'Was AU really a "charlatan", simply out for fame at all costs? Though he had an intellect far superior to mine, am I right in regarding both of us as being oppressed by the British Establishment?'[11] They shared a sense that they had been neglected by the literary world.

Edward had, I believe, a comparatively happy childhood, being close to his brother Mer, getting on well with his father but having increasing difficulty with his mother. In 1925 he wrote in his notebook: 'I never tell my mother the truth if I can help it. I dislike her but I like my father'.[12] He draws on quite a few childhood memories in *No Home but the Struggle* (1977), no doubt somewhat fictionalized.

CHAPTER 1: FAMILY AND CHILDHOOD

He did remember fantasizing about being hung upside down on a butcher's hook and also being scared by a rusted steam engine which he saw when visiting his mother's aunt, who had helped bring her up after her parents' death. In April 1947 he took his son Christopher to Romford to see the family sites, which he called 'a pilgrimage to ruined shrines'.[13] There had been the traditional class divisions in town life. Young Edward and Mer both admired and feared those they called the 'snipes', for guttersnipes. 'We were afraid of them. But we were envious of the skill with which they could spin acorn size wooden tops and keep them spinning by whipping them, and we were envious too of the ways they could keep their iron hoops thundering along the pavement with the aid only of a sort of iron stick with a hook at the end of it. Also they used old wooden packing cases and pram wheels to make cars they could sit in and propel quite fast with their feet'. His mother could be kind to the 'snipes' in a lady-of-the-manor way. Edward once discovered four of them in the dining room, eating bread and dripping provided by Isa. 'The four boys gave me a strange look, not at all hostile. Then I walked out of the room. I never thought of trying to get to know any of the "snipes" better, or to make friends of them if I could'.[14]

He found his father very supportive and reassuring and his mother too encouraged him to write. When his father became fatally ill in December 1958, Edward wrote in his notebook, 'He is the last link with true happiness'. He noted on the day of his death, 4 January 1959, 'One day I will write about this. I shall never forget it'. But as far as I know, he never did. And he noted the following April: 'Have been in a more or less constant state of tension since D died four months ago. Now there is nowhere left in the world where I can be completely at ease'. He also felt grateful to his father for his good health, his father once remarking to him, 'I've given you a good body'. Rather in contradiction to his previous statement about not having a location where he could feel comfortable, he seemed nevertheless to have a strong sense of place and family continuity. He was very pleased that he had come to live in the family house in Sandown and particularly that it connected him with his father. As he wrote on an anniversary of his father's birth: 'How have I been able to go on living without him? Only by living in his house. This gives me a kind of reality. I know who I am & who my grandfather was & that he too lived in this house. Otherwise I should have less place in society than a gypsy'.[15] Although he found his mother socially pretentious, he was reconciled with her in his own mind after her death in 1951 and came to mourn her passing. He wrote about her a few days after her death on Christmas Eve in 1951: 'She was an exceptional woman and she required but did not get a wider field than the family for the exercise of her powers. All of us were deeply under her influence even when, like myself, we tried to assert our independence by doing the opposite of what she wished ... She was a Romantic'.[16]

For his education he first went to a small kindergarten run by Mabel de St Croix, daughter of a stockbroker, at Kingswood Lodge in Romford. In the tradition of many in the English middle classes and most of the upper classes, he was then 'brutally' sent away to a prep school, Sutherland House in Windlesham, at the age of nine along with his brother Mer who was then seven.[17] In Mer's case it may not have been ultimately too painful, as he went on to be a

CHAPTER 1: FAMILY AND CHILDHOOD

teacher and headmaster at prep schools. But they were both deeply homesick at first, Mer crying day and night, writing to his mother pleading to be taken home, and Edward only at night. He had enjoyed the kindergarten he went to previously as 'the only school I have ever – as a pupil or a teacher – longed for during the holidays'.[18] Edward himself was rather scathing about the prep school. 'It was a school that was going downhill. We didn't realise this. We went to it because a friend of my mother's had a boy there and he came to see us and my mother noticed he took his coat off to wash his hands before lunch and was impressed by this. My father visited the school and was told the staff were qualified. Oxford and Cambridge. It's true the sewage system was rather peculiar but my father thought it was all right'.[19] At the time it had only twenty-seven pupils. Years later in 1970 Edward remarked about the school in his notebook: 'The main point about W was that it was a preparatory school. It prepared us for the true hell of the public school'.[20] He became captain of his dormitory and was called Cap'n Flase after his middle name. They had to wear bowler hats and Eton collars. Just before taking off for school their mother made them dress up in those clothes and go to show their kindergarten teacher. On their way they were mocked by the 'snipes'. There must have been a sense that one might be physically attacked, but in training to be a gentleman one had to ignore it and simply walk as fast as one could without running.

At their school the brothers formed a club of two known as the Red Brotherhood after a film they had seen. They communicated with one another through invented Egyptian pictographs. Edward also started to write and read to a greater extent. Among the earliest

CHAPTER 1: FAMILY AND CHILDHOOD

books he remembers were *Black Beauty* and *Pilgrim's Progress*. Like many children he had a conception of an imaginary country. In his papers in the British Library there are several notebooks dated 1914 when he was eleven. One consists of fourteen chapters, quite short, dealing with the adventures of one General Pict with an emphasis on battles. A second notebook also dated 1914 contains thirteen chapters. It has a title page, *The Invasion of Ritare* by E. F. Upward, Author of *Jason's River*. Also stated is 'Printers E. F. Upward Romford'. The stories and drawings within the notebook mostly, and unsurprisingly, depict battles. In the same group of papers there is a listing of favourite books and poems recorded in the last year of the war, 1918, when he turned fifteen and was at his public school. It consists of not unexpected names: Kipling, Burns, Herrick, Byron, Newbolt, Browning, Shelley, Wordsworth and Cowper. He announced in this list that Browning was the greatest English poet. His favourite books were *The Elusive [sic] Pimpernel, A Christmas Carol, Tale of Two Cities, Alice in Wonderland, A Study in Scarlet, The Jungle Book, Kidnapped, Quentin Durward* and *The War of the Worlds*.[21] In *No Home but the Struggle* he goes on at some length about the school, his fellow pupils, the bullying, the teachers, but it does not come across as a particularly negative experience. On the contrary, in the reading that was done, particularly poetry, and the colourful stories that some of the teachers told, it sounds as if it helped to build up Edward's imagination.

The school had its desired effect. Although he didn't do particularly well in the Common Entrance Examination, allowance was made for the fact that his father was away at war. He was admitted to a well-known public school, Repton. The headmaster at his prep school had a connection with a housemaster there. Perhaps his father's Cambridge contemporary, George Auden, had recommended his old school. So began what in many ways was the most formative experience of Upward's life. Repton continued his education as an English gentleman. It also made him a rebel.

Chapter 2: Repton

REPTON IS ONE OF THE MORE prominent public (fee-paying) schools in England although not quite as famous as Eton, Harrow and Winchester. (Coincidentally, it was used as the location for the filming of that classic sentimental depiction of public school life *Goodbye, Mr. Chips* in 1939 as well as for a later television version.) Edward's mother was determined that her sons (and ultimately daughter) would go to 'posh' schools. But the choice of Repton was somewhat arbitrary. Edward arrived in the autumn of 1917. His first memory as a 'new bug' was being given an exam about the local publicans and pubs, not that any of the boys could go to them. He also remembered never being so hungry, which may partially have been because the war was still going on. Edward went to Latham House, one of the then eight Repton houses. It turned out that its housemaster was asked to leave shortly after Edward arrived because of sexual improprieties with the boys in his charge. Years later Edward remarked about this, giving a rather strange explanation for the housemaster's actions. 'If it hadn't been for the war I doubt whether my own housemaster would have allowed himself to go so far as to interfere sexually with some of the younger boys in his house. He left the school abruptly at the end of my second term there, after the house prefects had been to see the headmaster about him, and the reason officially given out for his departure was that he wanted to join the army'.[1]

CHAPTER 2: REPTON

Sexuality does rather mark the beginning of his life at Repton. He recorded in *No Home but the Struggle*, which is a fictional account, that there was someone from his prep school at Repton, which he calls Rugtonstead in the novel, one year senior to him who was interested in him physically but when rebuffed became an enemy. Edward also makes the rather startling statement that in his second term at the school 'young Shant & I became lovers'.[2] But he probably does not mean this literally. In *No Home but the Struggle* he called him 'young Jib'. In his novel the narrator commented: 'My love for him was the only romantic love in my life that has ever been mutual. No doubt if we had been together in a day school instead of in a Public boarding-school segregated from ordinary life, and if we had been able to meet girls, we shouldn't have fallen in love with each other ... Kissing him or holding hands with him would have seemed as abhorrently sentimental and unnatural to me as it would have to him, though I was very conscious of his physical beauty'. In his novel he was crudely teased by others in the house about his 'keenness' for young Jib, one contemporary remarking, 'I bet your handkerchief is so stiff that you could stand it up on the mantelpiece as an ornament'.[3] In writing about the school he certainly captures the intense nastiness boys in a group were capable of. Elsewhere he commented presumably about this relationship: 'My best memory is of my romantic and reciprocated but entirely innocent love for another pupil who was my contemporary'.[4] He despised the filthiness of language with which the boys joked and teased about sex. As he remarked in an interview in 1993 with Peter Parker, Isherwood's biographer, 'Everyone was homosexual, up to a point, at Repton'. But actual physical sex was comparatively rare. 'It did happen and then, of course, the Head expelled the chief offender and gave a very severe beating to the less guilty one'.[5] Rather oddly, in 1998 he describes this romantic passion as being connected with a teacher and that his political sense, his intense hatred of the system, most vividly represented by fagging, was shaped by his sense of being persecuted. 'There was one master, he was a sort of amateur editor, poet, he also painted. We were very close. It was the only romantic affair in my life. Something quite innocent. I mean, it wasn't anything sexual or physical. He shouted at me across the field "Coward Upward!", and I think that this, in a way, was the moment in which my persecution feeling started'.[6]

He got on quite well with the new housemaster, W. M. Hooton, who recommended that he read Thomas Hardy. His refuge from his unhappiness at school was writing out in a notebook poems by poets whom he liked, his two favourites being at that point Shelley and Herrick. When he went home at Christmas his falling out of love was compensated by falling in love with a Romford contemporary of his whom he calls in his novel Christine. But he still had apparently platonic attractions at Repton, having preserved among his papers, along with notes on his readings in history, what he described as 'love prose pieces' but without any indication to whom they were addressed.

> If I could sink my personality unconditionally into yours, I should come as near to heaven as any man has attained ever ... I would like to curl up and go to sleep in the corner of a firelit room. I would like to feel music, like reviving new blood, flowing through my veins. I would like to attain to that

something in you which is so utterly inexplicable. But because of your laughter I know in my heart that it exists . . . As it is impossible to speak to you seriously, I have decided to write. Whenever I have tried to talk to you alone, someone else has come along and everything has been spoilt.[7]

In *No Home but the Struggle* he writes that in his last year at Repton he fell in love with a boy whom he calls Stafford who was in his first year. He wished for no physical contact other than possibly holding his hand. This was combined with his reading of Walt Whitman and writing two poems about being parted from Stafford. Shortly after leaving Repton, when at Cambridge in January 1923, he wrote a series of rather callow aphorisms. He makes a striking juxtaposition: a comment about public school boys following an odd statement about homosexuality, implying that he might dislike homosexuals, at the time that Isherwood was his greatest friend. He was fully aware of Isherwood's sexual interests. 'I have only hated one person in my life – myself . . . What shall we do for the homosexualist? We'll guard him from the fangs of respectability, then we'll give him a severe horse-whipping. The average public school boy is a human being, but public school boys collectively are brutish, disgusting and inhuman'.[8] It is unclear whether he approves or disapproves of the beating.

The expulsion of his housemaster introduces a dominant note characteristic of English society that would play a significant role in Upward's work.[9] In many ways boarding schools are among the most conformist of English institutions. Yet they are full of boys with raging hormones who are the charges of frequently unmarried masters. At these schools sexual scandal was frequently brewing very close to the surface of school life. Boys were certainly beaten (now beating has been forbidden in English schools) and often expelled for sexual misbehaviour. As the thoroughly heterosexual Lord Grantham remarked in the TV series *Downton Abbey*, when he was far less shocked than his servants by one of them being homosexual, he couldn't remember how many times he had been kissed at Eton. At a later point, Upward coined the term 'tea-tabling' with specific reference to the writings of E. M. Forster. The term stands for a recurring theme in English fiction and life: decorum and conformity on the surface, as at a tea party, but raging events and thoughts taking place, so to speak, under the table. Public school life was crucial in making clear how important this element was in English society. Strict politeness on the surface, one might say a form of gamesmanship, while possibly dreadful events and hostility lay just below. The English schoolboy can put lots of hostility into the use of 'sir'. The public school classroom was a battlefield for dominance between pupils and their teacher. And how passive-aggressive the use of the phrase 'I'm sorry' can be in England. It frequently conveys that the person being apologized to is the culprit. Perhaps this sense of warfare was intensified by the First World War. Upward acquired a sense of there being an enemy, the other side, early on. And later it would fit in with his Marxist analysis of society.

Repton, an Anglo-Saxon town on the banks of the Trent in Derbyshire, has a long history. It was the capital of the Kingdom of Mercia. An abbey was established there around 660. In 1172 it became a priory, which was dissolved in 1538 during the reign of

Henry VIII as part of the English Reformation and the dissolution of the monasteries. The priory, parts of which still survive, provided the original physical location for the school, established by the will of Sir John Port in 1557. The school, somewhat unusually for the time, did draw a few students from outside its locality. But then in the nineteenth century, like many other secondary boarding schools, it went 'national', open to boys from any location whose families could pay the fees. This was responding to the desire of members of the middle class. They were anxious to send their sons to prestigious public schools that would provide the education, contacts and veneer to ease their careers whether in Britain or in the empire. Schools such as Repton emerged as attractive and successful places of education. It generally required a dynamic nineteenth-century clergyman to be the force behind such a change. In the case of Repton the appointment of the Revd Steuart Adolphus Pears in 1854 began the period of growth and transformation. During the thirty years he was head, he made Repton a school of national prominence. In the twentieth century the two most famous headmasters were clergymen who went on to become Archbishops of Canterbury. First was William Temple (whose father had been Archbishop of Canterbury as well), headmaster from 1910 to 1914, appointed when he was twenty-eight. He was an impressive figure but not a very good administrator. Geoffrey Fisher succeeded him, at a similarly young age of twenty-seven, and remained headmaster until 1932 when he became Bishop of Chester on his way to becoming Archbishop of Canterbury. Fisher reinforced his connection with the school by marrying Pears's granddaughter. He was the powerful headmaster when Upward was at the school. Upward thought well

CHAPTER 2: REPTON

Repton School

of him. 'He was extremely capable and self-confident, and he had a good knowledge of Divinity. It was said of him by one of us Sixth Formers that his religion was not Christianity but Divinity'.[10] Upward also admired his humanity. Years later he recalled one of his talks as one of his most vivid memories of his school days. 'I remember Fisher speaking from the pulpit of the death of Muller who had been Repton's German master for many years, and I heard it said afterwards that he had died of a broken heart because of the hostility of ultra-patriotic colleagues in the Masters' Common Room'.[11] Although Fisher expelled two boys for homosexual practices, rather surprisingly he encouraged the boys to read Alec Waugh's *The Loom of Youth*. It was published in 1917 and had caused something of a scandal in its mentioning the significant presence of homosexuality at a public school.[12]

Another future Archbishop of Canterbury, Michael Ramsey,

was a year behind Upward as a pupil at Repton, but it doesn't appear that they were particular friends there or later at Cambridge. He too was something of a rebel at school, arguing with a master on the other side in a debating society that Britain should not send troops to Russia to suppress the Bolsheviks. Ramsey also refused to join the Officer Training Corps. Also at Repton he changed his religious denomination. His Cambridge family was Congregationalist but at Repton he chose to be confirmed in the Church of England. (His older brother, Frank Ramsey, a renowned philosopher and mathematician who died at the age of twenty-seven, was an atheist.) Fisher may not have thought well of Ramsey as a schoolboy, as years later he opposed him as his successor as archbishop.[13] There were in effect three Repton archbishops in a row, although only Ramsey had been a schoolboy there. One indication of a school coming into its own is when it would appear, as seems to be so often the case in England, although obviously it can't be true, that 'everyone' was at school together. The literary critic Humphry House and Vernon Watkins the poet were contemporaries of Upward's as was Harold Abrahams, the famous Anglo-Jewish athlete commemorated in *Chariots of Fire*. Other well-known Repton 'old boys' though not contemporaries of Upward's were Basil Rathbone, Roald Dahl, Denton Welch (who ran away from the school) and Stuart Hampshire. Dahl recorded that the school uniform was pinstripe trousers and long black tailcoat, a stiff butterfly collar, a starched shirt with studs and a twelve-button waistcoat.[14]

Parts of the priory still stand. It served as the oldest house for boys at the school for many years before part of it was turned into the school's First World War Memorial (the rest becoming a library and classrooms) dedicated on Armistice Day 1922 while Upward was a pupil. Three hundred and fifty-five 'old boys', more or less the size of the school at the time, were killed in that war. Many boys who were at school during the First World War but were too young to serve had conflicted feelings about not having taken part in what Isherwood referred to as 'The Test'. George Orwell, born the same year as Upward, had similar feelings while at his prep school St Cyprian's and also at Eton. When the war ended, Upward remembered: 'I was only just too young to go ... We had a bonfire on which we flung almost everything inflammable we could find. I danced wildly round it'.[15] Upward's growing commitment to be against the established values of his society manifested itself at Repton in his leaving the Officer Training Corps (OTC). In 1993 he provided a vivid memory of an encampment attended by various corps groups from other public schools as well. 'We went to a camp, and the really smartest schools were the least important. Eton misbehaved themselves in the most disgraceful manner. [One wonders if Orwell were there.] We used to have concerts in a big tent, and before it started they'd be singing all kinds of lewd songs, and they were almost the most slovenly on parade. It was a post-war reaction. And I in the end decided to be as slovenly as possible'.[16] He also refused to be confirmed in the Church of England. Even when he was at his prep school, encouraged by his father's religious position rather than his mother's, he deliberately wore his braces crossed when reciting the Anglican creed to indicate that he didn't believe in it, although he did have a brief period of religiosity under the influence of one of his prep school masters.

Rather oddly, perhaps, there are only a few references by Upward to the rather dramatic political events that took place at Repton during his first year. Perhaps he was too much the new boy to absorb what was happening. Victor Gollancz was fired from the staff because of his course on contemporary politics which he gave with another master, D. C. Somervell, who was also dismissed. In later life Gollancz went on to become one of the most prominent of English publishers. He was a central figure in the political activities of the 1930s, being the founder of the Left Book Club and deeply involved with left-wing politics. In fact, as recollected in an interview in 1969, Upward at first took rather the official view that what Gollancz was doing was too propagandistic, as the headmaster ultimately argued.[17] In *No Home but the Struggle* the narrator is writing a novel, *The Book of Eitna*. In that text he discusses 'the dismissal by the Headmaster of two young assistant masters who were said to have been carrying on pacifist propaganda among members of the Sixth Form. My sympathies at the time were far from being with these two masters whom I made Eitna describe as men of evil character'. But some time later while still at school he decides that he had been wrong about them.[18]

Gollancz, born in 1893, was a brilliant student at Oxford. He was anxious to join up when war broke out but couldn't persuade the army to take him until October 1915, and he was limited to home duties because of his poor eyesight. Then in 1916 he secured permission from the army to become a classics master at Repton and also to be involved with the OTC there. It was an unusual appointment as the number of Jewish masters at English public schools was few. He also persuaded the headmaster, Fisher, that he and D. C. Somervell, later a distinguished historian, should give a class in civics, that is, the contemporary world, a quite neglected topic at public schools. Introduced as a course in January 1917 before Upward arrived in the autumn of that year, it continued during Upward's first year and caused a great deal of turmoil. There was increasing talk in England of what would happen when the war was over, how would society be reconstructed. This question was to be the dominant theme of the class, to consider 'the great movements that were battling everywhere around ... militarism and a League of Nations, capitalism and socialism'.[19] Fisher approved of the course, particularly as traditional connections with the classics were not forgotten. The class was an extra. It was not held during regular teaching hours but in the evening of the weekly half-holiday. Forty-one sixth-form boys signed up, mostly from one house, the Priory. As the war was still going on, those pupils' likely next stop after Repton might well have been the trenches in France. Starting in June 1917, the class even put out a publication, *A Public School Looks at the World*, known as *The Pubber*. Among its contributors was the future playwright Benn Levy. It was sold in London at the radical bookstore Henderson & Sons, nicknamed 'The Bomb Shop', on the Charing Cross Road. Apparently the War Office was aware of it and may have complained to Fisher that it was a somewhat subversive and unpatriotic gesture at the time of war, taking particular objection to a piece in the third issue in November 1917 that raised the question of a negotiated peace. There were even two short books about the course by Gollancz and Somervell, *Political Education at a Public School*, published by William Collins in the spring of 1918, and *The School and the World*. It was a very exciting and engaging class.

Fisher came to feel however that through the class Gollancz was becoming too close to his students – he much enjoyed taking them to plays in London – and that he was not maintaining the proper distance. There were also associated activities in the debating society where Gollancz spoke in support of guild socialism, and such issues were discussed as women and the vote and what the state should do about the poor. It is not surprising that the whole project irritated quite a few of Gollancz's fellow teachers who tended to be more traditional. It's hard to believe that there wasn't some element of anti-Semitism involved. The first sentence of *Political Education at a Public School* read: 'Judged by the highest standard – and those who love them will not care to use any other – the Public Schools must be said to have failed, largely through having neglected worrying about the state of the society in which the students lived'.[20] Gollancz also believed, rather illogically, that an increased interest in current events lowered the level of vice and masturbation at the Priory.[21] There was much debate among the masters about the course, quite a few of them opposed to it, as well as signs of concern by the Governing Body and others. Fisher felt that he had no choice but to take the rather extreme step of firing Gollancz. He received his notice three days before the beginning of the summer term and was quite devastated. He loved being at Repton and now felt that he was being evicted from paradise. Shortly thereafter he would embark upon his extremely distinguished publishing career.

It is hard not to think that the situation ultimately formed at least a small part of Upward's political education. But he might have missed some of the excitement. In the spring of his first year, in 1918, he went home for several weeks. In the austere conditions characteristic of such schools, he had developed chilblains. This had two

CHAPTER 2: REPTON

Geoffrey Fisher in 1922 when Headmaster of Repton

important consequences. It was when he was briefly back home that he started writing poetry. Also, when he returned to school he was because of his health temporarily excused from fagging, so he could not be beaten, as many fags were, by the senior boy whose fag he would ordinarily have been, the so-called study-holder. Somehow this made him particularly conscious of the brutality of the system in which he found himself. The period of non-fagging did not last long. Years later he gave an interview to the school magazine in which he said about being a fag:

> One of the duties of the fags was to dust the mantelpiece in their studies, as coal was used in the fireplaces. Sometimes after a fag had done the dusting efficiently, the Study Holder would sprinkle dust over the mantelpiece in order to give a pretext for beating a fag. Fags must be kept in their place. Hitler is said to have admired the English public school system because it taught subordinates not to complain even when they were punished unjustly by their superiors. My Study Holder, Colburn or Colby by name, was more amiable than most, but he discovered that I was 'incomp'. I more than once, in spite of desperate stirring with a spoon, burnt the porridge I was heating in a saucepan for the study's supper . . . Colby felt he had to beat me for that.[22]

It was the arbitrariness of beating that he said made him a rebel 'throughout his life' and turned him against the system. When he was a study-holder himself he refused to beat anyone ('bumming'). He felt that not only was that the right thing to do but more important to him it was a seditious act of revenge against the system. He made one exception and beat one boy for taking a shortcut while running an errand, as he wanted to know what it felt like to beat someone. It happened to be one of the few Jewish pupils. '(Nor had I any anti-semitic feelings towards him, at least nothing comparable to those which many members of the House . . . showed towards the two or three Jews amongst us) but I wanted to find out what it was like to beat someone, and I did not do it again'.[23] His brother Mer who also attended Repton agreed with him about beating. When he became a prep school headmaster he gathered the sticks used for beating students and burnt them. When Upward was a schoolmaster, on one occasion he beat a student and felt intensely guilty about it. For him, both factually and symbolically, it was the essence of the evil of the world in which he found himself and that he would dedicate his life to change. It was the world of 'tea-tabling', decorous and proper on the surface, full of rage and irrational violence just below.

For these reasons Repton was such a formative experience for Upward. He firmly believed that it was his loathing for his school that turned him a decade later into a political radical of the far left. That was his mind-set. He had little or no interest in politics until after he left Cambridge some years later. Yet he felt that it was at Repton that he became a rebel, although he never attended any of the debates at the school, which were generally on political topics. (Under the influence of his reading then of Turgenev's *Virgin Soil*, he was pessimistic about the possibility of social progress.) Repton was the great shaping experience of Upward's life, in ways both negative but also possibly in ways more positive than he allowed. As he remarked in his 1969 interview, 'I absolutely loathed my public school ... [It] very definitely turned me in the direction I went'. In quite a few ways it was an excellent education and provided him, as it had for many writers of the period, as well as no doubt before and since, rich fodder on which to feed. Why were these schools such shaping experiences? They took boys at about the age of thirteen and put them in a total environment removed from their parents and the 'ordinary' world. Not only learning was literally beaten into them, with an emphasis on the classics, but also how to be English gentlemen, how to take commands from older boys, and eventually how to give orders, how to run a small community firmly with a rich assumption of authority. These schools grew to their greatest importance when they were training young men to go out and run or indeed rule the British Empire, or to remain at home as civil servants or politicians to run, indeed one might say to rule, the state. They were not taught to question the rightness of the state but rather to be part of its governing structure. In many ways it might appear as a seemingly benign authoritarian state with an attractive veneer of civilization: Athens above and Sparta below. The school was ultimately designed to send its pupils out into the world in order to run it. Although later than the Jesuit age of seven for the shaping of youth, it taught boys in a total environment as they were coming to intellectual, social and sexual maturity, and left powerful marks upon them. It was the great shaping experience.

But for some, such as Upward and Isherwood, the world that they were inadvertently part of by birth came to be the enemy. Fighting what public schools stood for was the way, they felt, to create a better world. Upward saw his later Communism as a total revolt against this society, most particularly as it was represented by the English public school. Years later, in 1970, he wrote in one of his notebooks: 'The public school as a model of imperialist society. The remote housemaster & remoter Head. The rule by subordinates, prefects. The piety above, the foulness beneath. It's true that the school gave poetry prizes, but this was to contain the impulse within the system & to tame it. Poetry easing a sense of revolt, but an inner revolt. It was like a priesthood, a turning away from the world'. Later that same year he wrote: 'Life at R when I look back at it seems almost wholly hateful, except for the time when I revolted against it. And for the imaginative time'.[24] Some of the reviewers of his novel *In the Thirties*, with one of its main themes his joining the Communist Party, felt, perhaps rather meanly, that the book was somewhat in a public school spirit, as if one were involved with a club for poor youths in the East End. Rather strikingly, the philosopher Stuart Hampshire, who had also been at Repton, wrote in his review: 'Joining the Communist Party still seems an innocent, schoolboyish gesture, like refusing to join the OTC and joining the Scouts instead'.[25] In many ways Upward was to all outward appearances a fairly conventional schoolboy, other than his leaving the OTC and his refusal to be confirmed. These decisions did not appear to cause any trouble for his career at the school. He was sufficiently good at sport to meet that crucial way of being accepted. 'I was a good footballer. I was in the 2nd XI, and I think I could have got into the first XI, but I didn't like the idea of frequently having to go away to play other schools. I didn't enjoy cricket, nor was I a good runner, jumper, swimmer or diver'.[26]

Perhaps the single most important event in Upward's life that happened at Repton was Christopher Isherwood's arriving at the school the year after him. Ultimately they became each other's closest friend for the rest of their lives. The relationship is somewhat paradoxical. The continual interest in Isherwood has helped keep the reputation of Upward alive. Yet Isherwood has overshadowed Upward. The purpose here, although obviously their very close friendship will be an important part of the story, will be to present

Upward as an important figure in his own right. Isherwood had been at the prep school St Edmund's where he came to know Auden, who was some years younger. His father, Frank, had been killed in the First World War at Ypres in May 1915. Isherwood and Upward did not become close friends at first as they were in different houses, and friendships were not encouraged across houses. Isherwood was in Hall, where Fisher lived, also serving as its housemaster. But they were both in the history sixth form in their last years where they were taught by G. B. Smith, favourably depicted as Holmes in Isherwood's *Lions and Shadows* and much liked by Upward. He was at Repton only from 1919 to 1926 when he left to be a reforming headmaster at Sedbergh. He had read history at King's College, Cambridge. He took the young men in hand and groomed them to apply for history at Cambridge, probably to Corpus Christi College where Repton had strong connections. Upward preserved the notes he took at Repton on standard historical questions and texts, as well as his copy of Smith's *Scenes from European History: A Companion for the Middle Forms for Schools*. At the same time, he was reading extensively in literature as well. He became particularly fond at Repton and later at Cambridge of a rather eclectic group: Emily Brontë, Wilfred Owen, Katherine Mansfield (after whom he would name his daughter) as well as W. N. P. Barbellion, Mark Rutherford and Robert Tressell. Smith stimulated his pupils' minds through startling generalizations, impressing upon them the necessity to grab the attention of those who would read their entrance exams at Cambridge as well as interview them.[27]

Upward enters literary history at this point under the name of Allen Chalmers, as described in Isherwood's *Lions and Shadows*:

> Chalmers was a pale, small, silent boy, a year older than myself, strikingly handsome, with dark hair and dark blue eyes. On the rare occasions when he got excited and began to talk, his face became flushed; he spoke so quickly and indistinctly, with nervous fumbling of his fingers against his lips, that it was very difficult to understand what he was saying ... No sooner had I come into contact with Chalmers than I determined to get to know him well. Never in my life have I been so strongly and immediately attracted to any personality, before or since. Everything about him appealed to me. He was a natural anarchist, a born romantic revolutionary ... Above all things, Chalmers loathed the school, which he invariably referred to as 'Hell'. His natural hatred of all established authority impressed me greatly.[28]

Upward records his friendship with Isherwood, whom he calls Richard in his *No Home but the Struggle,* and their bonding on the discovery that they both wished to be poets. Isherwood, according to Upward, only completely admired two lines in the innumerable poems that Upward had written. Citing them, he wrote: '*But from the sea, silent, far-glimmering there, / Sadness commemorates a child's desire* ... We had no romantic feelings at all towards each another, but in the course of interchanging our poetic ideas and enthusiasms we created a shared imaginative world which grew larger and richer the more we were together and which gave me a deeper and less inconstant pleasure than any romantic love affair I was ever to have'.[29] (At a later point Isherwood went through a group of Upward's poems written at school and at Cambridge and graded them, giving out among other grades five As and nine Ds.[30])

CHAPTER 2: REPTON

Whatever Upward thought of the school, in the 1960s it became proud of them as 'old boys'. It may have been that the institution was pleased by those who became well known, without necessarily agreeing with all that they said about their old school. As Upward informed Isherwood, the headmaster at that time, John Thorn, wrote to him in August 1962 wanting them to speak at the school to combat the natural philistinism of schoolboys. 'I regard you & Isherwood as among the few really distinguished people the place has produced – though many Reptonians would probably not have heard of either of you, being saturated with the C. B. Frys [a famous cricketer] of this life. I wonder how much the place has changed since your day. There's still plenty of athletics, & precious little interest in things of the mind. I have the job of trying to change this, but it won't be easy. It would certainly please me if one or two people like yourself could be prevailed upon to put in a brief appearance'. Upward commented to Isherwood, 'Does this mean that not only buggery but even Marxism has become respectable in this extraordinary country?' In the draft of his reply to Thorn in his papers he wrote, while declining to visit because of the illness of his wife: 'It seems quite inadequate for me to begin by merely thanking you very much indeed – for a letter that bowled me over completely. I hope that you like my novel [*In the Thirties*, published that year], in spite of its anti-public school bias. I must confess that though I was far from happy during my years as a fag at Repton I did enjoy being rebellious during my last year there, and I have since then felt admiration for the tolerance & understanding shown to me by the authorities at the time. I shall always remember with gratitude my housemaster W. M. Hooton and my history master G. B. Smith'.[31] Isherwood commented in a letter to Upward, 'Perhaps the last act of Mortmere will turn out to be our joint address to the boys and the subsequent destruction of Repton'. In the same letter he recognized that being against one's society was much easier if one had some money. The income that English society might give to its gentlemen made it possible to work for its change, indeed perhaps its wished-for destruction.[32] A decade later Upward feared, however seriously, that after what he had written about Repton in *No Home but the Struggle*, the school might want to expunge his name from its records.[33] The English frequently have a love-hate relationship with their institutions. Thinking back about the school in 1987 he remembered leaving for what he thought was the last time. 'I am in the train leaving Willington station. Others from the school in the carriage. "I shall never see that hateful place again". Their silent reaction. A little shocked. Had I no sentiment for the place? But in fact I came back within a week, at GB's [Smith's] request'.[34]

Repton played the crucial role in shaping Upward's conviction that there needed to be radical political changes in English society, although such ideas would not take firm hold until quite a few years later. It was also crucial that it was at Repton that he started to write, first as a poet. Perhaps it was triggered by the contrast between home and school when he came back to Romford for three weeks during term suffering from chilblains. He saw writing poetry at that time as the way to triumph over what he thought of as the vileness of the school, mostly to be found in the filthiness in speech and to a degree action of his fellow pupils. It was also a way to idealize his home in contrast to the school. 'The impulse to write it came to me as I was sitting alone in the morning-room looking out of the window at the honeysuckle'.³⁵ Robert Nichols, a now largely forgotten war poet, came to give a talk at the school on Wordsworth, was impressed by one of Upward's poems and corresponded with him for a while. Born in Shanklin on the Isle of Wight, he might have known and been intrigued by their common association with the island. Nichols inscribed a copy of his rather feyly entitled book of poems *Ardours and Endurances, also A Faun's Holiday & Poems and Phantasies* to 'the poet E. F. Upward' which must have been rather flattering to the schoolboy that he was.³⁶ Upward's style as a poet was then rather gloomily romantic and reinforced his sense of isolation and rebellion; he was steeped in the poetry of Rupert Brooke. He rather enjoyed his cult of gloom and his commitment to have his values be as far as possible the reverse of the school's.

Surviving in his papers is a jejune 1919 essay on 'Modernism in Poetry' full of sweeping and condescending misjudgements. 'Modern poetry has entirely degenerated from the grandeur of Shakespeare and Milton. We sink down out of sight. There are, of course, one or two exceptions. For instance Henry Newbolt, George Meredith, even Kipling at times, are moderately efficient in the art of poetry. Of course there is no doubt as to the greatest modern poet, the only one who can even claim to be compared with Tennyson, Browning and other poets of that time, is Rupert Brooke. In reading his poetry we can feel he is a true poet, he is inspiring. It is not without faults though, and the chief of these is his crudeness'. He had preserved a miscellany of his schoolboy notes, mostly on rather conventional historical topics that would be part of his studies. Elsewhere in this collection of reading-notes and drafts of poems there is commentary on individuals and the school. The following, with the name

Edward in the sixth form at Repton

CHAPTER 2: REPTON

left out, is probably Upward's comment on Smith. 'I believe — to be one of the world's great men. He, like Browning's Pictor Ignotus, is capable of effort in the great world, and yet he had confined himself to the insufficiencies of Repton. He is happy because he believes that his wonderful personality and spirit is imparted to us over whom [he] is placed... He is a prince among men, because, although he has reached middle age, he's not blind to instinct and idealism'.[37] His condescending comment about 'middle age' is amusingly ironic considering the great age he would attain himself and his continuing interest in ideas.

Upward did well as a poet at Repton, winning the Howe English Verse Prize in 1920 with a poem published in the school magazine. (He also wrote some fiction. During the Easter vacation in 1920 he wrote forty-five pages about one Hubert de Tracey who died in a chalk pit on the Isle of Wight.)[38] Isherwood's first mention of him in *Lions and Shadows* is as a poet.

> He had recently won the school poetry prize on the set subject: 'The Surrender of the German Fleet at Scapa Flow'. Chalmers' poem began: 'The Prussian watched the sombre winter sea'. This was its first and last reference, throughout, to anything German: as for the fleet itself, it was never mentioned at all. Chalmers filled the remainder of the six Spenserian stanzas with his favourite properties: wan blood-red mists, meaningless cries of invisible sea birds and the inaudible moanings of the drowned. But his entry was so unquestionably the best that it got the prize, nevertheless; despite the suspicion that it was merely one more expression of the

author's limitless quiet contempt for the authorities and all their works.[39]

In fact Isherwood misrepresented the poem. In it the Prussian is observing the 'dimly moving ships'. The poem deals rather directly with the set subject. 'These remnant vessels tell / Of worlds projected once and steadfastly, / Yet sunk in evil hands to worse than hell; / And heaven leaves him, in her irony, / A bitterness that knows no parallel'. The poem continues to be the ruminations of the Prussian as he contemplates 'the ruin of a mighty dream' and deals with his coming to terms with defeat. Upward's early published poems had been three unsigned ones, 'A Dream of the Ramayana', 'Summer Lost' and 'After Reading in Chatterton', in the school magazine, *The Reptonian,* in February 1920. In an interview in the same publication in 1994 he mentioned, '[I] remember vividly a happy moment when I, for the first time ever, saw a poem I had written in print. It was printed in *The Reptonian* and it was entitled *A Dream of the Ramayana*'.[40] These poems were rather lush and romantic. After the triumph of the prize he published in May two short poems under the name Falaise, one 'The Last Chance', a sonnet and a bit gloomy, and the other, 'Elfin Song', which began quite positively: 'Out in the summer woods away / My fancy stepped a fairy's way'. In October there was another rather gloomy poem, 'The Downs', and in December 'Gloom' itself. Its last of three stanzas read: 'And I loved Gloom, and dreamt with him, / And loved the tales he had: / Oh! And I've happiness with him, / For we are sad'. In June 1921 he again won the Howe Prize with a poem on presumably the set subject, 'Westminster Abbey (On Armistice Day)'. It is a long poem with a rather

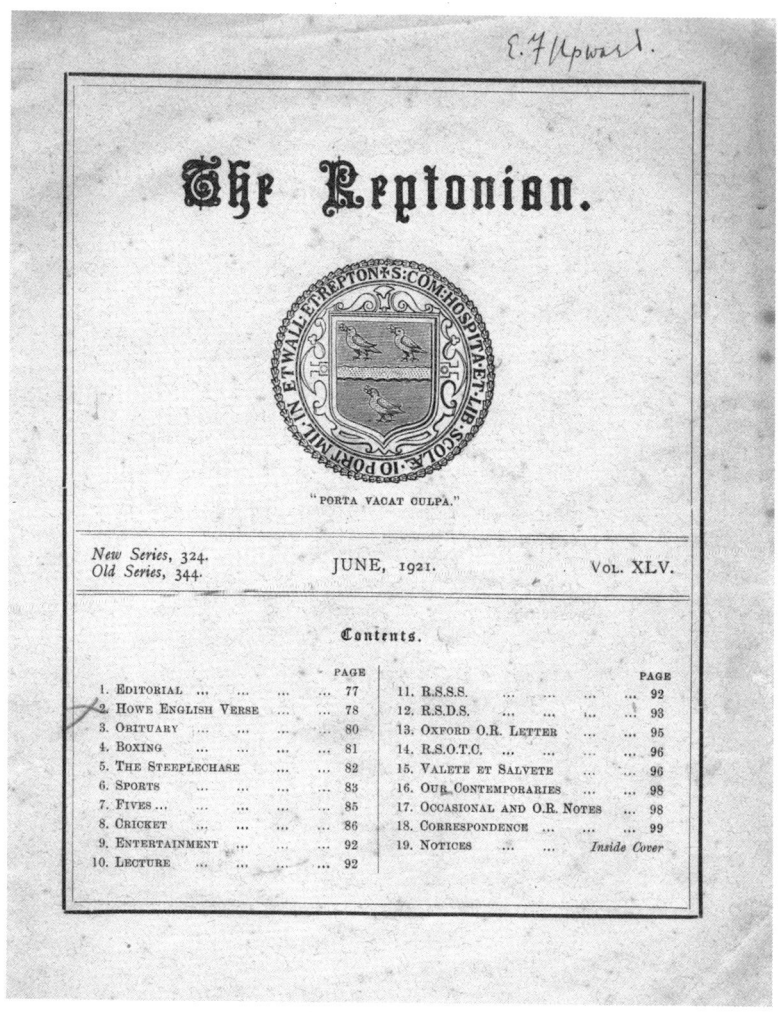

The Reptonian, *June 1921*

convoluted vocabulary that raises the question whether organ music in the abbey can be helpful. 'Music and dream shall shatter words and wars / In your glad hearts with thought stranger than stars. / Ah, what has Life to do with war?' And then in the next issue, in July

1921, there was a four-stanza poem, 'Departing', which might be construed as being rather sentimental about Repton, so contrary to what he later thought. The first stanza went: 'Going away, – how bitter then this is, / Since I have loved the quiet hills so long, / And found so strange a comfort in the skies, / And known so fair a song'.[41] That may have been more a public presentation of what he thought his feelings should appear to be. Between February 1920 and March 1922 he published twelve poems in The Reptonian.[42]

A contemporary of Upward's at Repton, Vernon Watkins, two years behind him, became a distinguished poet. He also went to Cambridge, to Magdalene College, in Upward's last year there. There is no evidence that they were particularly close. Yet he is in both Lions and Shadows and No Home but the Struggle and Upward later said that he was a model for Moxon in the Mortmere stories.[43] Both he and Upward were much influenced by Rupert Brooke and like Upward he won the Howe Prize. Like Upward, he felt that the atmosphere at Cambridge and perhaps at his college in particular where I. A. Richards was a fellow, emphasized language and criticism rather than actual writing. He left Cambridge after one year, a decision he always regretted. He was happier at Repton than Upward. Though bullied as a poet, he was eventually popular as an excellent tennis player and cricketer. For the school's quarter centenary he wrote a sequence of poems, 'Revisited Waters', that celebrated the happiness of his last eighteen months there. Yet he clearly had mixed feelings about the school, demonstrating how powerful that experience can be. In 1927 he was living in Swansea, employed as a teller, which he hated, in a bank where his father worked as well. Suffering a nervous breakdown, he travelled to Repton, attended chapel, and then burst into Fisher's study, physically assaulting him and accusing him of 'destroying youth'. Upward recalled that he told Fisher he was taking over the school. 'This crisis brought about what Watkins called a "revolution in sensibility"'. From that point on his life's work would be preoccupied with 'the conquest of Time; by which he meant the immortalization of his memories of Repton and the validation of all that he had known and valued there'.[44]

It is hard to tell how deeply Upward's youthful rebellion went at the time. Yet in retrospect it had been extremely important, what he regarded as the turning point in his life, what made him a rebel. He wrote to Isherwood in November 1922 when he had just arrived at Corpus. 'All institutions are damnable . . . Yes, Cambridge is damnable – as you anticipated – but in rather a different way. My God, if Repton was unmitigated Hell then Cambridge is insidious Hell!! Everything is so "nice", comfortable and perfect up here . . . History, History, Hysteria! It is hell. Nevertheless, mind you get a scholarship in history and come up here . . . I am glad that you are initiating a rebellion at Hell the greater. Wreck it! Smash it! Prostrate and prostitute it!' And then the following month he wrote: 'My bitterness against Repton can never die, but time has a mellowing influence and disgust fades into the mist of indifference . . . I believe that all classes and societies of men are despicable but that individuals are almost all lovable & human. I am never happy unless I am either hating or loving; here there is nothing to hate, so one has to fall back on love'.[45] Either while still at Repton or when at Cambridge he further reflected on the nature of the public school. 'The fault of the public school system consists primarily in its contempt for originality . . . The system, because it is suited to the majority, cannot be condemned. Fools flourish and are raised to mediocrity; the genius is persecuted and his individuality is often extinguished . . . Those who suffer most are the boys who excel in compliance with the system. House-prefects come under this category, and more particularly those whose one ambition has consisted in desire for vacuous authority'.[46]

Upward continued the career path expected from a member of his class. It was far from universal then that those who went to strong secondary schools, such as Repton, would then go on to university. They might go directly into business, financial or otherwise, particularly if there was a family business, or possibly into the military. And of course it was only a few years since that they would have risked their lives, as expected and required from the well-off young, as officers during the First World War. But particularly the brighter students were likely to go to university. Upward sat the entrance exam in December 1921 for Corpus Christi College, Cambridge, and succeeded in winning a scholarship. But he had some time before beginning at Cambridge in the autumn of 1922. This was spent mostly in France, including five months in Rouen from March until July, a period that he remembered as among the very happiest of his life. Before going to France after leaving Repton at the end of 1921 he was at home, where he asserted his religious freedom against the wishes of his mother. As he later wrote to Isherwood, 'I have not viewed the interior of a religious emporium since I left Hell'.[47] In Rouen he lived at Le Vert Logis, run by a retired schoolmaster, where he worked on his French. During this period he also went on an Alpine walking tour in the summer along the Swiss-French border with three other Reptonians, including Isherwood

CHAPTER 2: REPTON

Edward photographed in Rouen

(his first trip abroad) and Charles Smyth, who was already at Corpus from Repton and would go on to a distinguished career as a historian of the church as well as a canon and rector of St Margaret's, the prominent 'parish' church for the Houses of Parliament. He was the sort of 'official' person whom Upward disliked. The third was Geoffrey Kingsford, who appears in Lions and Shadows as Queensbridge. The trip was led and arranged by Smith, their highly regarded history teacher. (For some reason Isherwood eliminates Smith in his account of the trip in Lions and Shadows.) Isherwood and Upward decided that it was too conventional to be impressed by mountains, and in any case Mont Blanc was covered by clouds. But when they saw it the next morning, they couldn't help but be overwhelmed by the 'arrival' of the mountain, conquering their youthful cynicism. Isherwood provides a quite ecstatic description of their trip in Lions and Shadows: the joy of walking along the mountains and lakes. The high point is when Upward reads him what he regards as his best poem so far, 'Stranger in Spring', of nine stanzas. And Isherwood agrees with his judgement, that he is really cut out to be a poet. While at Rouen Upward wrote twenty-five poems. The sense of gloom that he had felt at Repton left him during this glorious period in France. Rouen was a liberation and a discovery; he loved being in the city of Flaubert and Maupassant and reading Charles Baudelaire there. The two of them made a return trip to the same area in 1926.

Also extremely important at Rouen was not only that Upward was writing poems but that he started to write stories. In his papers in the British Library there survive drafts of some of these earliest efforts. There is a quite short one about a dinner party at a bishop's house at which Christ, dressed in greyish-white rags, appears. He has some wine and bread and then leaves. Another one concerns a dinner party where a schoolmaster is a guest. He remarks, ironically considering Upward's future career, 'Schoolmastering is monotonous beyond words; it is sheer murder of intellect and keenness.

CHAPTER 2: REPTON

Christopher Isherwood's Lions and Shadows, 1938

When I was young I determined that I would not give way to monotony. My eyes were open. I had read Charles Baudelaire and believed, as he did, that monotony is worse than all immorality, all outrage – worse even than death. And yet I went the way of every schoolmaster. I fell into the snare and was held fast'. He also started a novel about Repton, *Equipment before Voyage: The Romance of a Public School Education*. His central figure is Alan Hardayne, a prefiguring of Alan Sebrill in his trilogy of novels, *The Spiral Ascent*. Alan is at a school called Purleigh. His father is very unsympathetic to his desire to moon around on the South Downs: 'What he wants is a good dose of public school'. The narrator remarks about public school boys: 'They are far too busily occupied with games and with sexual problems . . . Friendship was not allowed here: they specialised in immorality. Alan felt pleased by the ironic cynicism of his thought'.[48]

Repton had prepared Upward for the next step in his life: Cambridge. It had also shaped his future life. As he remarked in an interview in 1980: 'By the time I'd left Repton I'd been marked for life, as it were. I think everybody who goes to a public school, the large ones, is, and I think it's been the major influence in everything that's happened to me since. But by the time I left Repton I was a sort of conscious decadent. In other words, one did the opposite of whatever one thought was the right sort of public school thing to do, and so when I went to Cambridge I was determined to cling on to this. I didn't work. In those days one didn't'.[49] Repton had provided him with the education of an English gentleman. It had turned him into a rebel against the system. It had introduced him to Christopher Isherwood. There he became a poet. And at Rouen he began to write fiction.

Chapter 3: Cambridge

IN MANY WAYS Cambridge is the best-known moment in Edward Upward's life. Although the idea of that imaginary town, Mortmere, had been brewing in his and Isherwood's minds while at Repton, it was at Cambridge that it came into full bloom and marked a significant moment in English literary history, the shaping of a new approach. It was an aspect of modernism, a beginning of the most characteristic writing of the 1930s. And for Upward himself, whatever he might eventually think of it as a perhaps youthful folly, it remained an extremely important aspect of his writing. Although elements of Mortmereish fantasy were much less present in Isherwood, it was also significant for his literary career. And there is no question, although the degree is hard to assess, that through friendship it would form an important part of W. H. Auden's early sensibility. Although Upward and Isherwood did not know about surrealism, which was becoming part of cultural life in France around the same time, their invention of Mortmere has been taken as the precursor of its English version: fantasy conveying a greater reality, the 'real' reality behind the apparent reality, a crucial element in modernism. Commenting on surrealism years later in a notebook, Upward remarked that it was a method that he and Isherwood used long before they had heard about it: 'Surrealism – at its best – tries to create the most startling effects possible, regardless of objective reality'.[1] What is not mentioned perhaps because it is so obvious is that Mortmere also may draw upon the frequent standard situation in a classic English detective story. What would appear to be a totally respectable English village or country house has unspeakable events taking place just below the surface. In the detective story order is restored at the end. In Mortmere it is not. It was also a perverted version of the world of *Alice in Wonderland*. The Mortmere stories were full of the obscene imaginings of youth with the various characters representing twisted components of a village: Religion, Sport, County Society, Education.

It may also be a version of 'tea-tabling'. Upward coined that term as applicable to the writings of E. M. Forster, inspired by his reading of *Howards End* in November 1925 when he acquired both it as well as *Where Angels Fear to Tread* and *The Longest Journey*.[2] As with many literary positions Upward held, he would also express doubts about them. The decorous taking of tea covered but ultimately did not hide dramatic and traumatic events and strongly held beliefs. Upward's vision of English life encompassed both the genteel tea table and more absolute beliefs and actions, both good and bad. He felt that his writings were a nightmare about the English. Yet the tea table was also a sign of gentility, of being a gentleman. In 1929 Upward noted: 'The teatable must go into the fire. It was a justification of my failure to extract myself from a situation which I loathe. I am forced to be a teatable – does it follow therefore that the teatable is valid? I'm not sure that it doesn't. Probably the teatable is the best solution. Be moderate, be mild, condemn nothing and accept nothing absolutely. Yes, but I am only able to adopt this attitude because subliminally I have strong absolute beliefs. Atheism, free love, communism . . . The teatable denies all absolute names. Don't burn it'.[3]

CHAPTER 3: CAMBRIDGE

In *Lions and Shadows* the concept is presented in a rather benign way. 'Instead of trying to screw all his [Forster's] scenes up to the highest possible pitch, he tones them down until they sound like mothers' meeting gossip'.[4] It was part of the nature of English writing. Change often happens in England on a seemingly small scale. Small events frequently have significant ramifications in English novels. This may have rather conservative implications as in Macaulay's famous peroration at the time of the Great Reform Act of 1832: 'Reform, that you may preserve'. It may also be one explanation why in modern times there is unlikely to be revolution in England. Yet in Mortmere the contrast between appearance and reality could be stark, violent and possibly absurd. In literary terms, Mortmere was the most important part of their time in Cambridge.

Upward and Isherwood took the examination for admission to Corpus Christi College, Cambridge, at the same time in December 1921. It sounds quite formidable with several history papers, French and Latin translations and an English essay. Charles Smyth, now in his first year at Corpus, showed them around Cambridge. Upward won the £60 Mawson Scholarship and Isherwood a £40 one. Isherwood did not come up until a year later, appropriately, as he was a year behind Upward at Repton. He returned to Cambridge in December 1922 to take the examination again, this time winning the top scholarship of £80. Upward was very anxious that Isherwood join him at Corpus, writing to him the following March, 'If you were not coming up I should deliberately get myself sent down'.[5] Upward matriculated at the college in October 1922. At the time, most Cambridge colleges had comparatively few students, about a hundred and forty undergraduates at Corpus and eleven fellows as well as the Master. In some ways he liked the atmosphere of the college. 'Corpus was more liberally run than some [colleges]. Some other Colleges were more like a public school, but we were given a great deal of liberty – which was abused'.[6] Upward had a part-time position as a sub-librarian at the college library which he inherited from Smyth. His task was to open the library at a certain hour in the morning to show visitors its famous collection of illuminated books given to the college by Archbishop Parker. But he lost the post through oversleeping! In retrospect he felt that he had spent most of his first year in drinking and playing poker. He and Isherwood had specialized in history at Repton, inspired by Smith's teaching, and both read history at Cambridge. But after doing Part One in the History Tripos (the Cambridge general examinations at the end of the second year and third year), Upward in his third and last year read English. He felt that Smith was a better teacher of history than the Cambridge dons. In his view they dwelt too much on details without consideration for the larger picture. Years later he denounced history at Cambridge because of 'its fact-grubbing passionlessness, its dull indifference to human suffering, its lack of love, generosity, beauty and poetry'.[7] He nevertheless and perhaps paradoxically liked his history supervisors, conservative as they and the college itself might be: there was Kenneth Pickthorn, only eleven years older than he, a constitutional and Tudor historian who later served as a member of Parliament for the university until the seat was abolished in 1950. He was also fond of the other history Fellow, also staunchly conservative, Sir Geoffrey Butler, who went into Parliament as well. He liked Sir Edwin Hoskins, Baronet, who taught divinity and was dean of the chapel and librarian. Upward did badly in Part One of the History Tripos, receiving a Third. For his third year he had to be sent for supervisions at Pembroke next door, as no Corpus fellow was an English don. Even though he had mumps while taking Part Two of the Tripos in English, he did fairly well, receiving a 2–1.[8] In some ways he had quite a traditional student experience. Yet at the same time he regarded Cambridge like Repton, as a version of hell, an accursed institution.

Isherwood's relation with the exams was much more notorious. He had wanted to change to English early on but the college wouldn't let him until after he had taken Part One of the History Tripos, particularly as he had the top history scholarship. At the end of his first year in the preliminary informal exam, relying on the history he had learned at Repton, he received a 2–1 rather than the First expected of the leading history scholar. The situation was dire in his second year when he was faced with the formal Part One exam. There was no way, he felt, that he could receive a First. If he crammed he might get a Second, but that was beneath him. And he was very unhappy at the idea that Upward would no longer be in Cambridge the next year, so he did practically no academic work, although he did need to write essays for his supervisions. He frequently just copied out what Upward had written the previous year. Presumably they had different supervisors or the supervisor didn't notice! Isherwood's mother visualized his becoming a history don, and his growing dislike of her was likely to be another reason he was turning against his studies. He decided to defy the authorities by sitting the sets of three-hour papers that made up the examinations but answering the questions either with a few lines of irrelevant material, such as commenting on the ugliness of the room where

CHAPTER 3: CAMBRIDGE

'*Eddie on the Cam!* 11.08.23'

the examination was taking place, or by composing some lines of verse, perhaps a sonnet in response to a question about Charles II. When the examiners read his papers, he was summoned back to Cambridge. As a punishment, Upward later thought, Isherwood was not only expelled from the college but his name was also removed from its records. Isherwood depicts the interview with the college tutor, William Spens, as gentler; he was allowed to withdraw his name from the college register.⁹ Years later, when he became quite famous, he was back in the college's good graces and his name restored. Upward supported him in this escapade and enjoyed its subversive nature but in retrospect regretted to a degree that he did not discourage him. According to Isherwood, Upward didn't actually believe that he would do it.

Upward's greatest interest at Cambridge was his own writing. In 1922 he abandoned his novel with its presumably ironic subtitle: *Equipment before Voyage: The Romance of a Public School Education*. His greater commitment was still to his poetry, although he did in 1923 try his hand at a play, *After Six Years*, about a curator who wanted to burn down his museum. Preserved in his papers are innumerable drafts of poems as well as notes on his history readings. He was beginning to write stories. He also submitted poems to the *Cambridge Review*, one a Repton poem; three were published. In 1923 a further three poems appeared in *Benedict*, a college publication, one a reprint of a Repton poem. A poem was printed in both the 1924 and 1925 issues of a Cambridge chapbook, *Fanfreluche*. The 1925 poem had a characteristic opening line: 'How desolate the bridge against the sky'. Two poems were in the *Cambridge Mercury*, another local publication, in 1924. Isherwood thought sufficiently highly of one, 'Introduction', originally entitled 'To the Historian', to reprint it in *Lions and Shadows*. The first stanza of the twenty-eight-line poem combines history and poetry: 'You who must ponder cause and act / Historian, from the quag of fact / Search out, propound a cause for this – / The cross of life we bear who miss / Life's truth, and grope with baffled hands / About a stage none understands'.¹⁰

It was also in Cambridge that he began to write notebooks on the same day that Isherwood also started to keep a journal. Both he and Isherwood were partially inspired to record their thoughts by the so-called futility poems that they jointly composed at the time – 'twenty-one and nothing done'.¹¹ Or as he wrote in the notebook on 6 November, 'I remember that I am twenty-one and have done nothing'. They also modelled their journals on the recently published work by W. N. P. Barbellion, *The Journal of a Disappointed Man*. They had considered writing a joint book about their literary lives, *The Diary of Two Shapes*. Upward's notebooks were not diaries (he did not write in them every day). Although he did occasionally record events, they were more reflections and thoughts. Their dominant theme was his struggle to be a writer. In the ensuing seventy-five volumes of uniform size continuing until 2002, seven years before his death, can be found what one might call a dialogue, a conversation, a conflict, about the relationship of art and politics. The first volume covered three years from September 1924 to September 1927. He started recording his thoughts close to the time of his twenty-first birthday, the day of achieving one's 'majority'. That occasion tends to be taken quite seriously and festively in England, although there is no evidence that Upward had any special celebration. It's striking that his early entries are rather sweeping generalizations: 'Perfection is my aim'. 'I am in love with all beautiful women, and in my imagination I believe my love is returned'. 'I have one aim only, that is, to write down my emotional life in poetry'. Influenced by Villon and Baudelaire, he wished for his poems to have a sense of gloom, a theme going back to his Repton days.

CHAPTER 3: CAMBRIDGE

Edward in Christopher Isherwood's room at Cambridge, 1923, photographed by Isherwood

Perhaps somewhat perversely he was worried at first that Cambridge would not be sufficiently awful and hence would not inspire him. Years later in *No Home but the Struggle* he wrote, 'This really meant I was already confident that Cambridge wouldn't prevent me from writing the kind of poetry I had been thinking of'.[12] In his journal he noted: 'I have hopes that this term will be different from others. It will be filled with inspiration, passion and light'. 'My art is still in the womb. Endurance to deliver it. Nothing else matters'. In the same volume but some time later, in December 1925, he wrote about a potential biographer. 'I wonder what inferences my biographer (if I should happen to have one) would draw from this book if he should happen to discover it. "An intellectual prig and a misanthropist". But as a matter of fact I am warm-hearted and eager to love people. The biographer would have made the common mistake of confusing ideas with life'. Or as he had written the previous July (the choice of words is significant): 'What a cad you appear in this diary. In life, however, you are a gentleman'.[13]

His most notable public achievement at Cambridge was in the spring of 1924 while he was still reading history. He won the Chancellor's Medal for English Verse for a poem about the Buddha, the set topic. Six others competed for the prize. He read out part of his winning entry on 7 June at one of the ceremonies at the end of the academic year. Years later he wrote to his son Christopher about the event. 'You are right in thinking that one of the few things that brought my parents together in their later years was their pride in my writing. They came up to Cambridge to hear me read a passage of my Chancellor's Medal poem in the Senate House. (I think). I remember that my knees were trembling violently though (luckily) not visibly but my voice was firm when I read'.[14]

His poem was also printed in *Prolusiones Academicae* along with other prizewinners of the year, including essays by two men who went on to eminent academic careers, T. R. Henn the literary critic, and Herbert Butterfield the historian. There were also prizes in Greek and Latin. The poetry prize had been established in 1813 and was awarded most years, although there were considerable gaps when presumably no submission was deemed worthy, or for some other reason the competition was not held. Most of the winners are now forgotten names or distinguished in other ways. Thomas Babington Macaulay, Alfred Tennyson and Edward Bulwer-Lytton were among the winners in the nineteenth century. It was also won by academics who went on to distinction in other fields, such as Goldsworthy Lowes Dickinson and A. C. Pigou. Rupert Brooke and Siegfried Sassoon submitted entries, unsuccessfully. Lytton Strachey received the medal in 1902 for a poem on Ely Cathedral. There was then a twenty-year gap; the next time the prize was awarded was 1922. Until comparatively recently a topic would be set for the aspirants to submit a poem on anonymously. Years later Upward remembered that he had consulted only two books for background, one about Hindu and Buddhist myths and the other on religious systems of the world. He was very optimistic about winning.[15] The poem is long, about two hundred lines, and presents the Buddha's life in elegant verses with an emphasis on his earlier days. It begins: 'Deeper in time than the mind understands / Were shaped the crumbling contours of earth's lands, / And from a wilderness of mist and night / The still Himálayas rose in scarps of light'. And ends: 'Once in Benares' Deer Park when the day / Waked the still town, came in the blossoming way / A teacher who had knowledge of life's land, / And spoke this word, that men might understand'. Winning the medal gave him the right, unlike other third-year students, to continue to live in college. It was also commemorated at Repton by his name being listed on a plaque on the wall with others who won honours, more commonly athletic, at university. Isherwood clearly felt winning the prize was a form of selling out, as Upward found in his room a note from him that was not one of congratulations:

CHAPTER 3: CAMBRIDGE

'Goodbye my poor Hynd'.[16] (Hynd was Upward's fictional name in Mortmere.) On the other hand Isherwood wanted to be present when he read out the poem but Upward forbade him from attending. There is a nice irony that the poem should have been about the Buddha, considering that years later Isherwood became committed to Vedanta and published the poem in the magazine *Vedanta and the West* in 1950, as well as reading it to a Vedantist congregation in Los Angeles.

The poem can also be seen to mark Upward's transition to the study of English. The 1920s were a very exciting time for English studies at Cambridge, when they were established in their modern form. The most important aspect of Upward taking up the subject was his attending I. A. Richards' lectures. He found them intensely interesting and he regarded Richards as 'a great man'.[17] Up until then, writing poetry had been his primary commitment. He had been fairly prolific and had won prizes both at Repton and Cambridge. In retrospect the activities at Cambridge were less likely to be noticed than the more glamorous poetic ferment at Oxford later in the decade. It was with the Oxford poets that the somewhat older Upward and Isherwood would be associated: W. H. Auden, Stephen Spender, C. Day Lewis, Rex Warner and Louis MacNeice. There were promising poets at Cambridge at the same time: William Empson, Kathleen Raine, Richard Eberhart, Julian Bell and John Lehmann. Of them, only Lehmann was associated with the Auden group. The Auden circle would go on to be what might loosely be construed as a movement, what was held to be the most characteristic British writing of the 1930s. At Cambridge the most conspicuous and certainly the most influential literary event was the revolution in the practice of criticism led by I. A. Richards. Indeed one could go so far as to call it the birth of modern literary criticism. Richards had been recruited as a teacher for the newly fashioned English option. The subject arose out of the more philological traditions of Cambridge and more specifically from the Medieval and Modern Language Tripos. Mansfield Forbes and H. M. Chadwick were teachers of Anglo-Saxon, but nevertheless they were moving in the direction that English should be taught more as literature than as language. It might have been a reaction after the First World War against the older study of language associated with a Germanic tradition of scholarship. E. M. W. Tillyard and Arthur Quiller-Couch, the popular professor of English, played important roles in this development. But certainly a crucial, perhaps the most crucial, figure was Richards. He had read moral sciences at Cambridge, taking his degree in 1915. He had returned there in 1918 in order to study medicine and psychology. But he was about to give this up and was considering becoming a mountain guide when Forbes asked him to be a lecturer in English, to give courses on the modern novel and principles of literary criticism. Richards published three immensely influential books in the 1920s, *The Meaning of Meaning* in 1923 with C. K. Ogden, *Principles of Literary Criticism* in 1924 and *Practical Criticism* in 1929. They emphasized the analysis of text, shorn of its biographical implications.

Although Isherwood was still officially studying history, he went to Richards' lectures and described them in *Lions and Shadows*:

> Poets, ordered Mr. Richards, were to reflect aspects of the World-Picture. Poetry wasn't a holy flame, a fire-bird from the

moon; it was a group of interrelated stimuli acting upon the ocular nerves, the semi-circular canals, the brain, the solar plexus, the digestive and sexual organs ... We became behaviourists, materialists, atheists. In our conversation, we substituted the world 'emotive' for the word beautiful . . . But if Mr. Richards enormously stimulated us, he plunged us, also, into the profoundest gloom. It seemed to us that everything we had valued would have to be scrapped.[18]

Upward went to the lectures in his third year, and they had a profound and disconcerting effect upon him. He didn't agree that the emotional truths to be found in poetry could not refer to anything outside of the poems themselves. He regarded Richards as 'an amazing genius' with whom he profoundly disagreed even as he was heavily influenced by him.[19] Hearing his lectures led him largely to abandon poetry despite the accolade of having won the Chancellor's Medal the previous year. He describes the message of Richards' lectures in *No Home but the Struggle*: 'They dealt with poetry not just as something achieved in the past but as something still to be achieved in the present . . . He thought that poetry ought not to be regarded as referring to anything in the external world'.[20] Through Richards' influence he and Isherwood read T. S. Eliot more carefully and became more interested in psychology, reading Freud's *Introductory Lectures on Psycho-Analysis*, recently published in English. At the same time Richards convinced him that he was, as a poet, too concerned with rhythm and words and not enough with meaning. At one point he spoke to Richards after a lecture but their exchange was not a success; he felt he was being somewhat patronized. Among his miscellaneous papers in the British Library along with drafts of various poems there are thirty questions for I. A. Richards, written quite a few years later and presumably never sent. They nevertheless suggest why Richards led him to give up writing poetry. He still aimed to think poetically and to aspire to lead the poetic life and even write an occasional poem. The first question was: 'If a feeling, in contradistinction to a thought, is merely a state of mind and does not imply an object (as you assert on p. 330 of 'Practical Criticism') are we to assume that it has no physical basis in the nervous system?' And the twenty-sixth: 'Isn't it plain that if poetry is nonsense that criticism of it is also nonsense, and if poetry is a divine revelation then criticism of it cannot pretend to be scientific?'[21] The questions concerning Richards and the nature of poetry continued to plague him. He did not feel that he had resolved them until the early 1930s when he read Lenin's *Materialism and Empirio-Criticism*. For him it made clear the existence of the real world that, according to his understanding, Richards felt was not a necessary component of poetry.[22]

What was Upward's life like at Corpus? For his first two years he lived in rooms on the ground floor near the entrance to the college where he enjoyed passing drinks to a policeman on the street. In his third year he moved to a room in the Old Court that was allegedly haunted by the college ghost. Who were his friends? One, Boris Ord, was older (born in 1897) and had already studied at the Royal College of Music. He came to Corpus as an organ scholar and took a Mus.B. degree. In 1923 he went across the street with a fellowship at King's, eventually to be a legendary director of the King's choir. He greatly

CHAPTER 3: CAMBRIDGE

Corpus Christi College, Cambridge, Old Court, with 'Eddie's rooms, 1924–1925' indicated

enriched the musical life of Corpus before departing. There were also a fair number of Reptonians at the college with whom Upward was friendly in varying degrees. Of course his greatest friend was Isherwood, who credited Upward rather than Cambridge with his education. Or as Upward put it, they educated each other through endless talk, reading to one another various texts and the exchange of what they were writing: poems and, of growing importance, short fictions. Despite regarding Cambridge as hell, in July 1956 he went to an old boys' dinner at the college, although he didn't enjoy it: 'A painful experience'. Yet he must have been pleased when the following December his son Christopher won a major scholarship at the college.[23] Had he re-established contact in his son's interest? As with Repton, the college was quite proud of his having achieved a certain reputation as a writer, particularly in his later years. After his death, the college bought 112 books from his library, including

CHAPTER 3: CAMBRIDGE

multiple copies of his writings. He was also asked, perhaps partially on the basis of being one of the few survivors of his period, to contribute to a book about the college, published in 2003.[24] As is probably usual in such pieces, he emphasized the social rather than the intellectual. He enjoyed the pleasures of youth. He played poker. He went out a bit with town girls and recorded that he managed to kiss one called Milly, who may have been the first girl he kissed. He described the event to Isherwood in embarrassingly purple prose but perhaps he is being ironic. 'I have tasted her lips, and felt the smooth contour of undulating surfaces'.[25] He was also pursuing another town girl, Doreen, as well as others, at least according to his fictional account of these days: Doris, Edna and Molly. He remarked in his notebook on 31 October 1924, 'My relations with women are the mere experiments of a boy – sickly but innocent'.

When Upward had arrived in the autumn of 1922, Charles Smyth took him under his wing, a particular kindness as Upward disliked him and he was the model for the villain Laily in the Mortmere stories. The name came from a worm in an English ballad and may have dated back to his and Isherwood's days at Repton and been based on a housemaster there. Smyth may stand for what they regarded as the loathsomeness of the public school ethos. Years later Upward commented: 'I don't know why we had it in for him so much. He was so earnest and he was also tricky... He canvassed for people to vote for him for the Union – that's illegal. We just didn't like him. I don't know why we made such a bogey of him'.[26] Nevertheless he helped Upward's career in a social sense, judging with that acute English social awareness of class nuance that he wasn't quite up to the grandest Corpus organization, the Chess Club, but rather the one next down in rank, 'The Young Visiters', named in honour of the novel by the nine-year-old Daisy Ashford, recently published in 1919. In order to join it one had to answer questions on the rather cloying text about the adventures of the seventeen-year-old Ethel, her admirer and eventual husband Bernard and Mr Salteena. It all sounds rather camp. According to Upward, Smyth felt he was eligible for membership because of his good looks, that he had been to a public school, was a good soccer player and had a history scholarship. 'He tactfully avoided alluding to my lack of good family connections'. The club was devoted to dining and drinking. Unfortunately Upward remarked to some of his fellow members that he found the club rather silly. This was a factor in an episode that Upward remembered vividly. (The violence associated with such clubs at Oxford and Cambridge was depicted in a recent film, *Posh*, based on a play about a dining club at Oxford. It all begins with some decorum but ends with extraordinary mayhem and destruction.) The 'poshocracy' was Isherwood and Upward's term for the grander members of college, some of whom of course were members of 'The Young Visiters'. The 'poshocracy', also known as 'The Other Side', was the enemy. In an event seared into Upward's memory they invaded his rooms after a college feast at the end of term and wrecked quite a few of his possessions. Earlier in the evening Upward and Isherwood had visualized themselves standing on a table in Hall during the feast, shouting out a phrase from Villon, *'J'en appelle!'* that they thought of as a challenge to the enemy. According to Isherwood, Upward participated in the mayhem in his room, as drunk as anyone else, writing verse on the starched dress shirts of the 'poshocracy'. As they were flipping butter all about the room, Upward put butter on a broom and, using that, spread it on the backs of the 'enemy's' dinner jackets. According to Upward, Isherwood did nothing to stem the trashing of his friend's set and spent his time chatting calmly with Boris Ord. Upward was so furious that he wrote a note saying they were no longer friends but then tore it up in the morning. Isherwood went back to Upward's room the next morning to discover Upward dozing in a chair, still furious at him, informing him about the letter he hadn't sent. But they quickly made it up.[27]

The two years Isherwood and Upward were together at Cambridge were extremely important for both of them. In Isherwood's first year in particular they spent most of their days and a good part of their nights together. As Upward wrote, 'I respect him and often love him'.[28] Their determination was to be artists. They created their own private world although they continued to function in the public world of Cambridge more than they might care to admit. Through their class and education they were fully part of a society that they came to loathe. At this point their attitude had no political dimension. They had no interest in politics, regarding it all as being bogus, and did not bother to read newspapers. Other than being a 'natural' rebel and having a profound conviction that the entire system, as represented by Repton and Cambridge, was thoroughly corrupt, it is a little unclear why Upward hated his world so. It had treated him well. At Repton he had hated its institutions: fagging, beating, the chapel, the OTC, the profound sense of hierarchy, the hypocrisy of being 'clean and upstanding' while at the same time there was an atmosphere, not surprisingly, of sexual raunchiness and homosexuality. Yet he had received a good education and enjoyed sports. So many aspects of the school, particularly fagging, represented for him England's class system, which he came to detest so passionately that he believed it must be overthrown to be replaced by a better world. A revenge against the world that he and Isherwood saw as perpetuated at Cambridge was their joint invention of Mortmere. It was also known as 'The Other Town', reached through a door on Silver Street in Cambridge that they discovered on one of their evening walks; or as 'The Rats' Hostel', inspired by looking down into the Cam from the Garret Hostel Bridge. At first they wanted to call their imaginary town Mortlake but as that was a real English place they didn't use it. Surprisingly they didn't seem to dwell on the implications of 'Mortmere' meaning 'dead mother'. Or perhaps they didn't mention it as it was so obviously Freudian, for both at this point rather hated their mothers, Isherwood even more than Upward. Upward wrote to Isherwood in an undated letter some years later, 'Mortmere is of course Cambridge in everything but name'.[29] The darkness of Cambridge's streets, the penetrating cold and damp of its being close to the Fens, contributed to the necessary atmosphere of gloom. At the same time Mortmere was an escape from Cambridge. It had elements of works from their childhood, *Alice in Wonderland*, *Grimms' Fairy Tales* and Beatrix Potter, but given a more sinister twist, perhaps under the influence of Edgar Allan Poe.

They created the world out of which their literary careers flowed. The stories were a way to create a private universe that removed them from the conventional surround of their being English gentlemen at the university. The characters who lived in Mortmere were caricatures of the English. There was the Reverend Welken, the vulgarian Ronald Gunball, subject to delirium tremens, and the headmaster Gustave Shreeve, among others. Isherwood and Upward thought of it as a sort of anarchist paradise but also a hell. It was unpredictable, fantastic and violent with elements of pornography and sexual perversion. It was an 'imaginative game' in which to try out their writing skills. The titles of the stories were both gloomy and somewhat adolescent: 'The Leviathan of the Urinals', 'The Horror in the Tower', 'The Loathly Succubus'. Isherwood's 'The Horror in the Tower' tells of an aristocrat who contrives a lavatory so he can eat the excrement of his guests. Upward's Leviathan is a creature who when urinated upon in a public urinal grows to be a monster. In a sense their writings were an expression of the English fascination with lavatory humour. In a poem about the Laily worm, Upward wrote: 'Always in Cambridge town it seems to me / Morning's like midnight in a cemetery; / Beneath these sooty spires that prop the sky / Death's sordid bones and pashy ordures lie'.[30] Laily also stood for the study of history that Isherwood and Upward came profoundly to dislike. In 1953, in an action he came to regret, Upward destroyed most of his own Mortmere stories, saving the copies of Isherwood's. Even so, quite a bit was preserved, resulting in the publication in 1994 of *The Mortmere Stories* with an introduction by the editor of Isherwood's diaries, Katherine Bucknell.

It is a vision of what the world might really be like, although presented in a rather juvenile way. The point of the fantasy was not to escape the real world but better to understand it. Here we have the quaint 'typical' English village with the squire, the minister, the pub landlord, the headmaster and headmistress. But the chances are that they are all mad. The fantasy behind the apparent reality is in fact the greater reality of what life is really like. Perhaps the authors were both influenced by having brothers who in Isherwood's case (Richard) was eccentric and nonfunctional and in Upward's case (Laurence) schizophrenic. The power and the fantasy behind the apparent reality were to be found later, for instance, in the plays by Auden and Isherwood. Upward and Isherwood became even closer friends than at Repton without being, apparently, sexually interested in one another. Upward approved of Isherwood's homosexuality as a form of rebellion. They seemed to take great pleasure in seeing enemies all about them and imputing, say, to a casual remark by a shop assistant or a waiter the most sinister implications. Mortmere was a place that they would use as the location for their stories. They would continue to do so for some time, with perhaps the climax being Upward's 'The Railway Accident', written in 1928. In theory but less in practice they wished to rebel against everything that was respectable while at the same time seeming to be highly respectable young men, Isherwood in terms of class somewhat more elevated than Upward.

They would write stories late into the night and leave them, frequently incomplete, on the table in the other's sitting room to be found in the morning. Upward favoured an atmosphere of gloom, as in his poems, supported by his reading of Baudelaire and Sir Thomas Browne and in the dark furnishings of his rooms: a skull, a black lampshade, and prints by Dürer, the favourite being his *Melencolia I*. Yet the writing of the stories gave them both great pleasure; they were having a wonderful time with the exuberance of youth, despite at times adopting a lugubrious tone. Isherwood was also at work on a novel, *Lions and Shadows*, never finished but its title adopted as the title of his memoir of these years. It was clearly a

Degree day at Cambridge, 23 June 1925: Edward with a friend, E. Woodward

phrase that Isherwood was very fond of, having picked it up from C. E. Montague, who had experienced and wrote about the First World War. Isherwood was somewhat obsessed by the war, the 'Test' that he had missed and that had killed his father. Montague had written about his contemporaries as 'arrant lovers of living, mighty hunters of lions or shadows'.[31] In a letter to Upward from London in March 1923 Isherwood wrote: 'London is a strange world of illusion. It has an extraordinary kind of attraction – a sort of heedless haste towards nothing – fit for mighty hunters of lions or shadows'.[32] In the Mortmere stories Isherwood was Starn and Upward Hynd and they were professional pornographers. They were most prolific in writing the stories in the winter and spring of 1925 when Upward should have been studying hard for his English exams and Isherwood for Part One of the History Tripos. 'Christopher and I have been writing Hynd & Starn stories – he about shit eating and I about necrophiles'.[33] Upward's story 'The Little Hotel' was about a brothel for necrophiles. It was modelled on Conan Doyle's Sherlock Holmes story 'The Red-Headed League'. Isherwood's is in the later publication of Mortmere stories and is quite memorable in its vividness. In 1926 Upward wrote to Isherwood about these two stories: 'We are the authors of the Horror in the Tower and The Little Hotel. Perhaps we will not have lived in vain . . . *It is always the same town.* Whether they wear surplices or corduroy breeches or black velvet coats, whether they swear art's shaking flame or a child's rocking horse whether they live in Kensington, Romford or Cornwall . . . the same boiling fraud'.[34]

In a letter written from Romford in April 1924 during the long Easter break between terms Upward sent Isherwood a poem, 'The

Air', a sonnet inscribed to Laily, signed Edfu. He then went on to write: 'Laily shall be called a Lava-Tory, and his doctrine Lava-Toryism ... Alas my poor Starn I miss you sadly, I am cut off from humanity and emotional truth'.[35] They drew a map of Mortmere, a village on the Atlantic. There lived the Reverend Welken, who had had an affair with a choirboy and was busy manufacturing angels; and also the drunk, Ronald Gunball. The Watcher in Spanish was the conscience of the place and others were listed as 'The Persons of the Tragedy'.[36] Except for the Watcher the inhabitants of Mortmere were either insane or monsters. It was what the authors regarded as the true nature of English society.

Upward kept returning to Mortmere throughout his life in a rather love-hate relationship. The surviving stories weren't published until 1994 although 'The Railway Accident' had established itself some years earlier. In 1953 he opposed their publication, feeling that they were too juvenile, writing to Isherwood, 'They are really no more than dim sketches faintly hinting at the tremendous marvel of the Mortmere in our hearts'.[37] It was the same year in which he burned his copies of his own stories.[38] In January 1959 he considered writing a Mortmere journal called 'The Last Days' set on the Isle of Wight. In the 1960s he had the idea of writing a Mortmere-like novel. 'It would be a satirical parody of the modern pornographic & sadistic novel ... It would be about a gerontophile, who wd be an ironical double of the hero of Lolita'.[39] Some years later in August 1977 he envisioned a series of letters between Starn and Hynd, Isherwood's and his alter egos in the Mortmere stories.[40] Yet in the late 1980s when the idea was being bruited about of publishing the surviving stories, he resisted the idea.[41] In an interview in 1993 he regretted his later rejection of fantasy yet seemed to discount the Mortmere writing at the same time. 'I did feel at the time we wrote Mortmere that it wasn't the real thing, it wasn't really serious. In one way – well, one could write absolutely irresponsibly and you could do exactly what you want, could experiment. So one learnt a bit about writing doing it. We spent an awful amount of our time at Cambridge when we should have been studying writing those stories for one another'.[42] Over the years he kept thinking about writing stories or novels that returned to Mortmere. There were certainly elements of that world in his late short stories. In the late 1980s John Lehmann was in touch with him for his reminiscences, particularly about Mortmere, for a short memoir he was writing about Isherwood. Although Upward didn't provide anything for the book, he wrote an essay entitled 'Remembering Mortmere' that was published in the *London Magazine* in 1988.[43] There Upward claims that he and Isherwood didn't see Mortmere as anything more than an imaginative game and not intended for publication as their stories were too obscene. The essay is a general reminiscence of Isherwood rather than a detailed discussion of Mortmere.

Mortmere would hover over them for the rest of their lives, more for Upward than for Isherwood whose writing did not have that fantasy/reality quality to be found in Upward's first novel and his late stories, though not, perhaps to its detriment, in his trilogy, *The Spiral Ascent*. Isherwood's prose was more light-hearted and less ominous. They both left Cambridge at the same time, Isherwood in disgrace but happy to be gone. He wrote while at Freshwater on the Isle of Wight a jolly poem of farewell to his Corpus tutor, that is the supervisor of students for the college, William Spens, as he and Upward departed, taking the Mortmere characters with them. The last stanza of twenty-five of 'The Recessional from Cambridge' reads, 'Yes, sir, we know the ingratitude is appalling / We know the nature of our indiscretion / We know that when one chooses a profession – / Pardon a moment, but our friends are calling – / Yes, yes ... Quite true ... Well, so long ... Best of luck. / May you, throughout your life, ne'er lack a friend or fuck'.[44] They continued to write Mortmere stories over the next year or two, but only fragments remain.

The one exception, 'The Railway Accident', might be regarded as the culmination of Mortmere and as possibly Upward's finest and most highly regarded story. Isherwood characterizes it as a 'farewell to Mortmere': 'This is the last contribution either of us ever made to the literature of Mortmere. Mortmere seemed to have brought us to a dead end. The cult of romantic strangeness, we both knew, was a luxury for the comfortable University fireside'.[45] Though written in 1928, the story remained unpublished until 1949 when Isherwood persuaded Upward that it should appear in a bowdlerized version in the United States in the eleventh number of *New Directions* produced by the adventurous publisher James Laughlin. And even then it would be published under the name that Isherwood coined for Upward, Allen Chalmers. The name 'Chalmers', Upward's subsequent pseudonym in Isherwood's work, surfaces in December 1922 with Upward writing to Isherwood about his trip to Cambridge to take the entrance exam. 'Chalmers is rather a problem. But I daresay we can direct him to Magdalene and lose him there while we have tea in Orpen's rooms'.[46] Chalmers was a Repton contemporary, John Rutherford Chalmers, as was Orpen, a nephew of the painter

Sir William Orpen, but it is not clear why Isherwood later chose the name to represent Upward.[47]

Upward worried that the publication of 'The Railway Accident' would be bad for his reputation at the school where he was teaching but also that what had happened in the world, particularly the horrors of the German concentration camps and the Holocaust, would make the story's exaggerated brutality unacceptable. 'I have been feeling more and more that the thing is only being published because its sadism has now become fashionable. It was written in innocence, before we had dreamed that Mortmere would become real in Belsen'.[48] Upward was his own most severe judge. He was even more critical of the story in a letter to a publisher in 1984: 'a verbally exuberant piece of modernist nihilism, devoid of human sympathy and no depth of feeling of any kind'.[49] Isherwood provided a brief foreword to the 1949 publication. He introduced Chalmers as 'a distinguished British prose-writer, not yet as widely popular as his admirers could wish, but profoundly and subtly influential ... Mortmere was the mad nursery in which Chalmers grew up as a writer, and no future evaluation of his work will be able to ignore it ... [It is] a dream, or a nightmare about the English'.[50] Upward wrote about the inception of the story in a journal entry in 1983.

> I wanted the RA to be the most richly extraordinary and verbally unrestrained story I was capable of in which I could really let myself go because it would not be intended for publication but only to amaze and amuse Christopher Isherwood and any friends he might show it to. Thinking around for a sensational subject I remembered a disastrous railway

accident that had happened near Ilford on the line between Romford, where my home was, and Liverpool Street [a London station]. I often travelled by this line, and the accident had a traumatic effect on my imagination, though I was not involved in it. The details that Shreeve sketches on his notepad of the four sets of rails which become two correspond partly to the reality at Ilford ... In the unexpurgated version of the R.A. the verbally extravagant passage describing the actual accident was paralleled by an equally extravagant passage describing the homosexual rape of a choirboy in a rectory garden. Auden said of this that it couldn't have been written by a homosexual (he didn't explain why not).[51]

The very first paragraph with its long sentences is a parody of Proust, and elsewhere there is a parody of Joyce, both authors whom Upward admired immensely. Looking back in 1965 he felt that the authors who had influenced him most were Wilfred Owen, E. M. Forster, James Joyce and Marcel Proust, in that order.[52] (When an undergraduate, he had cited as the greatest influences upon him Wilfred Owen, Katherine Mansfield and Emily Brontë, known to him as 'Wilfred, Kathy and Emmy'.) 'The Railway Accident' is narrated by Hearn, a character who fused Isherwood and Upward. He is the headmaster of Frisbald College in Mortmere. He meets Shreeve in his compartment on the train. The train passes various surreal sights on its journey as Hearn and Shreeve have their peculiar conversation. Then the accident.

> Exceeding sixty miles an hour it visibly left the rails, jogging the foremost coaches through spraying wood from ploughed

sleepers, mowing the reeds. A blinding jolt had us into the inverted rack, dazzled with glass showering like luminous fish, ricocheting between punching upholstery . . . Coaches mounted like viciously copulating bulls, telescoped like ventilator hatches. Nostril gaps in a tunnel clogged with wreckage instantly flamed. A faint jet of blood sprayed from a vacant window. Frog-sprawling bodies fumed in blazing reeds.[53]

Isherwood did cut out the more vivid aspects of the homosexual rape in which a choirboy is attacked by three other choirboys at the urging of the Mortmere architect. There is a bombardment from the air and a boiler room explosion. Yet life goes on afterwards. Shreeve and Hearn are driven to Mortmere. Unperturbed, the inhabitants of the village embark on the annual treasure hunt. Hearn finds the treasure and the story ends with a non-fatal shooting of Welken, the rector of Mortmere, and the arrest of Harold Wrygrave for wrecking the train. The English village had turned absurdist. And the whole tale may be a fantasy in Hearn's mind. The story has no political content.

In his notebooks in January 1934 Upward succinctly summed up his earlier writing career from its very beginnings.

> I began by writing love poems in my school holidays, at the age of fourteen. No, I began writing far earlier than that – stories about imaginary lands, kings and above all soldiers . . . I felt I had discovered my true vocation, the only thing really worth living for. When I was about fifteen some of my poems were published in the school magazine. That only

impressed me for a short time. Later I failed to get any of the poems I had sent to Public School Verse accepted ... I have never had a poem published anywhere except in school and University magazines. This continual failure mightn't have put a stop to my writing poetry if I hadn't attended I. A. Richards' lectures on poetry during my last year at Cambridge. He convinced me that all the poetry I had written was worse than worthless. I tried to write a new kind of poetry but couldn't even begin to satisfy myself that it was any good. Finally I found that I couldn't write poetry at all. In this appalling (to me) situation I painfully tried to write prose. But I no longer wrote with any real hope of publication. The Mortmere stories were in fact written in such obscene language and with such obscene or blasphemous situations that they couldn't possibly have been published ... I was too much interested in form for its own sake ... I wanted my writing to be true to life and at the same time I wanted it to be ideally perfect in form. That was impossible. Either good writing must be true to life and more-or-less faulty in form, or it must be faultless in form and untrue to life ... [Why write?] In the past I should have answered: because there would have been no other way for me to find life worth living, because there is joy in writing by itself, whether it is published or not. This is probably true. But if one hides writing from the world, shrinks from any risk of outside criticism, the joy is a twisted, a morbid one, a secret joy, mental masturbation. So I have always got to write for publication.[54]

CHAPTER 3: CAMBRIDGE

Upward and Isherwood: a rare photograph of them together, early 1920s

In the years after Cambridge Upward's interests turned increasingly political. On the basis of his experiences at Repton and Cambridge he had decided that English society was rotten. Now the question was how was it to be changed? His father would probably have been willing to support him as a writer. But Upward felt that he had to make his own living. To do so he turned to the frequent resort of those who had studied arts subjects at university and did not wish to enter business: becoming a schoolmaster.

Chapter 4: Out in the World

AFTER CAMBRIDGE, WHAT? First he needed to earn a living, but even more important to him he wished to write. He was also in pursuit of love or at least sex. From 1926 to 1932 he would have an extraordinary number of temporary teaching jobs until in the autumn of 1932 he found a permanent position at Alleyn's School in Dulwich in south London. There he would be a member of the staff until 1961. He entered the teaching field with limited enthusiasm and though he was quite successful in his career he rarely enjoyed it. He had looked into the possibility late in his time at Cambridge. As he recalled in 1993: 'I tried to put off the awful day. I went to the careers person at Cambridge and we went through all sorts of careers and inevitably came round to teaching. Secondary school teaching wasn't so bad in those days. You got a good salary and better holidays of course'. His first lead was an interview for a position at Kingston College, Jamaica. Then there was a possibility of a position in Brussels. He spent autumn 1925 at home but went frequently to London on weekends to visit Isherwood and to continue to work on Mortmere stories. His first job was being a tutor to the Nance family in Tallwater House, Carbis Bay, in Cornwall next to St Ives. He was to teach their two children, Phoebe and Dickon, starting in January 1926. He was there until July 1927. He enjoyed himself and liked his employers. He wrote in his notebook on 1 March, 'I am happier than I have been for three years'. He found time for reading,

Edward Upward, 1926

recording the next day, 'Shakespeare, Wilfred [Owen], Villon and E. M. Forster begin to drive down all other gods'.[1] Yet when he recalled the experience in 1993 he remembered it with less fondness as he felt it kept him from writing. He had some awareness of the artistic traditions of the area and that Bernard Leach, a prominent potter, was in the neighbourhood. And of course the location was about to be immortalized in 1927 with the publication of Virginia Woolf's *To the Lighthouse*. The Godrevy Lighthouse itself could be seen from Carbis Bay. He joined the Arts Club in St Ives, being admitted on the strength of having won the Chancellor's Prize for Poetry at Cambridge. There he became infatuated with a girl he calls Tessy in *No Home but the Struggle*.

He and Isherwood had spent the previous July at Freshwater on the Isle of Wight working on their writing. They would go quite frequently to a boarding house, Marine Villa, which is still there, now a private home, with a wonderful view over the sea. That immediate area had strong literary associations from the nineteenth century with both Farringford, Tennyson's house, just up the road as well as Dimbola, Julia Margaret Cameron's residence. In April at Easter time, on a break from Upward's tutoring job, they went to the Isles of Scilly. The ultimate product of that visit was Isherwood's first novel, *All the Conspirators*, published in 1928 and dedicated to Upward. On walks there Upward contributed his ideas for the plot of the novel, then called *Seascape with Figures*. Many years later when the novel was reissued in the 1950s Isherwood expanded on the dedication: 'Even if this were now its only interest, there would still be one thing about it which hadn't dated, as far as I was concerned; its dedication. After half a lifetime, Edward Upward is still the friend he has

CHAPTER 4: OUT IN THE WORLD

Isherwood and Upward in the mirror, Marine Villa, Freshwater

always been; still the judge before whom all my work must stand trial and from whose verdict, much as I sometimes hate to admit it, there is no appeal. I now extend my dedication to include Edward's wife Hilda, their daughter Kathy and their son Christopher'.[2]

In the novel the name Allen Chalmers appears for the first time. It is used for the character based on him as well as on Hector Wintle, their Repton contemporary and fellow writer, at that point a medical student as is the Chalmers character in the novel. (Isherwood himself would briefly study medicine after the publication of the novel.) It opens with the Isherwood character, Philip, and Allen visiting the Scilly Isles. The reader doesn't discover until Philip returns to London that he has thrown up his job in the City in order to be a painter and writer, in defiance of his mother. But on his return he is pressured to return to his job. As Isherwood wrote in the 1958 foreword to the reissue of the novel, 'It records a minor engagement

CHAPTER 4: OUT IN THE WORLD

in what Shelley calls "the great war between the old and young". And what a war that was! Every battle of it was fought to a finish, with no quarter asked or shown'.³ Although Upward had mixed feelings about his mother, there was rarely the same intensity of conflict as between Christopher and his mother Kathleen. In 1934 he wrote to Isherwood about staying with his parents. 'This house is as much Usher as ever. I had a row with my mother at breakfast this morning which is going to reverberate for two to three days. My father has left the house forever after tampering with one of the maids who started stealing and tried to blackmail him. And I doubt whether I shall come back to this house again'.⁴ His father did return and ultimately Upward was on good terms with both his parents.

Between Upward's periods of teaching, the friends would return to Marine Villa in Freshwater, Upward himself being there from April to September 1928. At the Villa he took a photograph of Isherwood holding his first book, *All the Conspirators*, and at the same time Isherwood took the iconic profile portrait of him.

At this point he was also working on an abortive novel that began at a golf club, drawing presumably on his father's close involvement with the club at Romford, and then the novel would move on to Cambridge and Cornwall. For the Cambridge part he commented that 'without doubt the pseudo visions connected with the Mortmere day dream are important' and that he would also write about his 'jealousy & contempt for the poshocracy'.⁵

After Carbis Bay he had an extremely brief teaching stint of two weeks at Worcester where his charge was to keep order, which may not have been so easy, the boys informing him, 'We killed the last

Christopher Isherwood at Freshwater holding a copy of All the Conspirators, *his first novel, just published May 1928, photographed by Edward Upward*

CHAPTER 4: OUT IN THE WORLD

Edward at Freshwater, May 1928, photographed by Christopher Isherwood

master we had'.⁶ Next he was a tutor to a family in Lockerbie in Scotland from February to April 1928. This provided the model for the family the tutor worked for in his first novel, *Journey to the Border*, not published until ten years later. At Lockerbie he wrote his best-known story, 'The Railway Accident'. From September 1928 until April 1930 he had a temporary position teaching French and maths in the Junior School at Loretto, a prominent public school in Scotland. The headmaster in a letter of reference rather implies that he didn't do too well at his assigned task. 'A pleasant and loyal colleague but is essentially scholarly and artistic and I am certain that if he were dealing with an Upper Form in English he would be an inspiring and successful teacher'.⁷ He felt he did not fit into the Scottish atmosphere. Also he thought he was disapproved of because he had taken

CHAPTER 4: OUT IN THE WORLD

The house near Lockerbie where Edward was a tutor in 1928

up with a Scottish nurse he had met when he needed to go to a nursing home for some inner-ear trouble. He tried to be as subversive as he could. As he wrote to Isherwood in February 1930, with a rather romantic vision of the Soviet Union:

> If we had been born in Russia it would have been different. We should have been able to write in the mornings and never spent hours, days, years hunting for sex or lying crippled on a sofa under a copy of the *Times Literary Supplement*. My one hope now is that in the six weeks before I leave here I shall at least be able to poison a few of the boys against Christ and their country. Two of the masters are already my dupes and one of them is trying to fuck the housemaid at his hostel. I give them

pamphlets on Communism and nudge them in chapel during the Lord's Prayer.

The next year he commented to Isherwood about buggery in Russia. 'As far as I know Lenin said nothing about buggery. Possibly there wasn't any in Russia. The problem of buggery in a communist state will depend largely on the number of buggers who are communists. In any case persecution of buggers is anti-Leninist. But Gide will not be approved'.[8]

From September 1930 to August 1931, the academic year, he was teaching in Scarborough at the Boys' High School. It was a job for only a year while a master was away but he looked back on it as the school that he most enjoyed, as the sense of exuberance in his letters conveys. In September he wrote to Isherwood about his time there, presumably with some sense of fantasy. 'I enclose a new frontispiece for Mortmere. I am also a member of the Folk-dancing club and a club for genteel whores. Beau Nash would be stunned. Other members of the staff inform me that I shall be able to get as much fucking here as I want. Most of them are already Communists'.[9] Although he probably never came to love teaching he nevertheless enjoyed it or tolerated it, at least to the extent that he was willing to commit himself to it as the career he would follow. He wrote in his notebook: 'Teaching is not to be regarded as something forced from outside, something which I submit to but determine not to be crushed by ... I've got to love my work, to do everything I can to make myself a really efficient teacher'.[10] In a letter of reference the headmaster commented on his 'intellectual qualities and gentlemanly nature' and that in his teaching of English and French he was 'a very useful

CHAPTER 4: OUT IN THE WORLD

member of the Staff. His manner with boys is tactful and he has no trouble with discipline'.[11] At the same time he was clearly in quite a volatile state and could change his mind about his future quite regularly. Although his writing was going slowly, he was enjoying himself at Scarborough. His thoughts for his future were going off in all directions. He wrote to Isherwood:

> My novel proceeds at crucifixion speed, but something is done. It is frankly feuilleton and based on Roger Martin [du Gard]. Rowlandson, Joyce, Gide mean nothing any more. Edward Shanks [a now forgotten writer of the period] remains. Have I utterly misconceived what a novel is? Yes I am a very good school master – so good you would be amazed . . . My plans are to stay on here for another term and earn enough money to retire for a year into extremely cheap lodgings on the Firth of Forth. But if you hear of anything in Berlin or elsewhere that is free from too much terror let me know. A whore in a taxi has stolen my winter gloves.[12]

These letters at the time to Isherwood were almost as if they were bulletins, written without salutation or closing phrase and signature.

He did not leave teaching after the year at Scarborough nor apparently leave the country. He probably went to live at home in Romford for the autumn. Then for two months, February and March 1932, he taught at Stowe, a new public school in a very grand country house built by the Temple family. John Cornford, perhaps the most distinguished student Communist of his generation who

CHAPTER 4: OUT IN THE WORLD

was to die in Spain, was still there as a pupil at the time. While there is no evidence that these two figures met, Cornford was very likely to have been in the history sixth form that Upward taught. In later years Upward deeply admired his poetry. They were both moving towards Communism at that moment. He wrote about Stowe:

> That was very interesting. Lordly buildings. The thing I remember most about it was meeting a desperate unemployed man in the Park – they had beautiful grounds – who stood in my way, threatening me and asking for money. I said: Have you heard of the Unemployed Worker's Union. By the end of it I made him ashamed of himself and he was going away without a penny, but I gave him some money. That stuck in my mind. The rather lordly headmaster [J. F. Roxburgh], who read Prayers. And very nice rooms I had, with burning, I think, logs... I was very scared of the VIth Form there. They were doing some history book and they obviously knew much more about it than I did... They were very polite.

In May 1932 he was at Ottershaw College in Surrey. The headmaster was

> a very strange man [J. G. Jeffreys], a spellbinder who founded, I think, Bryanston School [a progressive public school begun in 1928], but he was found out. The usual practices. But quite a number of the parents believe in him still so he got this house at Ottershaw – in those days it was remarkable, it had silver taps – and a very odd collection of staff gathered together. They

didn't pay us anything – we got free eats, and we had a very nice time – pretty idle: we didn't do an awful lot of teaching. All sorts of ages, public school age. Unfortunately he did the same thing again there, and so that was the end of it. That was after I left. This is one of the occasions Auden turned up . . . I was walking back from the village to the school and suddenly a voice spoke out of a tree saying 'Mr Upward' – and there was Auden, who had climbed up quite high. I thought it was Jehovah reproving me.[13]

Then finally that autumn he took up on the recommendation of a friend of his schoolmaster brother, Mer, a position on the English staff at Alleyn's, where he would be for the rest of his teaching career. On the whole he was an effective teacher. But he always resented the time it took and that it kept him away from what he thought was his most important task: to be a writer.

He also wanted to have a more active love life. While at Repton he had fallen in love with a Romford girl, whom he calls Christine in *No Home but the Struggle*. She inspired him to become a poet. He wrote in his journal in 1952, 'Ever since the writing of that sonnet to Christine, thirty-three years ago [when he was sixteen], I have desired to be a writer'.[14] In Cornwall he spent time with Tessy and noted as well the attractiveness of the fourteen-year-old daughter whom he was tutoring along with her brother. His romantic interest in Tessy was very strong and they spent time together, but nothing came of it. It may be she whom he wrote about under another name to Isherwood at the time, but also he mentions the girl he was tutoring.

CHAPTER 4: OUT IN THE WORLD

'Dossy is at Zennor. She sleeps alone in a large tent with a table and chairs in it and a campbed . . . I hid among rocks on a hill far above the village and watched her all Sunday afternoon . . . Phoebe is strangely well developed for her age. Perhaps the heat has done it. Arithmetic creates an atmosphere of pure unreality around the common decencies and I feel unsafe'.[15] When writing in 1972 of his alter ego Alan Sebrill in his trilogy, he remarks, 'After Cornwall, he had more or less given up hope of romantic love and he simply required sex. He is still virgin'.[16] That may or may not have been true about the non-fictional self. In any case he wrote in his notebook some years later on 15 August 1932 in the midst of his on-and-off-again affair with Jane: 'My earlier experiences were either with whores or with girls to whom I hardly dare speak . . . Love is not, never should be, the most important thing. But perhaps it is the second most important thing'.[17] Sex was on his mind in the mid-1920s; he claimed in a letter to Isherwood from Cornwall to be writing from Impotence Villas and asked him to 'tell me about dry-fucks'.[18]

He came home between positions, and writing to Isherwood on Christmas Day in 1925 he brutally remarked: 'My swine of my mother has just covered the table with Christmas excrement . . . Tonight I intend to saw my genitals off with a teacup'. Some years later he wrote from Romford to Isherwood, 'Back in this Strindberg menage' and concluded the letter, 'Take care of your cock'.[19] This was also when he was busy reading Freud, Isherwood having given him a copy of the *Introductory Lectures on Psycho-Analysis* on 26 August 1925.[20] His sexual life became more intense at that time. In the summer of

CHAPTER 4: OUT IN THE WORLD

1925 Isherwood had taken a job, introduced by a Repton contemporary, as the secretary for a prominent string quartet, the first violin and founder of it being André Mangeot and including the young John Barbirolli, later to be one of Britain's greatest conductors. Mangeot was then in his early forties. His wife Olive was English, a granddaughter of Sir Henry Cole, the founder of the Victoria and Albert Museum. Isherwood became very close to the family and according to André encouraged Olive eventually to divorce him, driven to do so by his numerous affairs. Through Isherwood Upward saw a lot of the Mangeots and became, as did another friend of Isherwood's and Auden's from Oxford, Gabriel Carritt, a lover of Olive's. (Carritt also became a Communist.) Upward wrote rather brutally about her to Isherwood: 'Frigging, though I indulge in it very much more frequently than before, offers no satisfaction. Nothing I can do can really get down to the core of the itch. I suppose I shall have to return to her lovely cunt. For Christ's sake procure me someone younger with yellow hair and XVIIIth century bubs like lemons'. And in a later letter, perhaps the next year: 'I am quite reconciled to Olive again – in fact she never knew that I'd sworn I had seen the last of her – but I'm going to make it a rule not to be trapped in bed more than once a fortnight'.[21] He did continue to see her, writing to Isherwood some time later: 'I've been fairly regularly to bed with Olive ... I've behaved as badly as I can ... Can't you convince her it's wicked of her to have relations with me?' But in his next letter: 'I forgive Olive everything. She is really very nice'.[22] Through Upward Olive later became a member of the Communist Party.

His love life became particularly intense some years later in the early 1930s at the same time that he was becoming a Communist. At

CHAPTER 4: OUT IN THE WORLD

Ottershaw he fell in love with the sister of one of his fellow teachers, the daughter of a bank manager in Tunbridge Wells. Her name was Shirley Munro but he insisted on calling her Jane; she for her part didn't like Edward and called him Falaise. Her brother referred to him as fallacy or phallus. His relationship with her was rather a roller-coaster one as can be seen in a series of entries in his notebook in 1932 as well as in her letters to him. 'July 22 She is far, far better than any before . . . July 26 She's undoubtedly double-crossed me . . . When drunk she'd sleep with any man who attracted her. I can put up with that, but not with broken appointments . . . July 27 I love her . . . Aug 7 I must find a substitute for Jane. There is no other cure . . . Aug 9 I do love her'. The relationship led him to a brief discussion of the need to be married. 'Aug 13 Above all the horror of the example set by my parents . . . I know I ought to marry a communist, and preferable one of bourgeois origin. I must get married. But I must not allow my contempt for anarchism to rush me into marriage'.[23]

At some point he acquired the rather charming letters that he had written to her, and clearly their affair served as the model for the fling that Alan Sebrill has with 'Peg' at the very beginning of his novel *In the Thirties*. It has all the enthusiasm and joy of a first love affair. He wrote in one letter: 'Let us go soon to the golden land. Why not this week-end?' In another letter: 'If we're the sort of people who ought to meet only in the summer let's make the whole year summer'. But he also shared his politics with her in a letter dated 11 April but without a year.

> Why not banners and processions and the Red Flag? Our birthright of joy has been stolen from us, and how else can we

protest and try to get it back again? Better people than ourselves have tried individualistic methods, and they have all failed dismally. D. H. Lawrence for instance. The time has come to offend against the canons of 'good-taste' and join with the militant working class who alone are capable of making any real change for the better in our lives. The difficulty for us is pat the beginning, because our upbringing has made us fastidious and silly, but once we have begun we shall lose our uneasiness about Red Flags and we shall be far happier and shall no longer feel worthless.

Planning another meeting after an estrangement, he sent a poem to her:

> Now that we're meeting on Wednesday again
> What's going to happen? There's the puzzle.
> Do you think I'd better wear a muzzle?
> ... Or shall I wear my schoolmaster's gown
> And look very prim and decline to sit down,
> ... Or shall I be my golden self
> And mumble my words like a muddled elf
> And fail to arrive at any decision
> About ourselves and our queer position.
> ... So the best thing to do is to go on in the same
> Fuddled way, and regard it all as a game.
> ... And possibly some wonderful day some bright
> Accident will put everything miraculously right,
> And in a golden land I'll saunter
> With you, my cool lunar haunter.

In a later letter from the Isle of Wight he wrote: 'My joy, . . . Darling, how exciting we are. It's as though I had very luckily landed on a beach from a small homemade boat and suddenly realised that I had landed not merely on a beach but on an immense continent . . . How I miss you, my bright and tender nymph. With warmest dreams and wishes, Your sultry fawn'. In another letter: 'My dearest, You are not a beast . . . I am not pleading against your new resolution, though heaven knows it cuts me to the quick. [that she might sleep with others?] . . . I can't do without you. The prospect of years of work in this super-reactionary spot [the school where he was teaching] makes the remembrance of the golden land like a taste of pure water in hell . . . Let me see you fairly often. But wait till you've had proofs of my good behaviour next Wednesday'. This letter was probably the result of Jane telling him that she would be marrying someone else but might still be able to see him from time to time, which is what Peg says to Alan Sebrill in the novel. He does write to her on 18 December in an unspecified year and in an understated dramatic way: 'It was good to hear from you again after all these months . . . I have, believe it or not, got married since I last saw you, and have moved to a new flat'.[24]

After reading his novel *In the Thirties* on its publication in 1962 Jane re-established contact, writing to him: 'I do think you might have let poor Alan have a bit more fun in his golden land . . . Alan Sebrill is so young, so *serious*. You weren't like that, were you? . . . I seem to be carping when really I'm full of admiration for your valuable historical work. Will you ask Hilda [his wife] if I may be allowed to meet you again? Now that I'm 51 & a grandmother twice over I'm ever so harmless and well-meaning! And I *would* like to see you &

talk & hear your news'.[25] There is no indication that they actually did meet. In their time, neither that relationship nor his continuing liaison with Olive was going well. He tended to regard these interesting women as primarily sources of sexual relief although his letters to Jane do appear to be genuinely affectionate or more. He may have rather taken on the pose of the young cynic when he wrote to Isherwood in October 1932: 'We are slowly becoming more estranged. I made a preplanned attempt to rape her [Jane] about a fortnight ago but it failed and nothing at all intimate has happened since ... I may say that Olive alone has preserved my sanity in this crisis. I suppose I'd better marry her in the end. But not till she's sixty. [She was then in her early forties, twenty years older than Upward.] I've told her that she's better than many a young whore'.[26] The following December he wrote again to Isherwood about these relationships: 'I have finally broken with Jane, not having seen her for six weeks. Olive makes me ill. Disgust supervened. But she is useful as a news agency. I think she is getting a little tired of me. I become more and more frigid as the winter advances'.[27]

Perhaps one should move forward to 1936 when he married Hilda Maude Percival. She was born on 11 April 1909 at 15 Geneva Road in Brixton, south London. The house had no bathroom; in the style of the time for poorer families baths were taken in the kitchen but there was a washstand in each bedroom. She was the fourth of six children, four of whom lived into adulthood. Her father, Frederick William Percival, a clerk, was born in 1868 and died in 1920 from tuberculosis. He had left school at twelve and went to work for a printer. He was a serious reader and a Swedenborgian. Her mother, Elizabeth Ann Slade, was a teacher. She married when she was thirty-one, left teaching to have her children, then returned to it at the age of forty-seven. The family was poor but they were certainly respectable. One senses that Edward would like to think of the Percivals as working class, but they were actually more lower middle class. Even so the class differences were considerable and were a source of tension. Hilda had something of a Cockney accent which she largely lost. She did not have a particularly happy childhood, not getting on well with her mother. Will, Hilda's brother, had a single bed in the children's bedroom, and his three sisters shared the other bed. Will moved to his grandparents' bedroom after they died. As the son, to Hilda's and her sisters' irritation, he was favoured and excused from housework. He joined the Communist Party first but left it before war broke out because he was involved with the early development of radar as a research scientist. Through him Hilda joined the party and was a canvasser, a distributor of leaflets and an occasional public speaker. In many ways she was a more clear-eyed Communist than her husband. The Percival children were bright and were helped in their schoolwork by their teacher mother. At eleven Hilda won a scholarship to Mary Datchelor School, Camberwell, and her sisters Gwen, older, and Kath, younger, attended the same school. Hilda was at the school from 1920 to 1927, taking the General School Certificate exam at the age of sixteen in French, English and History. She dropped Latin as she disliked ancient history. If she had done four subjects she would have qualified for university admission but it is doubtful that she would have considered doing that. She and her sisters also had piano lessons at home. In 1925 her mother sold the house and bought 154 Turney Road in Dulwich, and this ultimately became the Upwards' home.[28] Hilda next went to Furzedown Training College, Streatham, where she pursued her studies, and in 1930 she began her teaching career at the Rolls Road School on the Old Kent Road where she continued until her son Christopher was born in 1938. One reason she joined the party was that she was horrified at the contrast between the comparative gentility of her training college and the poverty of the school in which she was teaching.

Edward and Hilda met in 1932 through Edward's involvement with the Communist Party in south London where Hilda lived. 'The first time I ever saw my darling was at a public meeting advertised in one of the south east London newspapers by the local party branch. She was giving a report on the recent Brussels Peace Conference which the branch had delegated her to attend. Listening to her I thought, "That is the kind of girl I ought to marry"'.[29] In 1934 he wrote to Christopher while he was visiting his family in Sandown: 'I wish that the whole family was not circulating in this room. Otherwise I would give you some details of my sex life. All I can say now is that I am off for a few days of this holiday with a schoolteacher... I am hoping without much confidence that this will put an end to my relations with Olive'. He remarked in the same letter, 'Significantly enough the teacher is called Hilda', which he clearly regarded as a solid proletarian name, particularly in contrast to Olive.[30] He came to her cell meetings; they went for walks on Box Hill. At first she was unresponsive to his physical advances but soon they were going off on weekends together, hoping not to be seen as they would have lost their jobs. The relationship with Hilda was becoming quite intense as he wrote to Christopher the following February: 'I now feel I have to see Hilda every day. It has gone pretty far, and we are looking round for a flat to live in. I supposed this had to happen in the end, and in any case we can't get married because she is a teacher and the L.C.C. [London County Council] would sack her if we did'.[31] Presumably they were contemplating living together, but he turned out to be wrong and she continued teaching for two years after marriage. Yet in March 1935 he wrote in his notebook: 'I *want* to marry *someone* – but owing to my economic situation H is not the right person. Who would be the right person? Someone who would keep me in touch with the non-teacher world. That is, in the present situation I should do better not to marry at all. I am not fit to take on the extra responsibility . . . If I earned my living by writing then I should not mind taking on the extra responsibility, but to marry now would be to clamp myself down to teaching for good and all'.[32] In May 1936 he wrote to Isherwood, who was then in Portugal, an interesting letter that has a bearing on Mortmere's association with surrealism: 'I went with Olive to the surrealist exhibition . . . I infinitely prefer it to abstract art. It is much more literary. A fearful dream occurs to me. What if I dared to come out to Portugal with Hilda? No, no, no. But the dangers are so gaping that the idea is very alluring'.[33] In April 1936 he wrote Hilda an oddly dispassionate love letter.

> There are times when one doesn't want to make love, but there are also times when one does want to. You know that as well as I do. I don't like writing a love letter at a time when I'm not feeling that I want to make love. It seems a fake, and it is a fake. But if I write you the other sort of letter you are offended. You suspect I've been treating you as a 'convenience' and am not really interested in you. That's nonsense and you know it is. And

because I'm afraid that if I write you an ordinary friendly letter you will be offended I put off writing to you for a while. Then the time comes when I want to write you a love letter, but I can't easily bring myself to do it because I guess that you are annoyed with me for not having written sooner. If you wonder why I, after making love to you at the end of last term, didn't feel like making love to you by letter as soon as I arrived home – the only explanation I can give is that the term had made me tired and fed up and I wanted to concentrate my remaining energy on getting ahead at once with my book. I know it was stupid and thoughtless of me to have suggested in my last letter that if I hadn't written you wouldn't have written . . . I can't guess what you will think of me for writing this letter. If it seems cold and priggish remember that I'm upset and am trying to put things right without being carried away by my feelings. You know that I am fond of you. You are not only my girl but you are my friend and my equal . . . Love, E.[34]

As late as August 1936 he felt that perhaps marrying Hilda was all a big mistake, writing to her: 'You know that we should be anything but an ideal couple . . . The courageous thing would be for us to break off'.[35] Then in December after his marriage he wrote to Isherwood: 'The marriage is going very well. My colleagues are giving me a clock, but they are very annoyed that I didn't have a honeymoon and didn't tell them anything about my intentions long ago'.[36] It was ultimately a very happy marriage and he came to be profoundly in love with her. But it was a love that grew and was not fully there at the beginning. She had been a member of the Communist Party

CHAPTER 4: OUT IN THE WORLD

since 1930 and was of lower-middle-class origin. One almost senses that he felt it was a duty to marry such a woman. His attitude towards Hilda was rather patronizing. In May 1936 he noted, 'Am very fond of H.' and then in June: 'To-day H said she is ordinary. For some reason this disturbed me. Why? Rout it out'. And then the next day: 'What if H is, as she says, ordinary? All the better. But I'd prefer to call her normal'. By the end of July he is in a turmoil of self-doubt about the relationship and what he saw at that moment as its lack of 'beauty, colour, tenderness, grace – these are natural needs. But they cannot be satisfied under capitalism ... The fight comes first'. And a few days later, on 1 August, he drafts a letter to Hilda, possibly never sent, saying that they should get married but not to each other. The next day he wrote in his notebook: 'I don't "love" H. I here and now renounce "love" and decide to ally myself with H ... "Love" can be had, yes, but it is counter-revolutionary. There must be a new, a [sic] altogether changed love. My love for H. Communists cannot indulge in "love" of the old sort, or else they cease to be communists ... The fact is I can't spend the holidays without her'. A few days later he wrote: 'The personal life is an impossibility ... The real question is: shall I be able to write better if I marry H? No. I am very fond of H but I don't want to marry her'. On 8 August he listed her disadvantages: that her looks weren't good enough, that she lacked a university education and that she was, in his view, working class. She had a trace of a Cockney accent while his voice was distinctly Oxbridge. He was, like it or not, an English gentleman. Yet she was more articulate at meetings. He wrote (one hopes that he was being somewhat ironic; perhaps not): 'I need her ... I am marrying into the working class, and am proud of it ... We must use our flat for party purposes... Remember, all objections are simply bourgeois prejudices in disguise... Civil war – the class war – has been going on inside me, and, as was finally inevitable, the working class has won ... The workers have won in me all along the line. Previously they won an important victory but left the citadel of sex almost intact... Now it is under workers' control'.[37] There is the horrific scene in *In the Thirties* when the Upward character, Alan, tells the Hilda character, Elsie, that she is ugly, which is quite untrue. His class doubts were transformed into a question of looks. As he wrote about this scene years later in his notebooks: 'A & E falling in love. Then the act, which links them with the animal kingdom far beyond class or civilization ... How his bourgeois trained eye saw her as ugly. How he now sees her as more beautiful than anyone on earth'.[38] They were married on 23 October 1936 at Peckham, presumably at the Registry office. There is no indication of who attended the wedding.

At first he had rather diffident feelings about having children; indeed he seemed to have mixed feelings about virtually everything he did. As he wrote in his notebook in January 1938: 'If I had been just a little queerer than I am what wd have happened to me? That which may yet happen. Danger can be a stimulus. However I can't help being glad that I have not got a child ... To have or not to have children. What makes me hesitate? Not war, not famine, not heredity, not even loss of holidays, but only now the thought of my writing ... My desire to write is far stronger than my desire to have children. But this doesn't mean that I don't want children'.[39] And indeed he had two, Christopher and Katherine, and seemed to have had a very happy family life, although Kathy found him a rather difficult father. His love for Hilda grew and grew. In August 1936 he wrote in his notebook: 'The marriage seems more and more natural and inevitable and right'.[40] When she was seriously ill in 1964 he wrote in his notebook, 'Rather than leave her in the lurch I wd burn every wretched word I've ever written'.[41]

Certainly the most significant literary development in Upward's life during the late 1920s and early 1930s was his growing friendship with W. H. Auden. Isherwood had introduced them at a restaurant in Soho in 1927. Upward's most vivid memory of the evening was their discussion of toilet seats.

> ... he attacked, forcefully and loudly enough for other diners around us to become interested, the sort of person who wouldn't sit down on public lavatory seats for fear of getting clap. (I wondered whether he had been told by Christopher that I never sat down on lavatory seats, public or otherwise; and, if he had been told, whether Christopher had added the extenuating explanation that I had formed the habit at our public school where I found the wood of the earth-closet seats altogether too rugged to be sat on in comfort.)[42]

Isherwood and Auden had been at prep school together but hadn't known each other well as Isherwood was three years older. Now they had reconnected. In 1926 and probably because of Upward's enthusiasm for the Isle of Wight, the two spent time together at Marine Villa overlooking the sea in Freshwater. There they became lovers. The relationship was probably more important for Auden than for Isherwood. Although not written until 1935, two of Auden's best-known poems, 'August for the People' and 'Look, stranger, on this island now', may have been connected with this visit. Or the poems may have been inspired more immediately by Upward's story 'The Island', published in 1935. Also in an early Auden poem, 'Humpty Dumpty', the Watcher in Spanish, a character from Mortmere, appears. 'Words made the Watcher face about and turn / On Wonderland the backside of indifference, / To scrutinize a world of slag-tips, chimneys / More eloquent of Death than cypresses'.[43]

Auden and Upward met before Upward himself felt he was at all political. But in the early 1930s he would attempt to move Auden towards Communism.[44] Even before meeting they had been corresponding. When Upward was in Cornwall, Auden sent him some poems. The sense of a rather subversive schoolboy touch of fantasy and conspiracy that pervades the idea of Mortmere was an important influence on the early Auden. And at the more serious end of the spectrum Upward would be a political influence upon him as Upward became more and more interested in Marxism and Leninism, ultimately leading to his joining the party. One doesn't know how much of the texts he read but in his library he had twenty-one books by Marx and thirty-three by Lenin, not to mention five books by Stalin. There was a paradoxical situation. Both Auden and Upward were deeply aware of the desperate economic state of society after the advent of the Depression in 1929. In Auden's case there was a certain sense of playing with the idea of revolution. Upward would ultimately become convinced that it was necessary, as Lenin argued, for there to be a revolution if British society were to be changed for the better. Auden no doubt never went that far and in any case by the end of the decade he retreated from a more radical political position. He would not cross the border or the frontier, a prevalent image of the period, into a new political world. Upward felt it was necessary to cross or at least to come up to the border, to join the party to support the workers' struggle, or otherwise he would go insane. Ultimately Auden would feel that at best he would walk along the frontier. The frontier can also be taken to stand for what might be regarded as an English paradox: intense class consciousness and intense individualism. It made Auden and Upward particularly receptive to the possible transformation of both society and the individual. But the two transformations might be in opposition. Less than two weeks before Auden and Isherwood went to China in January 1938 Auden came to see him. And Upward wrote under the impetus of the visit, 'Literature must help to change the world'.[45] It may have been the last time they met.

During this decade Auden and Upward were having quite parallel careers, both teaching at prep schools, primary boarding schools. He visited Auden in Helensburgh near Glasgow in February 1931 and Auden would visit him when Upward was teaching at Scarborough in Yorkshire the following summer. Auden, for reasons best known to himself, put on a red beard before getting off the train. Seeing Auden's photograph in the *Times Literary Supplement* in 1942 made Upward remember that he too was a poet, perhaps a bit paradoxically, considering Auden's negative view of his poetry: 'How I had felt about writing in the days when I knew Wystan. I remembered Scarborough & Helensburgh "my youth". Poetry was my first love and it will be my last. Looking back I see that not Rouen, not Cambridge, not Cornwall, but Scarborough was my real poetic period'.[46] It's not really clear why he should have written this, as he

CHAPTER 4: OUT IN THE WORLD

Auden and Isherwood in 1928, photographed in Oxford by Eric Bramall

wasn't writing much poetry if any at the time. He had tried his hand at poetry again, writing a poem in September 1930 called 'Lost and Found'. When he showed it and another poem, 'One More Redeemer' to Auden, it was dismissed with the one word 'No'. In some sense this stopped his career as a poet, although in the ensuing seventy years he seemed frequently to consider returning to poetry. In retrospect Upward may have rather exaggerated this ruling by Auden. He frequently called the artistic life that he led as the 'poetic life' and referred to his writing outside of his novels as 'prose poems'. Even earlier Auden had been discouraging about his poetry, reinforcing what Upward had taken away from Richards' lectures. 'I was too much taken by the rhythm and the words and didn't bother with the meaning. I couldn't get both. I could have written satirical poems,

CHAPTER 4: OUT IN THE WORLD

but I got into an age that was beyond satire. I agree with Auden that you can only be satirical about a society that you believed in'.[47] He was writing some short stories at the time; two would be published in *New Country* in 1933. He had been working on a novel, the 'golf club novel', but he abandoned it and turned to a new prose project, tentatively entitled *The Border-Line,* subsequently published as *Journey to the Border.* In any case there was no question that he had an intense artistic relationship with Auden.

It is difficult to assess how influential Upward was upon Auden either directly or via Isherwood. Upward started reading Auden's poetry in 1926, preferring it to T. S. Eliot's. When in 1930 he started to write poetry again, he commented in his notebook on 1 September, 'Has the sperm arrived after five years of impotence?'[48] The question of whether to return to the writing of poetry would remain an open and compelling one for the rest of his long life. Years later, in 1958, inspired by rereading Auden's early poems, he bemoaned having abandoned poetry, perhaps forgetting that it was partially thanks to Auden that he had done so. 'This morning I began to look at Wystan's selected poems which we have given to K. [his daughter Katherine] for her 18th birthday. As I read some of the earlier ones I found myself momentarily in the feeling with which I first read them, and soon a grief came over me. How I have wasted my life, how irrevocably and how far I have gone astray from myself. How deeply the poet in me has been buried beneath years of uncongenial work'.[49] Indeed all through his life he kept thinking that he would return to poetry. He ends his trilogy of novels, *The Spiral Ascent*, with the statement that Alan is a poet 'with my completed poem in my notebook on the small table beside my chair'. Auden read the man-

CHAPTER 4: OUT IN THE WORLD

uscript of 'The Railway Accident' in 1928 and would read from it in lectures. When sending Upward a copy of his reputation-making *Poems* in 1930 Auden praised the story and added, 'I shall never know how much in these poems is filched from you via Christopher'.[50] In return Upward deeply admired the poems Auden was writing at the time and felt he was unquestionably the most talented member of the group.

Probably the most important direct influence may have been when Upward allowed Auden to read what he had written so far in the third volume of his notebooks. The volume itself ran from January 1931 to January 1934. Upward at some future date wrote in it: 'W. H. Auden read this diary, certainly as far as June 28 '31 . . . I think the diary influenced his Airman's Journal'.[51] This was Book II, 'Journal of an Airman', a work of prose and poetry, the longest section of *The Orators: An English Study* published in 1932. According to Benjamin Kohlmann the 'Journal' was written between August and November 1931. Its diary-like entries do recall the notebook, reflecting Upward's growing sense of commitment to Communism on the basis of his reading of Marxist texts and some political involvement. The section of the 'Journal' with diagrams has an air of scientific objectivity but also of the world of Mortmere. 'At dinner an imaginary telegram of regret from a guest who has left the hotel to die may amuse. In the hall a Highland reel will, of course, be attempted, lit up by pocket torches fetched hurriedly from the bedrooms'.[52] The airman is an ambiguous and difficult figure. He certainly seems to be a leader and antibourgeois. Might he be a Fascist? Perhaps. At the time the Italians were quite prominent as aviators, also identified with the Italian literary movement of Futurism. Hitler had not yet

CHAPTER 4: OUT IN THE WORLD

come into power when the book was published, but Auden was fully aware of him from the time he had spent in Germany. Was the airman a Communist leader? Perhaps. At this time Auden was writing 'A Communist to Others' which, whatever his own political opinions, was in the voice of a Communist. A poem of twenty-two stanzas, it was published in September 1932 in the periodical *The Twentieth Century* as well as in *New Country* in 1933. In a letter in 1932 Auden described *The Orators* as 'a stage in my conversion to Communism'.[53]

This was the height of Upward's influence upon Auden. Through mutual visits to the schools where they were each teaching, the two were in close communication with one another. Both the speaker in the 'Journal of an Airman' and those who are addressed would appear to be schoolmasters. Benjamin Kohlmann argues convincingly that the poem was shaped by Auden's visit to Ottershaw. (On this visit Upward remembers Auden asking him, 'Can you procure for me a boy or a master?'[54]) Indeed the uncertainties in the poem may reflect less Auden's positions than the starts and stops of Upward's progress towards Communism. Kohlmann points out the parallels between the poem and Upward's notebook. The dominant theme in the notebook is a growing commitment to Communism. Over the next three years Upward would become increasingly involved, working for the Communist candidate for Parliament in Bethnal Green in 1931, joining the party on a probationary basis in 1932 and becoming a fully committed member in 1934. Presumably at approximately the same time Auden wrote another poem, 'Comrade Upward', which was not published. It is a poem of eleven two-line stanzas, except for the first which has four lines. The Comrade is attacking a member of the bourgeoisie. 'Who *has* made you a bloody fool? / The masters of course at my public school'. It's not quite clear how the situation of the poem is resolved. The last two stanzas read: 'Suppose a man starving came your way? / I'd tell him to go to the church and pray. // Where will you go after you die? / To drink champagne with God in the sky'.[55] As Kohlmann suggests, the Comrade is challenging the bourgeois elements within himself.

The third and last section of *The Orators* consists of six odes and an epilogue. Four of the odes are dedicated to individuals, with the third to 'Edward Upward, Schoolmaster'. The poem itself reflects their visits to one another. Upward was very sensitive about his connections with the other 1930s' poets, particularly Auden, of whom he thought so highly but whose return to religion and his subsequent move to the right politically so distressed him. The relationship with Auden obsessed him and was most vividly expressed years later in his story 'At the Ferry Inn'. When the ode was included in a collection of twentieth-century British poetry that Philip Larkin edited for Oxford University Press, the dedication was omitted which Upward took to mean that Auden was disowning their association. The anthology had sixteen Auden poems, with the third ode included under the title 'The Exiles' which Auden had given it in the 1945 volume of his poetry. In early October 1973 Upward and Larkin exchanged letters about the removal of the dedication. Larkin responded that he selected the poems as they were found in the 1966 collection of Auden's shorter poems. No doubt the correspondence had a particular intensity as Auden had died just days before at the end of September. The same day that he wrote to Larkin he noted in his notebook, 'I can't believe I shall ever get over Wystan's death, and to

CHAPTER 4: OUT IN THE WORLD

try to suppress my grief is useless'. The eliminating of dedications, Larkin wrote, 'was certainly not a conscious decision on my part . . . Would you like me to try to reinstate the dedication in later impressions?' Upward promptly replied that he would like the dedication restored, in an intriguing letter about his relationship with Auden, particularly in the early 1930s.

> I would dearly like it, but only if I can feel convinced that he would have liked it. I do feel that this ode was written particularly for me. Not long before he wrote it I had spent my half-term holiday with him at Helensburgh – I was then teaching at Scarborough where he in turn visited me – and the ode (whose setting is Helensburgh and the Clyde) echoes the tone of a short story I had previously written about being a Prep school master . . . I had not at the time of writing it become interested in Marxism . . . I wonder too whether the restoration of the dedication might have been his way of telling me that though he had come to abominate the Marxist opinions which I perhaps more than anyone else had been responsible for his introducing for a while into his poetry, he did not abominate me as a person. I am quite sure that if I had posted that letter to him we would have become friends again. I had not written to him or tried to meet him since 1939.[56]

Some days later Larkin sent him a copy of a letter from Auden's executor, Edward Mendelson, stating that in the 1945 edition of Auden's *Collected Poetry* he had eliminated most of the dedications of individual poems. (The collection as a whole was dedicated to Isher-

CHAPTER 4: OUT IN THE WORLD

wood and to Auden's partner Chester Kallman.) The letter Upward refers to was one he wrote in 1970, a few years before, but which to his later regret he decided not to send. In a 1993 interview with Peter Parker, Isherwood's biographer, he showed him the letter still in its envelope with stamps on it.

> Dear Wystan, (If I may be so [?] familiar after our not having met or corresponded for more than thirty years.) I am writing to say how touched I am at the discovery I have just made that the dedication at the head of the second [actually third] ode of The Orators which was removed when the ode was printed in your 1950 Collected Shorter Poems has reappeared in the 1966 edition of The Orators. I want to say also how good I think the poems in your City Without Walls are. I know you must have a great many correspondents to deal with, so please don't put yourself out to answer this very short letter. All good wishes. Yours ever Edward[57]

Upward didn't take in that it wasn't that the dedication was restored but rather that as it was a reprint of *The Orators* the original dedications remained. His reservations about Auden's political position made him decide at that point not to send the letter. The unresolved nature of the relationship bothered him to the end of his life. The withdrawal of the dedication may have been to a degree a deliberate repudiation of Upward as well as a general removal of some of the other dedications. But Upward probably took the act as more calculated than Auden intended. Upward was unaware that Auden very much disapproved of his denunciation of Isherwood's turn

CHAPTER 4: OUT IN THE WORLD

to Vedanta and pacifism at the time of the outbreak of war. At that point Auden more or less ceased to regard him as a friend or acquaintance. It fitted in with Auden's separation from the 1930s, famously described in his poem 'September 1, 1939' as that 'low dishonest decade'. There is no question that they had been friends in the 1930s and that Upward was part of the same circle of writers with similar interests, approaches and styles and that to an extent they published together. But other than Isherwood, Upward never saw much of the other writers in the group, except for Auden in the early 1930s. In the *Letters from Iceland* that Auden wrote with Louis MacNeice, published in 1937, Auden did make Isherwood and Upward his executors. 'I here appoint my joint executors / To judge my work if it be bad or good. / My manuscripts and letters, all to be theirs / All copyrights and royalties therefrom / I leave them as their property in equal shares'.[58] At that point Auden was quite serious about that intention. Isherwood wrote to Upward at the time that Auden went to Spain in January 1937 that they were to be his executors.[59] It was Isherwood whom Auden adored, and including Upward may have been a way of pleasing him.

Upward spent much of the summer of 1930 in Buxted in Surrey working on his 'golf club' novel, and then abandoning it. He visited Isherwood in Berlin in August 1930 where he went to a 'bugger's ball' but was a 'wallflower' although he was propositioned by Karl Giese, the secretary for the Institute for Sexual Science. On his return to England he was summoned by Isherwood's mother to report on her son. In the letter to Isherwood in September 1930 he described the visit.

CHAPTER 4: OUT IN THE WORLD

> I went to see Mater yesterday and sat in your transmogrified room. I have betrayed everything, but very diplomatically. My only blunder was letting her know that you were paying for Walter. I was properly trapped. But I'm far from sure that I managed to convince her that buggery isn't unnatural. However I insisted that you were more terrific than ever in England. I am writing some really good poetry and am very frightened ... You shall have the first section of my Berlin Ode as soon as possible ... My mother is trying to get me to a mental specialist ... She knows I'm writing & is trying to smash me. She is now quite dangerously insane.[60]

In the Easter break of 1932 Upward made his one trip, of almost three weeks, to the Soviet Union. The visit was organized by the Society for Cultural Relations with the Soviet Union and led by Beatrice King, a Russian married to an English solicitor. It mostly consisted of teachers at schools and colleges. They went by train from Ostend to Leningrad under fairly Spartan conditions and in Russia they travelled on long train journeys with inadequate stops for food. On the trip there was a minor train accident, a derailment, ironic in the light of his short story 'The Railway Accident'. Also on the trip were two women who would become eminent economists on the left: Barbara Wootton and Joan Robinson. He was very impressed in particular by the visit to a children's theatre in Leningrad. The group did go to innumerable official sites: factories, clinics, institutes such as the State Institute for Scientific Pedagogy, the Hammer & Sickle Seven Year Factory School, the Kiev Academy of Science. They also had time for standard tourist sights such as the Hermitage. They had

CHAPTER 4: OUT IN THE WORLD

Upward with Barbara Wootton (to his left, with glasses and hat) and the delegation to Russia, 1932

to insist on seeing a collective farm as the authorities were reluctant to facilitate such visits because of the famine raging at the time. They were able to prevent the visitors from being aware of it. Wootton, although in favour of state planning, was less impressed than Upward, writing 'the black and white mentality, the reluctance to recognize shades of goodness or badness or of success or failure, the kindergarten children singing songs about achieving five-year plans in four, the inability to admit the existence of, or to talk over, the real problems of the present, were depressingly childish'.[61] Upward gave a talk about the visit ten years later in 1942 when any doubts he might have had were suppressed by the necessity to be pro-Russian, as the USSR was an ally of Britain. He admitted that it was not a democracy but claimed, erroneously, that there was freedom to criticize and that there was equality of opportunity and no class distinctions; and that there had been the successful completion of an industrial revolution through the Five-Year plan.[62]

Remembering the trip in later years, he was somewhat less enthusiastic. In 1979 he wrote in his notebook: 'Fields like the sea. The birchwoods. I did not expect to see a "workers' paradise" as the sneerers called it . . . I was not ignorant of the difficulties, and therefore the bad things did not take me by surprise . . . There was so much to admire'.[63] In retrospect he realized that the famine that was intense at the time was hidden from them.[64] Then in an interview with Peter Parker in 1993 he said: 'We insisted upon seeing a collective farm but they could only scrape up one miserable peasant to show us round – very suspicious. Of course, one saw drunks lying on the pavement – that surprised me at first, though of course you would have seen that in Paris'.

By the early 1930s, although he wasn't satisfied with his life it had taken on a shape that would continue. His career until his retirement in 1961 would be as a schoolteacher. But more significant for him and vividly present in his notebooks would be a dilemma: should he be a writer, a poet, even if he weren't writing much poetry, or be a political activist? How did the two relate to one another? Why should perceived literary failure lead to political activism? He continually changed his mind about which mattered most. And was one more important because the other was proving to be not as valuable as he hoped? For instance his 'Author's Note' for *In the Thirties*, published in 1962 (the year after his retirement), read:

CHAPTER 4: OUT IN THE WORLD

> *In the Thirties* . . . describes the experiences of a young man whose failure to live as a poet leads him to make common cause with the unemployed and with others frustrated by the social and economic conditions of the time, and to join the Communist Party of Great Britain. The second novel, *The Deviators*, [subsequently renamed *The Rotten Elements*] will show how and why, in the late nineteen-forties, without becoming anti-Communist he leaves the Party. The third novel will aim to vindicate poetry as having its own kind of truth, which the poet must not subordinate to political truth, and will show how he recognizes at last that his primary duty is to try once again to live as a poet.[65]

But then he vividly recaptures the central dilemma of his life – dealing with the eternal question of what is more important, life or art? – in his Author's Note at the time of the publication in 1977 of the three novels together as *The Spiral Ascent*. 'The trilogy as a whole has the form of two interlinked dialectical triads. In volumes 1 & 2 the "political life" supersedes the "poetic life" and is in its turn superseded by the "new poetic life", that is to say Alan Sebrill comes back to the "poetic life" on a higher level, and in volumes 2 & 3 the "new poetic life" supersedes the "political life" and is in its turn superseded by the "new political life", that is to say he comes back at last to the "political life" on a higher level. There is a spiral ascent in his development'. Or as he put it at the end of the Cambridge chapter in *No Home but the Struggle*: 'I recognise that the political struggle is far more important than poetry. Nevertheless, if I am to give of my best to the struggle, poetry must still come first for me'.[66]

CHAPTER 4: OUT IN THE WORLD

Isherwood and Upward in Berlin, April 1932, photographed by Stephen Spender

He combined his visit to Russia with a visit to Isherwood in Berlin on his way back home in April. There he met Jean Ross, the model for Sally Bowles. He had written to Isherwood an enthusiastic postcard from Russia: 'The place is utterly terrific. No daydream could give an inkling of it'.[67] Isherwood wrote about that visit many years later: 'Edward hadn't returned from his trip an uncritical raving Russophile; he was too British for that. But Christopher knew that he had been profoundly moved. What he had glimpsed in Russia lay much deeper than any visual impressions of Lenin's tomb and the Red Square and the parades. It was the implication of the revolution itself for the rest of the world, including England'.[68] Upward also saw their mutual friend Stephen Spender on that visit to Berlin, who has left a vivid account of their meeting, also written much later, giving

CHAPTER 4: OUT IN THE WORLD

Stephen Spender, photographed by his brother Humphrey Spender, 1930s

Upward's reactions to Russia and Spender's own reactions to him. 'He was a small, dark young man with a keen miniature-like beauty. He looked at objects steadily with the concentration of a bird-watcher, often fixing one intently with his eyes while he was talking or listening. He gave the impression of combining humour with high moral seriousness. When I asked him what the Russian landscape was like, he stared in front of him and said with an effect of mysticism mixed with irony: "The most beautiful in the world". In another age he would probably have been a country parson who discovered poetic inspiration in paradoxes of orthodoxy symbolized by flowers concealed amongst the hedgerows of an English lane'.[69] In his autobiography Spender presents Upward slightly differently and more romantically. 'He was not unlike the smiling

CHAPTER 4: OUT IN THE WORLD

young Comsomol hero'.[70] Spender thought sufficiently highly of him to give him some of his unpublished poems to read.

Paradoxically Spender and John Lehmann were responsible for both sides of what one might call the 'myth' of Upward (myths being not necessarily untrue). The more positive part of the myth was one of mountain peaks: that Isherwood was the mountain to be discerned behind Auden as a great influence upon him, and Upward was the mountain beyond Isherwood. The other side of the myth was that Upward had been ruined as a writer by encasing himself exactly at this period in what Lehmann called the 'iron maiden' of Marxism and loyalty to the Communist Party. Spender with his particular form of egotistical self-deprecation had a certain admiration for Upward. He saw him as remaining loyal to his Communist faith, having a far deeper commitment to the political far left, which was true, than any other of the iconic young writers of the 1930s. As he wrote to him in 1964: 'Your intuitive realization that the poetic life had to be fused with its opposite, a real life. I think your life has been realer than the literary life and think that in the end true poetry has gained'.[71] His attitude to Upward was both praising and patronizing. In his journals in 1960 he stated that 'on reflection I think that Edward Upward is the best of all the generation of the thirties . . . Thinking again about Edward Upward's career of schoolmastering. How decent, how entirely honourable'.[72] In an article about him in the *London Magazine* in 1987 Spender made the intriguing point about both Auden and Upward that their intellectual development was essentially religious: Auden returned to Anglicanism; Upward's relation to Communism was similar to a conversion.[73] When in 1951

Spender published his autobiography *World within World*, Upward liked it a lot and wrote on May Day to Spender to tell him so. But he also thought that 'Allen Chalmers' had been misrepresented in it to a certain degree. He did go to some length to take issue on how Spender had depicted him as being sympathetic to the purge trials in Russia. He admitted that at the time he thought the victims might have been guilty. But it was not the knee-jerk reaction that Spender accused him of. He also felt he was more nuanced than Spender credited him about how Communist and bourgeois characters were to be depicted in fiction.[74] Isherwood too found *World within World* 'exceedingly interesting' although he wrote to Upward, 'There is something in it to enrage everybody, myself and yourself included'.[75]

In his interview with Peter Parker, Upward remarked that he always found Spender rather two-faced in a somewhat paradoxical way: 'He'll say very nice things to you in private, then in public he'll say something very nasty'. Spender did try to help Upward's career along, being involved in supporting an Arts Council grant for the publication of the third volume of his trilogy and writing about him, at Upward's request, at the time of his ninetieth birthday as well as doing an introduction to a revised version of *Journey to the Border* in 1994. But this was in the future.

The Special Branch of the Police, concerned with security matters, and MI5 took note of Upward's trip to Russia. Upward had first become 'a person of interest', as such individuals were called, in June 1931 when he contributed to a fund for the *Daily Worker*.[76] The degree to which MI5 with the cooperation of Special Branch would track 'ordinary' members or in this case still just a sympathizer to the Communist Party was quite extraordinary and makes one believe

CHAPTER 4: OUT IN THE WORLD

W. H. Auden, Christopher Isherwood and Cecil Day Lewis at Dorland Hall, Lower Regent St, 1937

that Britain is much closer to being a police state, not to say paranoid, than one might have thought or hoped. It would appear that the object was that every known Communist would have a file, as well as many others who were seen as fellow travellers or in other ways as security risks. As either members of the party or fellow travellers this would include the members of the Auden group, such as Auden himself as well as Isherwood, Day Lewis, Spender and Lehmann. Edward and Hilda Upward have a joint MI5 file as she too had been under observation since 1931. In January 1934 Special Branch responded to MI5's request for information about her. Apparently it wished to know more about those who visited the

Soviet Union. The report stated:

> She is employed as a teacher at the Rolls Road, L. C. C. school, S.E.1., in the junior girls' department... Miss Percival first came under notice of Special Branch on the 19th June, 1931, when she contributed articles to the 'Daily Worker'. On the 27th August, 1932 she was present at the Anti-war Congress held in Holland [presumably the same meeting that Upward remembered having taken place in Brussels]. She was present at the London Conference of the London and District Educational Workers on the 12th December, 1932. On the 21st August, 1933 she returned from a tour of Soviet Russia. Her description is as follows: born 11-4-1909 in London, height 5ft 1in., hair brown, eyes hazel, fresh complexion, medium build; wears rimless glasses. Attached are copies of her passport photographs.[77]

The first substantial appearance of Upward himself in the MI5 records was on his return from Russia. Special Branch wrote to MI5 on 17 April 1932: 'I beg to report the arrival here [presumably Dover] at 7-15 p.m., to-day, coming from Ostend, of Edward Falaise UPWARD, age 29, a schoolmaster, of 'EDFU', Romford, Essex, travelling on British passport No. 11600 issued on 13th March, 1932. He had in his baggage a book entitled 'VOKS', which was published in Russia by the Soviet Society for Forming Friendly Relations with Foreign Countries, together with a number of pamphlets dealing with the social life in the Soviet Union. UPWARD said he had been on a tour through the U.S.S.R., as a member of the Teacher's Delegation, and had been away for about three weeks'. This letter

CHAPTER 4: OUT IN THE WORLD

precipitated a request from MI5 on 22 April to see his passport papers, which it kept for five days, and in May 1933 it requested to see Hilda's passport papers as well.[78]

Now, after his springtime in Russia and Berlin, Upward was to take up in the autumn the position that he would hold for the next twenty-nine years, being a schoolmaster at a prominent secondary school, Alleyn's, in Dulwich, south London.

Chapter 5: Schoolmaster at Alleyn's, 1932–1961

THE FOUNDER OF ALLEYN'S, Edward Alleyn, was a very successful actor, theatrical entrepreneur and manager of the Fortune Theatre. As such he was a rival to Shakespeare. He bought the Manor of Dulwich in 1605 and then established Dulwich College in 1619 as a school for a few poor scholars, Alleyn's College of God's Gift. It became a public school of very good reputation. Its lower school, known as Alleyn's, separated from the college in 1882 and transformed itself into a school that took boys from nine on, but it did not have quite the same social standing as its older part, Dulwich. It required an Act of Parliament to create Alleyn's, arising out of a desire of local parents for a more 'practical' school that was not committed to the classics. Alleyn's first headmaster, the Revd Joseph Henry Smith, was determined that the school should not be under the shadow of Dulwich and declared the separation through the adoption of soccer as the major sport rather than rugby. A separate girls' school, James Allen's, also emerged from the original foundation. (Alleyn's itself became coeducational in 1974.) Alleyn's had its own buildings by 1887. When Upward arrived there were about eight hundred pupils. It took pupils from nine to seventeen, many fee-paying and after the war a third on scholarships mostly given by the London County Council. Although a day school, it created a house system in 1907 with the names of each house's first head. Upward became the housemaster of Roper's in 1948. He was also in

CHAPTER 5: SCHOOLMASTER AT ALLEYN'S, 1932–1961

charge of the small Scribbler's Club for would-be student writers. R. B. Henderson, the headmaster since 1920, had Upward brought to his attention by a friend of Upward's brother Mer. He was the most transformative headmaster in the history of the school. In 1929 the school had officially become a public school when Henderson was elected to the Headmasters' Conference. He had begun his teaching career at Rugby and wished to make Alleyn's as similar to a traditional public school as possible, the masters to act as if they were at a boarding school and the boys to feel that even though they were living at home all their waking time belonged to the school. Upward, as a graduate of Repton and Cambridge, had excellent credentials. He was hired in the spring of 1932 to begin teaching the following autumn. He received a reassuring and friendly letter in June about his duties. He would be teaching the lowest form of the upper school

Alleyn's School, Dulwich, as it was when Upward taught there

CHAPTER 5: SCHOOLMASTER AT ALLEYN'S, 1932–1961

'oddments of history' and also English to the sixth form.

> Once in a form room here no one ever interferes in the slightest degree. There is a story that one man who used to drink beer in his form room only taught when drunk. I think you are in for a fairly light time as you are an extra man being added. Your no. of periods per week will be about 26. There are three half holidays per week Tues, Thurs & Sat when work ends at 1:15 except Sat when it ends at 12:30. On ordinary days work ends at 3:45, except Friday, when it ends at 3. Out of school duties are negligible . . . I hope that the Russian trip was a success. I gathered that Communism went over big and you still have hope for the Human Race. You are lucky if that is so. I have none.[1]

At times he enjoyed teaching and was on the whole good at it. But quite a bit of the time he disliked being a schoolteacher, regarding it as what he had to do in order to support himself and his family. As he wrote in his notebook in 1957 in two different entries: 'There is no harm in hating what makes the school what it is but I must never extend my hate to the human beings there'. 'Let me then face the new term with courage and with the thought that away from school I am doing what I was born for. Let me bear school as part of the hell I always knew I should be in for when I first realised I wanted to write'.[2] He was grateful that the school year provided the summers off, which he could devote to his writing. But the school was clearly not his major interest. As he wrote in his notebook in 1939: 'As an artist I hate the school from the bottom of my heart. It is mean and ugly and hypocritical. Yet I cannot – as I once could – be against it. I know I ought to make it better . . . What is my job? To spread

CHAPTER 5: SCHOOLMASTER AT ALLEYN'S, 1932–1961

communism, to spread poetry'. At times he was in despair. He wrote in August: 'School is destroying the best years of my life ... I shd have had money. That, at the present time, is the first prerequisite for serious work'.[3] It was the cry of the English gentleman: one should have a private unearned income in order to do what one wished with one's life. The paradox in Upward's case is that he would want to use the freedom that that would have given him to destroy the bourgeois society that had produced the income.

Even during the school year he hoped to devote three evenings a week to his writings, the other evenings to party work; he would also attend cell meetings. The police thought that he also had headed a teachers' cell in south-east London but I have not seen any indication of its activities.[4] But presumably he would also have to allow time for class preparation. His teaching style was quiet and not particularly dynamic. Most of his pupils thought well of him. In his journals he would frequently rail against the school as a prison and a torment keeping him from what was ultimately the most important thing in his life: art and being a writer. His notebooks are a continual dialogue – with very little discussion of his teaching career – about what is more important, art or life, the latter as primarily dominated by the need to create a better society through Communism. But should politics serve literature or literature politics? Ideally each would reinforce the other, but Upward could never resolve the dilemma. Teaching was a distant third. It supported him and, as did his wife's salary, his family. At times he was more sanguine, feeling that he held a socially necessary job that had both its rewards and its pains. He became head of the English staff in 1942. He was interested in school sport and played for the Wanderers, the staff

CHAPTER 5: SCHOOLMASTER AT ALLEYN'S, 1932–1961

football and cricket team, and umpired the under-fifteen sports. His attitude towards what he was doing was volatile. He hated the discipline side of school life, as he had hated fagging at Repton. Yet by the end of the 1930s he seemed almost positive about teaching. 'Now my daily work as a teacher becomes important, can do good instead of evil. I can be of use to the boys now; before, I was worse than useless to them. The hatred that existed on both sides has gone, I hope, forever. The accursed discipline has become friendliness'.5

Most but not all of the pupils who remembered his teaching were very enthusiastic about his abilities. There are scattered reminiscences about him, some gathered quite recently. The school has become aware of his eminence and has put up a display case about him. In a publication of 2011 about the school in the 1930s, among the five events mentioned as important in 1932, along with the teaching staff of forty-one taking a pay cut because of the Depression, and it being the fiftieth anniversary of the school, was that Edward Upward arrived as an English master. That same year, but before Upward's arrival, in a mock election the school voted for the National government, in effect the Tories. But the debating society, the 50 Club, voted for the Labour Party. In 1936 among the three items listed was that Upward established a junior League of Nations Union, in keeping with the Communist position to support the Popular Front. It was a cause close to the headmaster's heart. It was also recorded that in 1938 his novel *Journey to the Border* was published and that Christopher Isherwood visited the school, no doubt arranged by Upward, to give a talk about his trip to China. One might almost say that the school is now inordinately proud of him. One former pupil wrote, 'If there are any positive qualities in my prose, I am sure,

CHAPTER 5: SCHOOLMASTER AT ALLEYN'S, 1932–1961

looking back, that I owe them to the English teacher I had in the VIth at Alleyn's, Edward Upward'. Though the pupil, Pat Harvey, eventually became aware that Upward's own writings he 'found frankly dull or worse. He in my opinion fails utterly to rise to the importance of the fascinating autobiographical material he had there waiting to be exploited: a "liberal" Communist caught in the slimy trap of the Party discipline of the '30s and '40s. In his defence I should close by saying that his classroom teaching was devoid of any nonsense about "a Marxist interpretation of . . ." altogether'.[6] Upward was very self-conscious about politics in the classroom but he wished to do political work among the staff. Years later, in 1969, he reflected in his notebooks: 'It isn't quite true that I didn't try to get a Marxist line across in the school. Certainly I did among the staff, and even to some extent among my pupils . . . I did use literature when I cd to point a Marxist moral. Was my relation with the Sixth Form really so bad? It was certainly friendly. The real trouble was that I didn't want to be a teacher at all, was forced into it by economic need'.[7] He did manage to recruit two members of the staff for the party.[8] He felt that his politics might get him into trouble at the school but he probably exaggerated that worry.

He was not a dynamic teacher. He was highly conscientious about it but it was not at the centre of his being. He only seemed to be at peace with teaching when he was not happy or indeed in despair about his political or writing activities. He noted on 4 May 1953 that 'my job must be the main thing in my life . . . Politics took first place for me (as a revolt against the society which had not allowed me to live as a poet), writing second place, and teaching third'.[9] And then some years later he could write: 'So while I hate

CHAPTER 5: SCHOOLMASTER AT ALLEYN'S, 1932–1961

school like poison and love writing above everything I must nevertheless cope with school first . . . Writing is my solace and my only salvation'.[10] And yet quite a few years later he would remark, 'Slavery though teaching mainly was, how much worse trying to live by writing wd have been'.[11] He regarded the school with an attitude similar to the one he took to the world in which he found himself. He could hate it in the abstract but not the actual individuals within it. He felt he should do the best he could for his pupils. As Harvey relates, his pupils felt that he at times fell asleep during class. Once this was put to the test by inserting a scene of their own devising into a reading of *Coriolanus*. Upward did twig what was happening, confiscated the script but smiled and congratulated the pupils on writing Shakespearean verse that scanned quite accurately.[12] One of his former pupils, David Alexander, remarked about him that he 'was a very quiet withdrawn sort of man but with a wonderful understanding of English literature . . . He was a great influence *and* he was a card-carrying member of the Communist Party'.[13] Another former pupil was unenthusiastic about his teaching, feeling that his caution about indoctrinating his pupils made him too careful. 'The effect was that he would never express an opinion on any subject, including English literature. That limited his usefulness as a teacher'.[14] One pupil, John Crome, who went on to a career as a film director, had memories of his teacher from a different perspective, being, which was very rare, a young Communist at the school.

> Others will have written in praise of Mr Upward's sweetness, his schoolmasterly charm and his ability to inspire, but I want to tell a little about the aspect of his life that touched mine, and

CHAPTER 5: SCHOOLMASTER AT ALLEYN'S, 1932–1961

*The Upwards' house,
154 Turney Road, Dulwich*

which, to him, was the most important, his Communism. Mr Upward was described in one of the many obituaries as a typical schoolmaster of a minor public school, and so he seemed, and so he was. Let's face it, Alleyn's when I arrived there in the early fifties was, predominantly, what my mother would call a petit-bourgeois school . . . Mr Upward . . . fitted in perfectly despite his overriding political aim, that of eliminating the bourgeoisie and replacing 'bourgeois democracy' with Communism . . . It was comforting to know that there was a teacher who was on the same side. However, Mr Upward was scrupulous in keeping his politics out of the classroom.

Arthur Chandler, the historian of the school, was taught by

CHAPTER 5: SCHOOLMASTER AT ALLEYN'S, 1932–1961

him in the 1940s and remembered him 'as having a very laid-back style, but he was firm and you listened. It was a bit peculiar to have someone extremely left-wing teaching at an English public school. I was told that one teacher was advised to put an Upward book in a plain wrapper if he wanted to read it in the Common Room'.[15]

After his first year at the school he wrote with what one might call lighthearted despair to Olive when he was recuperating from the experience at the family house in Sandown. The teaching at

Above: Hilda Upward, April 1937
Left: Edward at Sandown, September 1938

CHAPTER 5: SCHOOLMASTER AT ALLEYN'S, 1932–1961

what was really his first regular job was quite exhausting. As he knew from Repton, the classroom could be a particularly difficult place. It could almost be a war of generations where behind the formal deference, the continual use of 'sir', there was something of a war going on about who would be in control of the classroom. The master had the sanctions of corporal punishment which Upward hated, and the pupils could employ the youthful techniques of adolescence. As Upward wrote: 'I haven't yet recovered – probably never shall – from the frightful wounds of last term. I dream every night of the dear old school. This won't do at all. Can't we start a profitable bookstore? To such daydreams does this temporary haven reduce me. I suppose when the time comes I shall be glad to return to the old war . . . I'm glad I'm not a headmaster. My brother has spent the whole holidays so far writing letters. My sister is acting in Northampton. There seems to be no C. P. [Communist Party] in the Isle of Wight yet'.[16]

The war years were perhaps the most dramatic time in the history of the school and also in the disruption that it caused for the Upwards as well as the other pupils and masters. In common with many other schools in the London area, it was evacuated out of the city. The day before war broke out, 2 September 1939, the senior boys went to villages near Maidstone in Kent while the juniors, after being there for a while, took off for Monmouthshire. In some senses Kent was a foolish place to go as it was more vulnerable than many other areas, not only to invasion but being under the flight path of German bombers who might choose to drop some of their bombs on their way home. The boys could stare up to the skies and observe the Battle of Britain. Once a Spitfire crashed a hundred yards from

CHAPTER 5: SCHOOLMASTER AT ALLEYN'S, 1932–1961

Edward at Rossall School, Lancashire; Hilda Upward holding her daughter Katherine, Cleveleys, Lancashire

where they were having a class. It was a difficult time in his family life as Hilda was expecting their second child. Jean Ross, the model for Sally Bowles, who had become a member of the Communist Party, came to the rescue and Hilda went to her house near Welwyn in Hertfordshire to have her baby, Katherine, on 2 March 1941. On 6 January 1941 the senior school moved to Cleveleys near Blackpool in Lancashire where it joined up with Rossall, a somewhat grander public school. The junior school ceased to operate for the duration.

While there, Upward enlisted in the Home Guard. When the war was clearly coming in August 1939 he had had no difficulty in accepting the Communist line that it was a war between rival imperialisms and that the Soviet-German pact was a way to prevent further British appeasement of Germany. He even naively thought

CHAPTER 5: SCHOOLMASTER AT ALLEYN'S, 1932–1961

Edward with his children Christopher and Katherine, Cleveleys

that the Soviet Union would send help to the Poles in their fight against the Germans. Rather amazingly, he wrote in his notebook on 25 October 1939 that 'Russia is and will remain a *peaceful* power, threatening no one', and in April 1941 that a 'B[ritish] victory would

CHAPTER 5: SCHOOLMASTER AT ALLEYN'S, 1932–1961

be an even greater disaster for the world than a Nazi victory'. When rereading this page in 1988 he commented that he was tempted to tear it out of his notebook, writing, 'How wrong mere logic can be when it becomes detached from reality'. Of course his view radically changed when Russia was invaded. He did praise Churchill as a consistent enemy of the Nazis.[17] The headmaster, C. R. Allison, making the best of the wartime situation, extolled the virtues of the boys having a boarding school experience, being schoolboys twenty-four hours a day.

In Cleveleys Upward became chairman of the local Anglo-Russian Friendship Society and was quite active in supporting the war now that Russia was in it. Perhaps paradoxically and bizarrely it was through these pro-war activities that he came under the close scrutiny of Special Branch and MI5. It began on 16 July 1942 when the Special Branch of the Lancashire Constabulary sent a 'History Sheet and Identity Form' to MI5, which noted among other features that Upward's hair was dark brown, that his complexion was 'fresh', that he was 'well spoken' and that his dress was 'usually grey suit, collar and tie, trilby hat, raglan raincoat. Respectable appearance'. In answer to the question, 'Is he a member of any Association, or Organisation, etc.?' the answer was 'Yes. Member of Communist Party, Blackpool Branch'. And to the next question, 'How does he spend his evening and spare time?' 'At home & attending local meetings of Communist cell'. The form also states rather surprisingly that he had an alias, 'T. Franklin'. Letters from Franklin, with a handwriting similar to Upward's but in my view not the same, are in the file about various Communist meetings in the area. There is also an entry for 'Remarks' where it is stated: 'UPWARD, as far as is known

CHAPTER 5: SCHOOLMASTER AT ALLEYN'S, 1932–1961

Edward and Hilda, early 1940s

bears a good character. He is well respected and holds a good position at the School where he is employed. He appears to lead a normal life but it is known that most of his political activities are carried out secretively and under cover. His associates are members of the Communist Party and persons connected with this political movement, in the district where he resides, mostly Civil Servants at present employed at Blackpool'. The last entry deals with 'Family Connections'. 'Hilda May UPWARD, wife of this man, who resides at the same address, is also an interested party in the Communist Move-

CHAPTER 5: SCHOOLMASTER AT ALLEYN'S, 1932-1961

ment. Apart from a son, who is only a child, no other relatives are known'.[18] For some reason his daughter Kathy was not noticed.

The misidentification of Upward with Franklin may have arisen as Franklin may have been a resident at the same address, 30 Whiteside Way, before the Upwards. There is an intercepted letter in Upward's MI5 file from that address, dated 1 January 1942 from Franklin in his role as treasurer of the Blackpool branch of the Communist Party. It is quite difficult to read but appears to deal with minor financial matters such as the collection of £6 for a Fighting Fund. The next preserved relevant document is a letter of 16 April 1942 from the Chief Constable of Blackpool to the Director General of MI5, Sir David Petrie, informing him that there is no evidence that Franklin resides at 30 Whiteside Way and that he would appear to be no longer associated with the Blackpool branch of the party. Both statements appear to be untrue. There is an 18 May intercepted letter from Franklin written from that address sending another £6 from the Blackpool branch to a party office in Manchester, mostly in the form of insurance fee stamps for 102 members. Also in the file is a list of letters sent to Upward but copies of their contents are not present other than a notation that one mailing was a magazine and another a printed paper 're the Women's Parliament'. On 16 June Sir David Petrie wrote to E. H. Holmes, the Chief Constable of Blackpool, about 'Upwood' (the name is corrected in the letter's last sentence), asking if he might be using 'Franklin' as an alias. He also notes that 'Upwood' had been the leader of the south-east London subdistrict of the party. Holmes replied on 22 June that 'Upwood' 'is using the name Franklin to cover up his Communistic activities. It has been ascertained that Upwood is using his house for the

CHAPTER 5: SCHOOLMASTER AT ALLEYN'S, 1932-1961

purpose of conducting lectures to prospective members of the Communist Party . . . At the moment Upwood is contacting and is interested in members of the Civil Service who are at present employed in Blackpool. A strict watch will be maintained upon Upwood's activities in this Borough. I am also contacting the Lancashire County Police concerning Upwood, since he resides and is employed just over the Borough Boundary, in the Lancashire County Police area'. On 20 July the Chief Constable's office in Preston confirmed to Sir David that 'observations are being maintained on this man's activities in my area', and it also corrected the spelling of his name. On 21 July the same office reported to MI5 that:

> a meeting was held at Cleveleys on 15.6.42., under the title of the Blackpool Civil Servants Current Affairs Discussion Group, which does not exist as an organised body, but is purely a cloak for recruiting Civil Servants into the Communist Party. Branch meetings are alleged to have been held at UPWARD's home where reference has been made to a Communist Cell in the Ministry of Pensions Office at Cleveleys Hydro and Norcross and the intention to form other cells in the various Ministries in the district to advance Communist policy in the Civil Servants' Clerical Association. UPWARD is also a member of the Anglo-Soviet Unity Committee at Cleveleys.

There are copies of further letters written in August in the file on the stationery of the party's Blackpool branch reporting at length to a party person, Pat Devine, in Manchester on the 'fiasco' of a meeting scheduled to be addressed by T. H. James, which through inefficien-

CHAPTER 5: SCHOOLMASTER AT ALLEYN'S, 1932–1961

cies and missed connections never took place. MI5 states that the letter is from Franklin and the handwriting looks the same, but the signature would appear to be different. The last Franklin letter in the file was written from Blackpool more than two years later, on 5 December 1945, after the Upwards had left the area. It made an inquiry of the unnamed educational organizer for the party in Manchester whether a 'District School' was to be held in January. So here we have a glimpse of how MI5 and the Chief Constable's office spent some of their time coping with the Communist threat.[19] To be fair, there was Communist espionage but it was extremely unlikely that Edward Upward was involved. The state wished to monitor Communist activity and particularly efforts to recruit converts to the cause. One further document of 16 November 1943 in Upward's file notes that a schoolboy at Alleyn's, one Geoffrey Norman Hancock, had applied for membership in the party but the police 'thought unwise to make direct enquiries at the school in this case, as one of the masters, Edward Falaise UPWARD, is said to be a member of the Communist Party'.[20] There is also other material in the file from the time that the Upwards were living in Cleveleys, intercepted letters that Hilda wrote to 'Dear C[omra]de' in Blackpool about who should be on which committee, about what room a meeting should be held in, and inquiring about a summer school, making sure that there would be enough milk for her children, aged three and five, whom she would be bringing.[21]

Although it was some years earlier, there is another set of letters in the MI5 file during the war concerning Edward's sister, Yolande. On 16 December 1939 Sir Vernon Kell, then Director General of MI5, wrote to the Chief Constable of the Isle of Wight to inquire whether

CHAPTER 5: SCHOOLMASTER AT ALLEYN'S, 1932–1961

she was a suitable person to be a member of the W.R.N.S., the women's naval unit, as she was a sister of a known Communist. He concluded his letter, 'I am of course anxious that she should not become aware that she is a subject of enquiry'. Yolande was then living with her parents in Sandown. In fact it turned out that she was already a member of the W.R.N.S although at that moment was on sick leave. The report, written by a Sergeant Butler, is rather interesting. He remarked that Yolande's father

> is well known locally and highly respected and is Vice President of Sandown Conservative Association... Although [her brother] is known to possess Communist views, there is no evidence that these views are shared by his sister, Yolande Upward. From enquiries made it appears that Yolande Upward does not openly associate herself with any Political party or express any extreme Political views and she is not believed to be sympathetic with Communist Views ... I am informed that shortly after the outbreak of war she joined the W.R.N.S. at Portsmouth and to have journeyed daily to Portsmouth from Sandown in this employment. She was later transferred to Ryde, Isle of Wight and, on or about 16th November, 1939 she suffered a breakdown in health and as far as can be ascertained she has not since been employed in that capacity. It would thus appear that this person is already a member of the W.R.N.S. This person is not known to me personally but, from enquiries made she does appear to be a suitable person to be employed in this branch of the Service. Nothing is known to her detriment in this district.[22]

CHAPTER 5: SCHOOLMASTER AT ALLEYN'S, 1932–1961

Alleyn's would be in Cleveleys until March 1945. Only about two hundred of the Alleyn's pupils joined the evacuation while about a hundred remained at the old school location. There they were joined by boys from other schools evacuated from central London. The time of return was a period of turmoil although there is no indication that this had any particular effect upon Upward himself. In the post-war spirit that British society should become more egalitarian there was a move, reflected in the Education Act of 1944 and the Fleming Report of the same year, that secondary education should be available to all without payment at schools that were receiving direct grants from the state. A compromise was worked out that direct grant schools could charge fees to the 50 per cent of their pupils who were not paid for by the London County Council. By a nice coincidence one of the figures who worked that out was Geoffrey Fisher, Upward's old headmaster at Repton, who was at this point Bishop of London. But the exact status of Alleyn's was cloudy and it was uniquely in the category of a 'Transitionally Aided School'. It became a direct grant school in 1957, with the fee-payers being charged £99 a year but with many free places available to boys from Greater London and also from Kent. In the 1970s direct grant schools were being pressed to become comprehensive schools, that is, less elitist, which Alleyn's did not wish to do. The Labour government in the 1970s dismantled the direct grant system. The Saddlers' Company, one of the City of London guilds, came to the rescue of Alleyn's with a considerable financial contribution, apparently the result of a former headmaster sitting next to the clerk of the company at a dinner.[23] So in 1974 the school became independent and coeducational. Upward was long gone, having retired in 1961, but to that date from 1945 he had taught at the school when it was likely to have been at its most egalitarian in the make-up of the pupils. I have not found any trace in his notebooks or elsewhere of his reaction to these questions. There is the nice Isherwoodian touch that in the 1970s Lord Wolfenden, perhaps most famous for the Wolfenden Report that led to the decriminalization of homosexuality in 1967, was the chairman of the governors of the school.

Much of the information about the post-war history of the school is found in Donald Leinster-Mackay's *Alleyn's and Rossall Schools: The Second World War, Experience and Status*. The ultimate paragraph of his brief study gives an excellent sense of what the school had become during Upward's time there as well as mentioning him as one of the school's claims to fame.

> Alleyn's today is a securely established day public school . . . It evinces many features of conventional public schools: extensive playing fields; handsome buildings: a wide range of extra-curricular activities including fencing, photography and fives; close Oxford (Brasenose College) and Cambridge (Gonville and Caius College) connections; a well-established Founder's Day, complete with blue cornflowers in the button-hole on that special day, a Founder sanctified by time, dating back to 1619; a chapel shared with two other public schools on the same foundation; a history of distinguished masters including Edward Upward (poet, novelist and former close friend of Christopher Isherwood), Sir John Maitland (gentleman and scholar), John Lanchbery (famous Sydney conductor and composer), W. J. Smith (musician *extraordinaire* for whom the school held in

CHAPTER 5: SCHOOLMASTER AT ALLEYN'S, 1932–1961

1989 a centenary concert) and Michael Croft (founder of the National Youth Theatre); a *national* reputation in at least three areas of school life – music, drama and cadet forces, and a national reputation on the sports field in soccer and cricket.[24]

To say a little more about Michael Croft: echoing Edward Alleyn's career, the school had something of a theatrical tradition. Croft was a master there from 1950 to 1955. Upward was one reason he had been attracted to the school. He wrote a powerful and successful novel, *Spare the Rod* (1954), which took place at a school somewhat lower on the social scale than Alleyn's although after the war there were more working-class pupils. The book was largely based on his earlier experience teaching in North Oxford; he thanked Upward for his 'advice and assistance' on the book. As Upward wrote about him, he came 'to stir things up . . . He accused us [the staff] quite rightly of, among other things, not visiting the boys in their homes'. Upward felt that his presentations of Shakespeare were at times too bombastic. He launched very impressive productions which were the origins of his National Youth Theatre. 'Shakespeare's lines seldom came "trippingly off the tongue", but at least the audience could hear every word they spoke'.[25] They were extraordinary large-scale productions, such as his first one of *Julius Caesar* on the school's playing fields, using the Cadet Corps as part of the cast. He is now memorialized by the state-of-the-art Michael Croft Theatre at the school. Shortly before his early death in his fifties in 1986, having established with a lot of difficulty the Youth Theatre, he wrote to Upward about visiting the school and how it had changed: 'The school itself has blossomed as a kind of centre for the liberal arts for those

CHAPTER 5: SCHOOLMASTER AT ALLEYN'S, 1932–1961

Edward as a teacher at Alleyn's, photographed by his pupil Eric Fray

who can afford to pay for the privilege. It seems incredible, going there now and seeing the youngsters sauntering about with an air of utter enjoyment, that the place could ever have been so reactionary and bigoted as it was when I was there ... Let others reap what we have sown!'[26] Recent graduates with distinguished acting careers are Jude Law and Sam West. The school has maintained its connections with Edward Alleyn.

Upward was not really a happy schoolteacher but it is fair to say that he was a successful one. It was also a necessary career and probably the best he could have chosen. He needed to have an income and with the short holidays during the year and the long one during the summer it provided him with time to write, although he

CHAPTER 5: SCHOOLMASTER AT ALLEYN'S, 1932–1961

was more prone to spend the time agonizing about his difficulties in writing. He took an academic year sabbatical from teaching in 1952–53, but more common than one might think on sabbaticals, faced by having unrestricted time to write, he panicked and had a nervous breakdown. He worried that the school might give him trouble because of his politics but in fact he never seemed to have any difficulty and might well have been able to proselytize more without dire consequences. The school treated him well when he was there and now it is touchingly proud of him as someone who sheds eminence upon it as one of its best-known figures and that he was there for twenty-nine years. When I visited some years ago there was in its main atrium a fine display in several cases about his career. As he wrote in his notebooks about whether his politics or his art was more important to him, so too he would frequently complain about how much he disliked his job and also feel that he wasn't good at it. Then more rarely he would grudgingly admit that he liked the pupils and his colleagues. On his retirement he didn't wish to say bad things about the school, but on the other hand he didn't want to lie and say how much he enjoyed it. He disliked the clock he was given as a retirement present. His career probably gave him more pleasure than he cared to admit. He was rarely happy in the situation he found himself in and his notebooks are full of railings against the awfulness of teaching. In many ways he had a good life, a good education, hate it as he might. He had a decent job, a happy marriage with two fine children and some standing in the literary world, though not as grand as that of the other writers of the 1930s with whom he was identified. He had a commitment to create a better world through Communism. He would appear to be a genial and friendly man. But beneath, as with the world of Mortmere, there was a seething angry person who profoundly hated the society that had helped create him. He held his position with the firmness of an assured English gentleman. He did not anticipate that now he was no longer teaching he would be happy and could devote himself full-time to writing. But he hoped at least that he would be *creatively* unhappy. Once he had achieved the longed-for point of early retirement, it was not, as he might have anticipated, as fulfilling as he had hoped. But it was also nevertheless a time of considerable accomplishment.

Chapter 6: Being a Communist and a Writer

FROM REPTON ON, Upward was very conscious that he was a rebel, against the system, opposed to its values, its hierarchies, its religion and how it was structured. But it is unclear why. He certainly benefited from it. As a son of a doctor he had the advantageous education of his class, a boarding prep school, a prominent public school and then further study at one of the ancient universities, in his case Corpus Christi College, Cambridge. He did not appear to be particularly unhappy. Though he regarded both Repton and Cambridge as hells he nevertheless had a good education there, made friends, most particularly Isherwood, did well and was quite a good athlete. In his mid-teens he became aware that his chief ambition in life was to be a writer, preferably a poet. After finishing at Cambridge he was obligated to earn a living, and as many had done in his position before, turned to schoolteaching. He had little interest in politics while a student. He was a rebel first and then discovered, via Marx and Lenin, how and why. But as the 1920s progressed he became more and more political, intensified no doubt at the end of the decade by the Great Depression. Britain had never really recovered from the First World War. But starting in 1929 its economic situation, as in the rest of the world, became increasingly desperate. Although there was a Labour government in power from 1929 to 1931 it was not able to cope. For quite a few of the brightest in British society Communism seemed the only solution. It provided

CHAPTER 6: BEING A COMMUNIST AND A WRITER

hope. In many ways a commitment or flirtation with Communism set the tone of the 1930s. It was both earnest but, particularly in Auden's work, leavened with irony and wit. How serious were they about revolution? Auden seemed to give a call for action. 'If we really want to live, we'd better start at once to try; / If we don't, it doesn't matter, but we'd better start to die'. The advent of Hitler in 1933, much more than Mussolini, made the threat of Fascism to democracy and world peace much more present. These writers were caught on the frontier, on the border, by the characteristic English combination of intense class consciousness and intense individualism.

Upward increasingly committed himself to an absolute repudiation of the bourgeois system through becoming a Marxist and his growing belief in the necessity of a Communist revolution. He turned to a reading of Marx and Lenin and it became clearer and clearer to him that he must join the cause of the workers. He was also reading Engels and Feuerbach. He wished to put the world to rights. As a self-conscious member of the middle class he also felt, with some sense of diffidence, that he must join the British Communist Party. In July 1931 in his notebooks he recorded the course of his reading. 'How gradually I have become converted to dialectical materialism I am not certain of myself even now. Marx's historical materialism was instantly convincing, but memories of Jung and disagreements with Richards kept me from really understanding the more fundamental theory . . . In the beginning was the deed. And the deed cannot take place in a void . . . Being forced to earn my own living has exposed for me the old lie: in the beginning was the word . . . The word is an aristocratic conception, suitable to an age of leisure & slavery . . . The deed will grow and it will kill metaphysics'.

Some months later he made clear how he felt writing and his movement towards Communism were connected. 'If I had never been a poet I should never have noticed anything wrong with my surroundings . . . There is only one way to escape – by revolution. Fire and blood, bishops floating, arse upwards in the ruddy river . . . The liberation of the working class is the liberation of poetry'.[1] This makes it somewhat clearer what was driving Upward, why he so detested the system that on the whole had treated him well. He did not have any personal experience of the Depression. He managed to find employment and he was not in much contact with what the working class was suffering. It was, however, a totally legitimate intellectual journey to a conviction that Britain should become a socialist, Marxist state. He seems to hold contrary views, as we all are liable to do, to his endless dilemma of whether art or life is more important. The question is well caught in a recent comment about William Morris by David Latham: 'For Morris, then, art is not merely the revolutionary dream of a "glimpsed alternative"; it is the full embrace of a revolutionary commitment to the potential of each individual life. Art must draw us beyond the threshold, across the sundering flood that rises between the hellish reality of how we live and the heavenly dream of how we might live'.[2] In this period Marxism became central to Upward's being and outlook on the world. Yet although he would from time to time condemn the outlandish conceptions of Mortmere he would not really abandon them. His object was to socialize them, to deepen them from manifestations of the corruptions of English society to symbols of its social ills. As Isherwood wrote in *Lions and Shadows,* the attempt was 'to find the formula which would transform our private fancies and amusing freaks and bogies into valid symbols of the ills of society'.[3] Not only to understand society but to change it. Upward thought that he found in Marx and Lenin the way that this could be done.

He went so far as to think that if he failed to be politically active, he might go insane. The paradox of his situation was that he felt he needed to be politically active in order to write, but as it turned out the period of his political commitment after the publication of *Journey to the Border* in 1938 until he left the party in 1948 was the time when he couldn't write at all. He felt that as a member of the middle classes he would not be readily accepted by the Communist Party. He began by doing political canvassing on behalf of the party in Bethnal Green in London in the general election of 1931. The party succeeded in acquiring 10.7 per cent of the vote, a higher figure than in any other constituency in London where a Communist candidate had run.[4] He then joined the party in a provisional way in 1932 and became a full-fledged member in 1934. His wife Hilda had become a member of the party in 1930. He was a highly committed member, canvassing and selling the *Daily Worker*, which needed to be done by individuals as the newspaper distributors refused to handle it. But he was so much of two minds about what he was doing that he was in danger of driving himself to distraction. As he wrote in his notebook on 1 February 1931:

> There must be no regrets – only a determination to destroy and rebuild . . . Before anything can be hoped for our society must be turned inside out. Destroy what is known as Western Civilisation . . . Come now, what do I want? Leisure, leisure, leisure . . . I am willing to admire and submit to the practical

Communist, but I don't want to be too practical myself. I think it proper that I should do some useful work, but I don't think it proper that I should give all my time to useful work. I don't want to be forced into a position of greater responsibility than I occupy at present . . . I want to do something, I want to write, I want to make our lives less sordid, I want to come out in flower.[5]

He eventually became very active on the editorial board of *Ploughshare*, the publication of the Teachers' Anti-War Movement, as well as making quite a few contributions to it. He published one story, *The Island*, in *Left Review* in 1935. But he made little effort to move beyond being an ordinary member of the party or to work or affiliate with the various literary groups within it, such as the Ralph Fox (Writers') Group, or the left-wing literary organizations later associated with the Left Book Club, such as its Readers' Group or its Poets' Group. None of the Auden circle took part alongside the recognized Communist Party writers in the founding of the *Left Review* in 1934. Upward, having just officially joined the party, was not a known writer at that point so it is not surprising that he didn't participate. He published in an early number as did other members of the group, Auden himself as well as Spender, Day Lewis and Lehmann. Some members of the Auden circle did address these organizations: Rex Warner, Cecil Day Lewis and Louis MacNeice.[6] In 1938 Upward gave a talk to a writers' group in south-east London on dialectical materialism.[7] He did not seem to visualize himself as a leader of the revolution but rather as a humble participant alongside the workers. He would seem to prefer to identify with the 95 per cent of the party who were working class. His affiliation with *Ploughshare* also connected him with the considerable number of members of the party who were teachers. The leadership of the party, such as Harry Pollitt, was suspicious of both its middle-class and intellectual members; most of the intellectuals in the party suffered from that double taint. In any case the party did not encourage the formation of literary groups.

The Communist Party was established in Britain in 1920 and ceased to exist in 1991. The successor to the *Daily Worker* was the *Morning Star* and Upward loyally continued to subscribe to it. The British party was never large compared to others in Europe. It arose out of the enthusiasm in Britain and elsewhere for the possibilities represented by the great revolution in Russia in 1917. As with the French Revolution, it would appear that a new and better world was coming into existence. It is a hope eternally doomed to failure but in many ways noble, even though terrible actions are so frequently committed in the name of the vision those revolutions represent. The 1930s were the party's most successful period outside of Russia. To many Communism seemed to be a possible solution to the world's ills, particularly the economic consequences of the Depression and the dangers of the rise of Fascism, first in Italy and in a more threatening form in Germany. Although the majority of the party remained working class, it was in the 1930s that it would have its greatest number of middle-class members, indicated to a considerable degree by the great growth of membership among university students. The working-class members tended to be pragmatists, the middle-class idealists. There was the small group of hard-headed individuals who ran the party. In 1932 it had a membership of approximately 7,000 and by 1939 it had grown to almost 18,000. At its height, after the Soviet Union had entered the war, it grew to approximately 56,000. In 1931 about 60 per cent of its membership consisted of the unemployed.[8] There was not yet a full awareness of the extent to which the Communist parties in various countries were subject to Soviet control nor of the price that was being paid in the Soviet Union for Communism in terms of repression, famine and death. The knowledge of the full horrors of Stalin's regime, the deaths and the purges, was yet to come. Upward had become convinced of the truths of the Marxist-Leninist analysis of society, most particularly through his reading of Lenin's *Materialism and Empirio-Criticism*. In the years before Upward's joining, the party had some effectiveness in organizing the unemployed but it had had fewer members because of its policy of 'Class Against Class'. That argued that all to the right of the party were 'social fascists', particularly those who might be construed as social democrats. In the 1930s the Communist-dominated National Unemployed Workers' Movement, particularly through its hunger marches, was very successful. Later in the decade the party changed to a policy of the Popular Front, hoping to have some cooperation with other groups on the left, perhaps even the Labour Party, in the fight against Fascism. Upward was in search of a faith and the party became for him his religion. But he also felt, with some exaggeration, that by joining the party he had become a 'nonperson', ignored by his society as a writer. He had to a degree some sense of confidence as a well-educated member of the middle class. At the same time he felt he had made himself an outcast, even though in fact he continued to live a thoroughly respectable life.

CHAPTER 6: BEING A COMMUNIST AND A WRITER

Upward remained a Marxist Leninist but left the party in 1948 as he thought it had become too revisionist in its willingness to cooperate with the Labour Party – not that that party had much desire to cooperate with it. Both he and his wife were active party members but did not appear to be involved to any great extent beyond the level of their local group and its meetings and activities, although they did participate in rallies and demonstrations in central London. The Upward household was totally dominated by Communist activities as might be true in other Communist families. Christopher Upward did feel that party activities were the most central part of his parents' lives. When the family was living at Cleveleys, it was perhaps a bit much for the boy to be lectured by his

Kathy, Hilda and Edward, walking in the country

parents during his bath time about the necessity to open a second front. And his daughter Kathy remembers that during the crisis in 1948 when Edward and Hilda left the party there wasn't time to read to her as she wished, and by the time they could return to doing so, she could read on her own. Later she would feel somewhat excluded by their political discussions.[9]

As a proper member of the party Upward belonged to a cell and attended its meetings. As the main thrust of the party was to organize the workers in factories, middle-class members such as Upward occupied a somewhat ambiguous position. He felt an obligation to try to convert his fellow teachers to the cause but quite correctly did not wish to endanger his position at the school by doing so to any great extent. Loyalty to the decisions of the party was a very important consideration and to disagree with it publicly was a major sin. As the guidelines for being a member of the party anywhere in the world stated in 1921: 'The communist organizer regards every single party member and *every* revolutionary worker from the outset as he will be in his *future historic role as soldier* in our combat organization at the time of the revolution. Accordingly, he guides him in advance into *that* nucleus and *that* work which best corresponds to his future position and type of weapon. His work today must also be useful in itself, necessary for today's struggle, not merely a drill which the practical worker today does not understand. This same work, however, is also in part training for the important demands of tomorrow's final struggle'.[10]

Although the point for Upward of being a Communist was to create a better Britain and a better world, he seemed to be more involved with his own personal dilemma of the relation of politics

CHAPTER 6: BEING A COMMUNIST AND A WRITER

to his own desire to be a writer. He appears to be willing himself to be politically active and it seems that he would prefer to be at home writing. Yet writing was such an effort for him. It was so painfully slow and he was constantly revising, rarely satisfied with what he had written. As he remarked in an interview in 1976: 'There's hardly anything I less wanted to do than to be active as far as direct political activity goes. It isn't my cup of tea in a way, and yet I felt that I had to'.[11] His was a middle-class Communism of someone who was not working class, was not involved with organizing in factories, the mobilization of the working-class. This was the main and in Britain on the whole the vain purpose of the party, although it did achieve significant power for party members in some trade unions. He had a certain sense of diffidence, as if his middle-class status might deprive him of the right to be a Communist. In a review of *In the Thirties* his fellow Reptonian Stuart Hampshire remarked that the book 'is the record of the pursuit of a moral ideal . . . This is the Marxism of the Nonconformist chapel, and not of the learned doctors and dialecticians, with a week-end ramble, and a Victorian passion for flowers and shells, in place of café conversation'.[12] Upward had a characteristic correspondence with Hampshire about the review, writing to him that it made him uneasy, particularly as he thought so highly of Hampshire. Hampshire replied: 'I was both moved and distressed by your letter this morning. I had hoped that I had shown in my review that I had recognised the literary purpose and value of the quiet style and gentleness . . . I enjoyed the book immensely'. Upward replied: 'I re-read your review in the New Statesman and I couldn't understand why I had found it so unfavourable when I first read it. I think it is extremely fair'.[13]

Upward was a careful reader of Marx and Lenin. He came to Communism much like a religious conversion, out of despair in which the alternative might almost have been madness. And there was the eternal dichotomy between politics and writing: which was more important? He tried to resolve the dilemma through such statements as, 'My prime aim is to help the cause, and to help it primarily through the means I am best equipped to use – writing'.[14] It was also a big adventure. He wrote to Isherwood in 1930 about his intention to join the party. 'Couldn't we somehow take over that paper [the *Daily Worker*] and write articles exposing uncle [presumably a symbol for respectable society] and short stories about criminal buggery? Seriously I'm going to try to get involved in a really big bomb outrage'.[15] He was in touch with the *Daily Worker* about possibly having a reporting job with it during the 1931 general election but nothing came of that. As he remarked to Isherwood, he was amused that it used the proper English form of the time, addressing him as Edward Upward, Esquire, on the envelope.[16] Shortly later he would write to him: 'Don't believe a word you hear about the Communists. It is quite untrue that they falsify the news. All bourgeois news is false, consciously or unconsciously . . . All talk about communist extremism is trash. Babies either come out of the cunt or they are brought to the house by storks. No intermediate theory is possible. We knew all this at Cambridge . . . I'm going daily to the Communist committee rooms at Bethnal Green. It's very wonderful indeed. But soon I shall have to throw bricks at the police'.[17] By 1933 he was devoting quite a bit of time to the party, writing to Isherwood: 'Three nights a week I go regularly to party work – worthless to the party but will be very valuable some day to my writing. And on an average one afternoon a week goes to the party too'.[18] He did not necessarily find the work exciting, noting on 20 April 1938: 'Work for the cause seems worthy but dull ... The peace movement is so boring'. And the next day: 'I must somehow find the time to combine party activity and writing in the right proportions. Neither alone wd be sufficient'. He continually changed his mind, or to put it another way, continually debated with himself whether his writing or his party work was more important. Later on he cut down his commitment to three meetings a fortnight, and not surprisingly he found the endless meetings boring and mechanical. Members of the party were also expected to be out and about, going to demonstrations, selling the *Daily Worker,* knocking on doors on behalf of candidates, selling pamphlets, in effect working for the cause. The meeting of the cell might be devoted to the discussion of Marxist texts. Being a member of the party was not an easy commitment. And one had to be loyal to it and the party line with expulsion a possible penalty for deviance. It was a faith devoted in the view of its members to creating a better world through organizing the workers to bring about a revolution. But also with the growth of the idea of the Popular Front the cell would also support Labour Party candidates. Upward would not object at this point, although he would do so after the war.

He was active in collecting dues. He could still be enthusiastic about it all despite the tedious aspects of being a good party member. Looking back, he wrote in 1946: 'My subject is still the necessity of communism ... Reading Morris again. How excellent he is. Only he and Caudwell [the Communist literary critic killed in the Spanish Civil War] touch what is nearest my heart ... Teacher's group at last resurrected. This has taken nearly a year'.[19] It is rather surprising that during these years he says very little about the Spanish Civil War which had so captured the imagination of so many on the left. He was in the midst of writing his novel and was about to get married. He did collect money on behalf of the Loyalists. A month after the war broke out he wrote in his notebook: 'Spain. How it makes me rage. I want to fight for them ... But I must get on with my drivelling book'.[20] He does say that if the party had asked him to go he would have done so willingly and there are later some indications that he felt he had not been as involved with that cause as he should have been. In a draft of a story his fictional counterpart has a discussion with Hilda's fictional counterpart about Spain. '"I was ashamed that I did not go to join the International Brigade", Alan said. "Quite unnecessarily ashamed", she said. "The Party would not have expected you to go. You and I were doing useful work among teachers"'.[21]

As a member of the Streatham branch of the party he was out on the streets in Bermondsey and Islington demonstrating against Sir Oswald Mosley, the leader of the British Union of Fascists. He was an active party member and his writing was in many ways dedicated to the cause. But his activities as a party member did not reflect his being a writer. According to MI5 he was a member of the C. P. Writer's Group, but if so he wasn't a very active one as no mention of it appears in his notebooks. MI5 also tracked his membership in the Educational Workers' League and has in its files a copy of a letter from him cancelling one of its meetings.[22] He was aware of the difference between himself as a middle-class member of the party and a working-class member. As he wrote in his notebook in

CHAPTER 6: BEING A COMMUNIST AND A WRITER

September 1935: 'The worker who comes to communism comes to it as a result of bitter practical experience. But the middle class intellectual comes to communism through mental rather than practical experience. I am trying to describe that mental experience . . . The actual events of my life wd be quite uninteresting but the events of my intellectual life are interesting'.[23] He was still very much committed to being a writer, and in a letter to Isherwood the next year he was seething with ideas for what he called prose poems. And he added, 'Each of us helps the revolution best by using his own weapons'.[24] He would also in the 1930s be quite doctrinaire in terms of literary theory about how it was crucial to be a Marxist in order to be a good writer. Perhaps to the detriment of his imagination in his trilogy, *The Spiral Ascent*, he strove to write a flat 'socialist realist' prose. Over the years he endlessly debated with himself the dilemma of writing versus action, and at this point in the late 1930s he wrote in his notebook: 'Before I became a communist my problem was What shall I write about? Then having become a communist I asked myself Why write? . . . So – during term at any rate – I devoted myself exclusively to political work . . . I think I was justified in asking comrades to give me more leisure for writing. My mistake was, when I got more leisure, to belittle the importance of political work . . . Unless it [writing] helps the movement it will be *aesthetically* bad'.[25] He loyally attended cell meetings, and in the first novel of his trilogy, *In the Thirties,* he recounts one at which a member is expelled for arguing that the party is descrting its Leninist principles, forecasting what Upward would do himself in 1948. But he wished to convey how he felt when he became a member of the party. When he was working on his novels, a very long process, in the 1950s he sent what

CHAPTER 6: BEING A COMMUNIST AND A WRITER

he had written so far to Stephen Spender for his comments. Spender found the conversion to Communism by the central figure, Alan Sebrill, too sudden. In reply Upward wrote: 'The effect I was trying to get in this first novel was of a convert's fresh and innocent enthusiasm for the Party. Disillusion comes in the second novel, and I can see no artistic reason whatsoever why it should pervade the first in the form of hindsighted irony. I aimed to write about the Party members in the same sort of spirit that Hazlitt wrote about Coleridge in his marvellous essay on his first meeting with the Lake Poets'.[26] There is a continual tension in his writing as he frequently aimed at a plain style to make it more accessible. Hence his writing might be flat because of his deliberate suppression of his imagination.

Perhaps this is the place to return to the central dilemma faced by Upward throughout his life: what is more important for him, writing or politics, or to put it in even more fundamental terms, art or life? One will inevitably return to the theme in discussing the third novel of his trilogy, *No Home but the Struggle*, and it has already been brought up with reference to various didactic statements he made in that book. In one sense he resolved the dilemma – how satisfactorily is hard to say – by having the topic of so much of his writing be political life. Stephen Spender pointed that out in a piece he wrote about him on his ninetieth birthday stating, perhaps controversially (but Upward probably agreed), that his commitment to politics was a religious conversion. 'He is the only one [of the Auden group] who in his work and his life has remained consistently concerned with politics ... Sebrill [the Upward figure in the trilogy] is essentially religious, a visionary'.[27] Within days in his notebook for 1954 he could write contradictory statements about his writings. 'I am going to write again . . . *but not for publication* . . . I *need* to create'. And then two weeks later, 'The truth seems to be that I have no real desire to write at present'. And then the next day, 'The muse has deceived me'. At another point two years later he could declare, 'I was born to be a writer – that is my central conviction'. On the other hand, he could state in 1961, 'Writing must be an adjunct to & not a substitute for life'. Or later in 1963 he would attempt to combine writing and social purpose. 'While I'm writing I'm at least trying to be socially useful. Only the feeling that I still have a function in society can keep me sane'. But he could also remark that same year: 'Art . . . To hell with duty'. Or the next year: 'I have never doubted that politics are more important than poetry and that poetry can & should help politics indirectly. There's that vital word – indirectly'. The solution was to support his political cause through his writing. He kept tormenting himself, changing his mind so often within days about whether he was going to be a poet or not. Years before, in 1940, on the first page of a new notebook, he planned to entitle it 'Poems'. 'Then I shall write the poems. I don't know what they'll be about. I only know I want to write them. They must not be planned . . . This morning I put to paper the first bit of creative writing I have attempted since the war began . . . Writing is the only "happiness"'. Yet on 9 August he firmly announced that he was giving up poetry. Or as he tried to reconcile the dilemma in 1978, that his writing was an assertion of his humanity against capitalism. But he also felt that it was an assertion against death: 'Never again to regard writing as being primarily for the struggle, though the struggle is still what I primarily live for'.[28] He eventually worked out the dilemma in a rather schizophrenic way. The first two volumes of his trilogy, particularly the second, were written as political texts in a realist style. Then the third provided a transition back to the writing life: a prelude to the writing of his later short stories, which he generally regarded as prose poetry, a return to his earliest commitment to be a poet. Or as he wrote to Stephen Spender in 1956 when he was working on his trilogy of novels: 'The poet ought never to allow politics (communist or anti-communist) to dominate his poetry. Indirectly the trilogy is an attack on "commitment" in imaginative literature. However my main aim has not been to deliver a message of any kind but to use my political experiences as material for a work of art'.[29] He wanted his writing to be aesthetically satisfying but his commitment to politics may have undermined that intention.

What about actual writing in the 1930s? He was a central member of what was seen as a dominant group in setting the spirit of the decade. The phrase 'British Writers of the 1930s', or more particularly 'Young Writers of the Thirties', brings to mind the Auden group. An exhibition in 1976 at the National Portrait Gallery with the latter title had on its flyer photographs of Auden, Isherwood, Spender, Day Lewis and MacNeice. Upward was not there, nor were Rex Warner and John Lehmann, but they were represented in the exhibition itself. A crucial shaping of the group as such was the publication of *New Signatures* although it also included others such as William Empson and Julian Bell. The book was a new departure; its publicity statement read almost as a manifesto against T. S. Eliot:

> These new poems and satires by W. H. Auden, Julian Bell, Cecil Day Lewis, Stephen Spender, A. S. J. Tessimond, and others, are

a challenge to the pessimism and intellectual aloofness which has marked the best poetry of recent years. These young poets rebel only against those things which they believe can and must be changed in the postwar world, and their work in consequence has a vigour and width of appeal which has long seemed lacking from English poetry.

The slim blue volume, no. 24 in the Hogarth Living Poets Series, came out in the spring of 1932, created a mild sensation then and has since been taken to mark the beginning, the formal opening, of the poetic movement of the 1930s. In a sense it was merely a continuation, a sort of joint issue, of *Oxford* and *Cambridge Poetry*, for only two of the nine contributors, William Plomer and Tessimond, had not attended one or other of the ancient universities. Several had already published books of verse – Lehmann, Day Lewis (*Transitional Poem* and *From Feathers to Iron*) and Plomer – in the Hogarth Series. Auden's *Poems* had come out in 1930 from Faber & Faber, where T. S. Eliot reigned. He played, like the Woolfs at the Hogarth Press, an important part in sponsoring the new movement. It had already received a fair amount of attention. All the contributors, even those whose first books were still two or three years in the future, had published in periodicals such as the *Listener*, *Adelphi* and the *Criterion* (edited by Eliot). In short they were not entirely unknown and unrecognized, nor was *New Signatures* quite the succession of discoveries that its legend credits it with being. But Lehmann, working at the Hogarth Press, was entirely right in his intuition that the public, 'sluggish in its appreciation of individual poets', might be 'obliged to sit up and take notice' if they were presented as 'a *front*'.

CHAPTER 6: BEING A COMMUNIST AND A WRITER

> The reviewers were impressed [Lehmann sums up], the public bought it and there was a general feeling in the air that Something had happened in poetry. We even had to print a second impression within a few weeks. Several of the poets were already known individually; but the little book was like a searchlight suddenly switched on to reveal that, without anyone noticing it, a group of skirmishers had been creeping up in a concerted movement of attack. Some of us were, perhaps, as surprised as the public to find that we formed part of a secret foray . . . However, an impression had been made on the public that no amount of reservations or protestations on the part of individual contributors could efface, and from that moment we were all lumped together as the 'New Signatures poets'.[30]

The crucial point of difference between the writers of the 1930s and their immediate predecessors had more to do with history (content) than with literature (technique). 'Perhaps, after all', Spender decided some twenty years later, in his autobiography *World within World*,

> the qualities which distinguished us from the writers of the previous decade lay not in ourselves, but in the events to which we reacted. These were unemployment, economic crisis, nascent fascism, approaching war . . . The older writers were reacting in the twenties to the exhaustion and hopelessness of a Europe in which the old régimes were falling to pieces. We were a 'new generation', but it took me some time to appreciate the meaning of this phrase. It amounted to meaning that we

CHAPTER 6: BEING A COMMUNIST AND A WRITER

had begun to write in circumstances strikingly different from those of our immediate predecessors and that a consciousness of this was shown in our writing ... We were the 1930s.[31]

Upward had ceased to be a poet; otherwise he might have been in the collection. But the next year, when Michael Roberts edited for the Hogarth Press *New Country*, Upward contributed two stories, his very first publications in prose, 'The Colleagues' and 'Sunday'. The book was subtitled 'Prose and Poetry by the Authors of *New Signatures*'. In fact some of the original poets were not represented, most notably Empson and Bell, and it included exclusively prose writers such as Isherwood, with a story 'An Evening by the Bay'. It was based on the visit their fellow Reptonian and would-be novelist Hector Wintle made to Isherwood and Upward at Freshwater. It recounted their going to a nearby bar where Wintle tried to pick up a girl. Virtually all the writers in the anthology were at that point committed to the left. Roberts's introduction was their manifesto. Although the collection also included William Plomer, G. F. Brett, Charles Madge, Richard Goodman and A. S. J. Tessimond, the iconic writers were noticeably there: W. H. Auden, Stephen Spender, C. Day Lewis, John Lehmann, Isherwood and Upward. Among Auden's four poems was, arguably, his most left-wing effusion, 'A Communist to Others', the poem of his most influenced by Upward. Roberts's lengthy preface talks of the generation of writers represented in the book as having grown up under the shadow of the First World War but having been too young to participate in it. In Isherwood's terms, they are now setting themselves a new 'Test': coping with the crushing problems of the Great Depression and the rise of

Fascism. Roberts tended to lump these writers together, claiming that they all felt the need for revolutionary change even though they might well have mixed feelings about the Communist Party. He wrote of the necessity to declare one's politics and to move towards an English form of Marxism: 'If Marxism seems to us to be tainted with its nineteenth-century origin yet nevertheless to be, in the main, true, if, in the hands of its present exponents, the doctrine seems inelastic and fails to understand a temper which is not merely bourgeois but inherently English, it is for us to prepare the way for an English Lenin by modifying and developing that doctrine'. Rather extraordinarily, considering that the book was published by the Woolfs at the Hogarth Press, the preface attacks, inaccurately, Bloomsbury. 'Bloomsbury is absurd not because of its minor affectations, but because of its impotence, because it is an agglomeration of individuals wrenched out of their proper environment so that their abilities no longer serve or give pleasure to themselves or others'. Yet it is a very English manifesto, and it would seem that Roberts wants a revolution, the abolition of the English class system, in order to preserve village cricket, that it shouldn't be replaced by Test Matches. He felt that the impulse to write could no longer be purely literary and that it was necessary for it to identify with the working class. It is a very individualistic and English sort of Communism that he is advocating. 'Economic communism is valuable only in so far as it removes the vested interests which by enforcing standardisation, oppose all genuine education, the full development of the individual which might be possible in a state of social communism'. His preface ends with an example of what he means as he remembers, a distinguished mountain climber himself, the sense of community he found in a group of twelve schoolboy and undergraduate mountain climbers.[32] In the prose section of the anthology the first piece is Cecil Day Lewis's 'Letter to a Young Revolutionary', giving advice about joining the Communist Party. He argues that one must have faith in a new life. In the poetry section the last poem is Rex Warner's 'Hymn' with its concluding lines: 'All Power / not to-morrow but now in this hour, All Power / to lovers of life, to workers, to the hammer, the sickle, the blood. / Come then, companions. This is the spring of blood, / heart's hey-day, movement of masses, beginning of good'.[33]

In the prose section it is hard to grasp the leftist content of Isherwood's story other than some of its minor characters being working class. But certainly Upward's stories had social implications, the first presenting the problem and the second the solution. 'The Colleagues' is about a boys' scout troop at a school and the masters who run it. The story begins in the voice of the older master who wishes to co-opt the younger one into doing the proper thing in the handling of the scouts. The last pages of the story switch to the voice of the younger figure wishing that he had declined to be helpful. 'Why acquiesce for an instant? Decline utterly to be an accomplice. Queer the whole schedule'. But he realizes that he is likely to give in to the system. 'Never risk being thought to imagine yourself Shelley. Be passive. Be active. Be nothing. Be a schoolmaster . . . Nothing that happens in the school grounds has any connection with what happens in the town outside . . . I shall be here or in places similar to this for the rest of my life'.[34]

More dramatic was Upward's second story in the volume, 'Sunday', which Samuel Hynes regards as the most political piece in the collection.³⁵ The story is very brief, only six printed pages, written when he was still a probationary member of the party but announcing, in effect, his conversion. Spender, writing about the two stories in his 1935 study *The Destructive Element*, found them religious in tone. He thought sufficiently highly of them that he submitted them, unsuccessfully, on Upward's behalf to the *Criterion*, the literary journal edited by T. S. Eliot. Upward accepted Spender's statement that 'The Colleagues' was religious but felt that 'Sunday' was not. As he wrote to him: 'You did me proud. I'm afraid it's true that the Colleagues is religious, but I wrote that before I knew anything about communism. Sunday is expressly anti-religious'.³⁶ Spender also saw 'Sunday' as being Kafkaesque.³⁷ Upward is continually being compared to Kafka but in fact he was not very familiar with him, although he was perhaps by chance reading *The Castle* at this time. He was certainly not influenced by him. Some thought his prose was similar although he actually disliked what he regarded as Kafka's style of fantasy. (He has also been called more accurately a prose Magritte.)

'Sunday' is a much more 'modern' story than 'The Colleagues', written in a stream of consciousness style. It does have a sense of fantasy. 'This is a public path, no discrimination is made against persons not moving on a definite errand, against women without tennis shoes, men who aren't easily called Freddy by their colleagues'. The narrator goes to his lodgings for lunch, 'recognising the future, vindicating the poets, retiring between pillars as Socrates, desperate as Spartacus, emerging with Lenin, foreseeing the greatest of all eras'. The narrator's more immediate worry is using a duplicating machine for the first time. He is also concerned that he might be sacked without a testimonial, echoing Auden's poem 'A Communist to Others' which had adopted Upward's Communist voice. 'Epictetus would tell me that this is something outside my control, that I ought to be ready to accept it without complaint if it comes'. He concludes that 'history is here in the park, in the town. It is in the offices, the duplicators, the traffic, the nursemaids wheeling prams, the airmen, the aviary, the new viaduct over the valley . . . It is going to live with the enemies of suffering'. In the concluding lines of the story the narrator 'will go out into the street and walk down to the harbour. He will go to the small club behind the Geisha Café. He will ask whether there is a meeting to-night. At first he may be regarded with suspicion, even taken for a police spy. And quite naturally. He will have to prove himself, to prove that he isn't a mere neurotic, an untrustworthy freak. It will take time. But it is the only hope. He will at least have made a start'.[38]

In 1935 Upward published in *Left Review* a short story, 'The Island'. A monthly journal edited by Montagu Slater, Amabel Williams-Ellis and T. H. Wintringham, *Left Review* was dominated by the party. It also included pieces by sympathizers, the first issue having a brief symposium on 'Writers and War' with contributions by J. B. Priestley, Siegfried Sassoon, George Bernard Shaw and Stefan Zweig. The fourth issue, no. 4, January 1935, had Upward's story. It also included contributions from John Lehmann, Sylvia Townsend Warner, Winifred Holtby and D. S. Mirsky. 'The Island' takes place on the Isle of Wight which Upward knew intimately. It is written as an address to a workman embarked on a holiday on the island. In a sense the story was a prose parallel to Auden's well-known poem of the same year, 'August for the People'. The story has a fine sense of the island as it is and as it was. The speaker urges the recipient of his thoughts to enjoy himself like other visiting workers. Yet there are fears about the economic horrors of the real world not only on the mainland but on the island itself. Hunger and war are present. It is a meditation on the nature of the island that ends with the necessity of making it a fit place for men and women to live. Two years later the story was reprinted in a collection with a characteristic title for the 1930s: *In Letters of Red*. This anthology was an eclectic collection including among its twenty contributors Auden, Day Lewis, MacNeice, Warner and also Siegfried Sassoon and John Strachey with an essay, 'The Education of a Communist'. (Although he never actually became a member of the party Strachey was a dedicated fellow traveller.) In the introductory note about Upward in the volume, it is stated that he is 'the most interesting modern writer whose name does not show in the British Museum Catalogue'.[39]

Upward's next major bit of writing was the eighteen contributions he made to *Ploughshare* between 1935 and 1938. One was unsigned, the others were signed either EDFU or E.F.U. It was the publication of the Teachers' Anti-War Movement, presumably Communist dominated. Upward served on its editorial board from 1936 to 1939. His pieces were very brief and were mostly rather unsophisticated disquisitions on the cause of war – imperialism – and how to prevent war: the workers must refuse to manufacture its tools. The publication became *The New Ploughshare* in 1938 and in its July–August issue of that year there was a poem by Auden, 'James Honeyman', presumably secured by Upward. It fitted into the concerns of the publication as it told the tale of a brilliant young man who invented a bomb that, rejected by his own government, ended up destroying him and his family. He also published a piece by Isherwood, 'A Day in Paradise', a suitably ironic sketch contrasting the touristic version of a tropical island with the dreadful poverty that was there. It was based on a visit Isherwood had made to the Canary Islands in 1934. Hilda also wrote for the publication. Upward's first contribution, 'Peace Talk', in January 1935 was a didactic sketch about two schoolmasters listening to the headmaster's speech on Armistice Day. Mitchell, the Upward figure, tells his fellow teacher that the real causes of war are capitalism and imperialism. His frequent contributions over these years seem more dutiful than inspired; for example, a very short story in the April–May issue in which two schoolmasters are talking about the stories in 'Boys' Papers' and how their young heroes are embryo empire-builders or Fascists. In June–July 1935 there was a very short review of Ignazio Silone's *Fontamara*. In the issue of September–October he wrote a dialogue criticizing the Officer Training Corps at schools. In June–July there was a short review of the Communist Tom Wintringham's book *The Coming World War*. Upward agrees with Wintringham's view that wars are caused by imperialism and will end when the working class refuses to manufacture the tools of war. In November–December Upward makes suggestions for what would be a proper headmaster's speech on Armistice Day in which he would argue for taking action to prevent the war in Abyssinia from escalating. The issue of January–February 1936 contained a discussion of military toys for children. In April–May he wrote about the decline of truth in wartime and how teachers were co-opted during the First World War. In June–July there was a piece about a German girl, presumably fictional, who supported Hitler but had some doubts

CHAPTER 6: BEING A COMMUNIST AND A WRITER

about him. In November–December he returned to Armistice Day, arguing that Italy, Japan and Germany were causing the present war situation. His last sentence called for action on the Spanish Civil War 'to help the Spanish people to save their country from the agents of the German and Italian militarists'. His contribution to the January–February issue of 1937 was a review of *Spain in Revolt*. In a following issue, September–October, there is another brief review and in January–February 1938 a piece about treaties between nations increasingly reverting to pre-war aggressiveness instead of moving towards peace through the League of Nations. In the renamed *The New Ploughshare* of April 1938 he wrote 'Is Peace-Teaching Propaganda?' which argued in favour, not surprisingly, of teaching the virtues of peace in schools. 'The Armaments Scandal' of June 1938 was against the manufacture of arms for private profit. In July he wrote approvingly of collective security. In December his last piece was a reprint of his earlier one on military toys but with an illustration of Fascist items that included figurines of Hitler and Mussolini.

These were minor works of prose, some in the form of stories. Elsewhere, in 1937, he published perhaps his best-known, indeed, somewhat notorious essay, 'Sketch for a Marxist Interpretation of Literature'. In the mid-1930s he was at his most dogmatic about his Marxism, reinforced by his reading of Lenin. In 1935 he wrote firmly to Spender while commenting on his left-wing book of literary criticism, *The Destructive Element*, that he had no doubts about the correctness of the Marxist analysis.

> I see no reason why the communist's knowledge of the future should make him write badly about the present; on the con-

trary it should give him an insight into the present which a writer ignorant of the future could not have. No communist pretends to know the future in detail, but we do know the broad outlines of the political future, we do know that eventually the working class will overthrow capitalism – just as certainly as we know that eventually the light of the sun will give out. Our knowledge is a scientific knowledge ... I am convinced that though it is possible for a writer to write a good (from a literary point of view) novel from a non-communist standpoint, the same writer could write a very much better novel from a pro-communist standpoint.[40]

The 'Sketch' appeared in one of the most characteristic publications of the decade, *The Mind in Chains: Socialism and the Cultural Revolution*, edited by Cecil Day Lewis, at the time a member of the party and a leader of the cell in Cheltenham, better known as a genteel spa town. In his view, in the Soviet Union the workers were free, having broken their chains. He felt that for the same to happen in Britain intellectuals and artists must join forces with the workers. Among the eleven essays in the collection were Rex Warner on education, Anthony Blunt on art and J. D. Bernal on science. And Upward on literature. In it he was continuing, explicitly, his debate with I. A. Richards. He believed that literature and criticism must be firmly connected with the material world. 'The more nearly a critic succeeds in ignoring the objective world, the more limited and irrational will his practical criticism be. The more closely he approaches to the Marxist practice of explaining spiritual realities (i.e. thoughts and feelings) in terms of material realities (i.e. nature and human society) the fuller

Front cover of The Mind in Chains, *1937*

and more scientific will his criticism be'. The essay reflects a conflict within Upward himself and his desire to suppress his natural tendency towards fantasy. 'A modern fantasy cannot tell the truth, cannot give a picture of life which will survive the test of experience; since fantasy implies in practice a retreat from the real world into the world of imagination, and though such a retreat may have been practicable and desirable in a more leisured and less profoundly disturbed age than our own it is becoming increasingly impracticable to-day'. He discusses Proust, Joyce and Lawrence, writers he admires but feels ultimately fail and will not last (!), as they share, even Lawrence, the life of a social class that is doomed to extinction. For the Marxist 'no modern book can be true to life unless it recognises, more or less clearly, both the decadence of present-day society and the inevitability of revolution'. Later he admitted that these judgements were 'hurriedly written, insufficiently thought-out and very short and it was ridiculously over-simple'.[41] But in the essay itself he announced in no uncertain terms: 'A writer to-day who wishes to produce the best work that he is capable of producing, must first of all become a socialist in his practical life, must go over to the progressive side of the class conflict'. He recognized that this will not guarantee that one is a good writer, as the person must also possess talent. 'But unless he has in his everyday life taken the side of the workers, he cannot, no matter how talented he may be, write a good book, cannot tell the truth about reality'. He must also devote time to the struggle which may limit the time he can devote to being a writer, which was certainly true in Upward's case. But in the future, when the class struggle has been won, the writer will be able to devote himself exclusively to being a writer. 'Such a happy situation for the writer has not yet arrived, though in Russia it is on the way, and in Russia already writers are better off than anywhere else in the world'.[42] However much he may have regretted this article and however much it was attacked as being overly dogmatic, he really never wavered in his belief that in order to achieve truth, writing could not be hostile to Marxism.[43]

In a prominent essay in the *Times Literary Supplement* in 1937, 'Marxism and Literature', A. L. Rowse paid special attention to this essay as signifying the new trend in criticism, although he also cited the writings of Ralph Fox, T. A. Jackson, Christopher Caudwell, L. C. Knights and Herbert Read. He saw it as a reaction against more textual criticisms based on literary forms. He did not mention I. A. Richards but this was the literary position that Upward was reacting against. Rowse also argued that this approach is less original than its practitioners believe, that earlier there had been literary criticism firmly grounded in social and historical context. He cited as an example Leslie Stephen as a precursor of the Marxist point of view in his *English Literature and Society in the Eighteenth Century* published in 1904. 'It is the most explicit anticipation of this "Marxist" literary criticism that has appeared in this country. For not only does it relate, in the most systematic and satisfactory manner, the content of eighteenth-century literature to the social conditions of the time, but it goes further to apply the conception to literary form'. He criticizes Upward's standards as not being aesthetic enough and that he and his colleagues are rather addicted to a Puritan theology. He feels that this approach deals well with the history of literature but is not a means of literary or aesthetic criticism. But he is aware of the degree that this left-wing literary criticism is the new and powerful

CHAPTER 6: BEING A COMMUNIST AND A WRITER

note in the writings of the 1930s.[44]

George Orwell, writing in 1940, discussed the 'Sketch' in his 'Inside the Whale', his essay about contemporary literature that rather improbably begins with Henry Miller's *Tropic of Cancer*. In a famous paragraph full of those wonderful Orwellian generalizations he summarizes the literary situation.

> Quite suddenly in 1930-35, something happens. The literary climate changes. A new group of writers, Auden and Spender and the rest of them, has made its appearance, and although technically these writers owe something to their predecessors, their 'tendency' is entirely different. Suddenly we have got out of the twilight of the gods into a sort of Boy Scout atmosphere of bare knees and community singing. The typical literary man ceases to be a cultural expatriate with a leaning towards the Church, and becomes an eager-minded schoolboy with a leaning towards Communism . . . For the middle and late 'thirties, Auden, Spender & Co. *are* 'the movement', just as Joyce, Eliot & Co. were for the 'twenties.

Orwell specifically includes Upward in this group. As he points out, paradoxically these 1930s' writers were much closer tied by birth and education to the English Establishment than were the dominant writers of the 1920s such as Joyce and Eliot. He ascribes to Upward the influential idea that an author must 'either be actively "left" or write badly'. Orwell sees the move to the left being driven by both middle-class unemployment and the need for a belief system, in this case to be found in the Soviet Union and Stalin. 'It is the patriotism of the deracinated . . . They can swallow totalitarianism *because* they have no experience of anything except liberalism'. Orwell recommends, not a course he followed himself, that the writer keep out of politics, a major reason Miller is a central figure in his essay.[45] Upward continually wanted to revise his work and in an interview in 1977 he both accepted to an extent Orwell's criticism and modified his point of view. 'What I should have said and what I believe I intended to say but expressed myself badly was "no book written at the present time is likely to be good unless the picture it gives of reality is, intentionally or unintentionally, at least similar in the main to the picture a Marxist writer would give"'. He also regretted his attack on fantasy in that essay 'because it is the form that always came most naturally to me'.[46]

In later years Upward came to feel he overstated his case, commenting in an interview in 1969 that it was the worst thing he ever wrote. He also recognized in the interview that the party was rather like the Catholic Church.[47] 'It was meant to be provocative, and for that reason was rather silly. But many of the ideas in it I would still hold by. But some I wouldn't'.[48] In the same interview he mentioned that his father had known Orwell's father quite well, but he did not elaborate on how that came about and it is quite unclear where they were likely to have met. He disliked Orwell as a writer and felt that he was antisocialist in *Animal Farm* rather than, the more standard interpretation, that the fable was pointing out how easily socialism could go wrong. He remarked in an interview some years later about his Marxist piece: 'I think the essay's pretty awful . . . What I was trying to do – what hadn't been done at the time – was to establish some sort of connection between Marxism and literary value'.[49] In order to conform to the guidelines that he suggested in the essay, he tried to move to a plainer style, less immediately attractive than his more fantastic writing. After publishing his trilogy he developed in his short stories a synthesis of realism and fantasy.

Starting in the early 1930s, having put aside one project, the so-called 'golf club' novel, he turned to another writing endeavour which he referred to as 'The Border-Line', published in 1938 as *Journey to the Border*. It is his best-known work. As he said of it in 1934, 'The Border Line was conceived as an honest history of myself in transition from bourgeois to communist'.[50] The concept of the border and of the frontier tells us a lot about the literary world of the 1930s. The border or frontier must be approached – but can it be crossed? – in order that another and better world might come into existence. Auden and his circle in their early poems depicted a blighted vision of England, this country of ours where nobody is well, and called for a 'change of heart'. Coming to the border marked in Upward's case a commitment to the workers' cause. Although the idea of crossing the frontier and getting away from stultifying England was important for this group of writers, only Auden and Isherwood actually permanently left England for the United States. (After the war Auden did return to spend time at Oxford and also lived partly in Austria.) In the late 1920s and early 1930s, most famously Isherwood and to a lesser extent Auden and Spender literally crossed the border to live for varying periods of time in Germany, and in Portugal. Germany, before Hitler, was an extremely exciting place to be. So Isherwood presented it in *Goodbye to Berlin*, and particularly in its best-known story, 'Sally Bowles'. Borders presented the possibilities for a better future life as a writer, as a political being, as an

CHAPTER 6: BEING A COMMUNIST AND A WRITER

individual, as an Englishman. For Isherwood, Auden and Spender, Berlin was a place where they could live freely as homosexuals; as Isherwood later wrote in *Christopher and His Kind,* 'Berlin meant boys'. A homosexual life was possible in England but it had to be furtive; blackmail and jail were always threats, as homosexuality was illegal in England until 1967. Upward chose to regard Isherwood's homosexuality as partially a political act, a defiance of society. And these young men also found in Berlin the political fight between the Nazis and the Communists much more intense than politics at home. After the high drama of the General Strike of 1926, the conflicts between Tory and Labour, even between Communists and the British Union of Fascists, might be comparatively pallid and ineffectual although the battle against the British Union of Fascists did heat up. Upward was active in resisting Fascist demonstrations and in helping with the hunger marches. In England the Tories ruled for most of the period.

There was the Labour government of 1929 but it culminated in the sell-out by the Labour prime minister Ramsay MacDonald in 1931. That year a Tory-dominated national government took office that did not appear to offer any viable solution to the problems of the Great Depression. It became increasingly tempting to cross the border metaphorically through Communism into the promising new state of the Soviet Union and for some into the Fascist state of Italy and later Nazi Germany. But there were other borders to be crossed. Auden and MacNeice wrote *Letters from Iceland,* and Auden and Isherwood *Journey to a War* about their trip to China. Then with the coming of the war Auden and Isherwood crossed the border to the United States. The theme of travel was incessant,

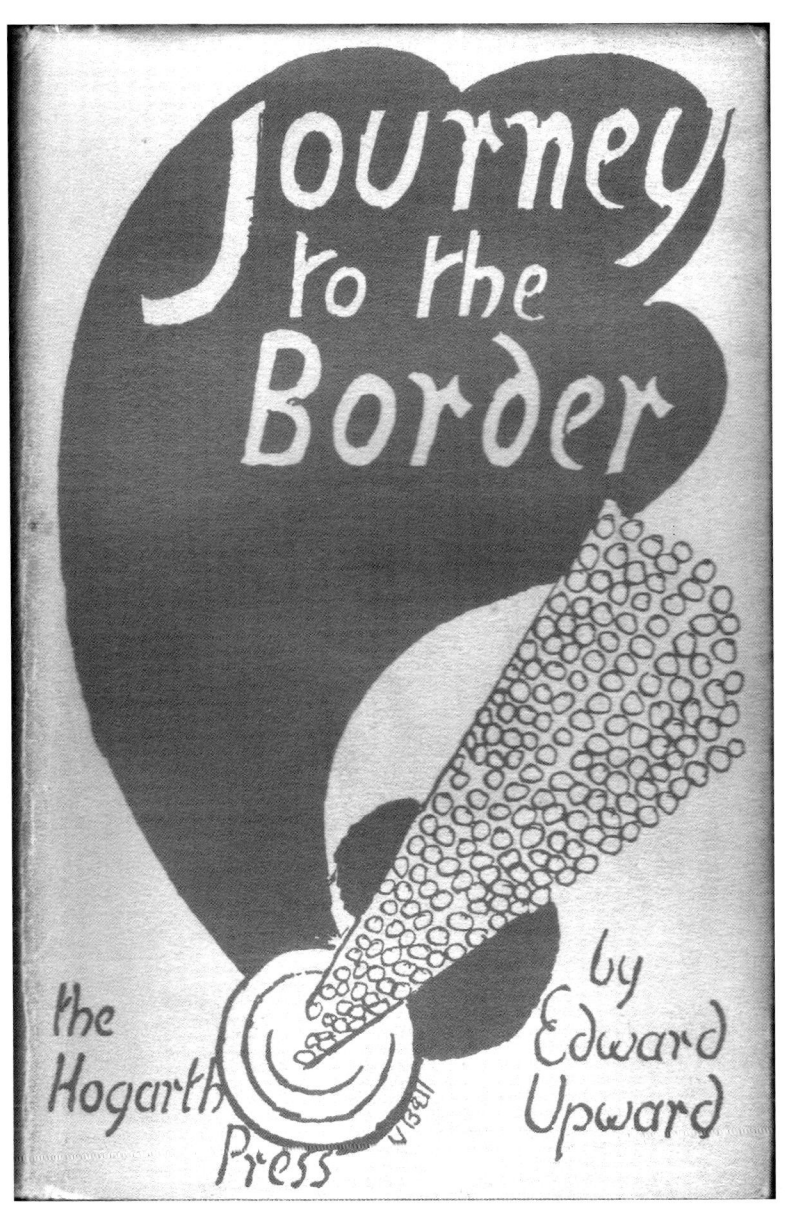

Journey to the Border, *Hogarth Press 1938, dust jacket by Vanessa Bell*

and it would seem that quite a few of the 1930s' writers were forever on the move, living for varying periods of time in foreign places. Going abroad was a way of finding a more interesting life and also a way to pick up some income through travel articles and books.

Journey to the Border is in so many ways a characteristic work of the 1930s. The material is realistic yet in quite a bit of the narrative there is the world of fantasy, the world of Mortmere. At the same time it is something of an anti-Mortmere book. Although there is fantasy in it, it is also a polemic against fantasy, Upward turning on his earlier self. Much of the book is in the mind of the central character, the unnamed tutor, and at times Upward referred to the book as an allegorical fantasy. His principal aim in life was to be an imaginative writer, but at this point he felt it was necessary to do that through a commitment to politics. Could Upward in effect turn against fantasy, using fantasy? He wanted to write in a way that was comprehensible to the working-class reader, a style that he saw as comparable to the poems of Wilfred Owen. Yet he was full of continual doubts about his writing and unease about Mortmere. It was difficult and almost perverse for him to keep his high imaginative skills suppressed. He started to work on the novel, as he noted with customary precision, on 24 January 1932.[51] As usual he was pessimistic with some justification about how his writing was going. He wrote extremely slowly and continually revised. Isherwood was the only person to whom he showed the manuscript. He wrote to him in 1934: 'In some ways it seems very good and in others monumentally boring. The Mortmereish part that I have now arrived at falls very flat, I think. I have lost the art of working up a romantically

CHAPTER 6: BEING A COMMUNIST AND A WRITER

John Lehmann in the 1930s

sinister atmosphere with conviction'.[52] At last he recorded in his notebook on 6 September 1937, 'Twenty minutes to twelve. Have finished The Border-Line'.[53]

Now he needed to face the issue of having it published. Here a central figure was John Lehmann. At Cambridge Lehmann was a very close friend of Julian Bell's and through him met Bell's aunt, Virginia Woolf, which ultimately led to his working for the Hogarth Press. He also published with the press, not only in *New Signatures* but two books of his own poetry, their titles suggesting the transition to left-wing politics that was taking place in the 1930s: *The Garden Revisited* in 1931 and *The Noise of History* in 1934. Lehmann figured in the Woolfs' both confrontational and cooperative relationships and friendships with the young writers of the 1930s. Lehmann introduced them to the Woolfs and they were happy to publish

CHAPTER 6: BEING A COMMUNIST AND A WRITER

them. In 1936 he launched the first issue of the semiannual *New Writing*, in effect a continuation of *New Country*. Margot Heinemann has characterized both the *Left Review* and *New Writing* as having between them 'introduced much of the seminal writing of these years. To study them provides a context for the most characteristic thirties writing'.[54] 'New' was such a characteristic term of the time, yet harkening back to Ezra Pound's modernist cry, 'Make It New'. *New Writing* was not published at first by the Woolfs at the Hogarth Press but rather by John Lane. Lehmann had left the press at that point in part because Leonard Woolf was so difficult to work for. (He was later to return.) The Manifesto for the first *New Writing* announced that 'NEW WRITING is first and foremost interested in literature, and though it does not intend to open its pages to writers of reactionary or Fascist sentiments, it is independent of any political party'.[55]

MI5 took note of the forthcoming publication and Upward's possible connection. In his file there is a paragraph from an intercepted letter from Paris of 23 November 1935 from John Lehmann to Claud Cockburn, the prominent Communist journalist. 'I shall be home fairly soon now, and collecting material for the first number of the periodical I told you about. It's now almost certainly to be called The Bridge, and will appear twice a year, book size. Christopher, Edward UPWARD, Stephen SPENDER, AUDEN, Ralph FOX, a couple of Left Reviewites, some Germans and some French, will, I hope, almost certain be represented in Vol. 1'.[56] The volume contained the first of Isherwood's Berlin stories, 'The Nowaks', poetry by Stephen Spender and Boris Pasternak and the first chapter of Upward's novel, still known as *The Border-Line*. Lehmann published in the second issue one of George Orwell's most famous essays, 'Shooting an Elephant', which he had especially written for Lehmann, his fag at Eton. And then subsequently he published Isherwood's 'Sally Bowles', Isherwood writing to Lehmann that it 'had unexpectedly passed Edward Upward – so I am sending it to you'. A second excerpt from Upward's novel appeared in the third *New Writing*, now issued by the Communist press, Lawrence & Wishart. But it was actually Isherwood who persuaded the Woolfs to publish the novel. In November 1938 Upward signed a contract for it with an advance of £20. The title was changed as it was discovered that another novel with the same title had been published by Heinemann. Its publication date was 10 March 1938. Vanessa Bell designed its dust jacket for which she was paid £3. The press also tried, without success, to find an American publisher, being in touch with Knopf and W. W. Norton among others. Donald Brace of Harcourt Brace liked it but felt it wouldn't have enough of an audience in the United States.[57] By the standards of the time it was moderately successful. It was recommended by the Book Society. The very well-known photographer Howard Coster did a publicity portrait of Upward. It received on the whole good reviews. Fourteen hundred copies were printed at the price of seven shillings and sixpence and 438 were sold in the first year.[58]

Isherwood had written to John Lehmann: 'Edward's book is being published by the Hogarth in early spring. This after a terrific putsch on my part. There was a wonderful dinner party given by the Woolfs to the Upwards, a great success. Virginia is really the nicest woman I know: she was so nice to Mrs U. Elizabeth Bowen came in afterwards [as did Isherwood himself], so Edward got a real glimpse of Bloomsbury, and quite enjoyed it, in his chilly way'.[59] 'Chilly' seems an inaccurate word to describe Upward who was generally friendly and outgoing in conversation. He might have been somewhat reserved on this particular occasion, meeting the Woolfs for the first time. Upward remembered vividly that Virginia smoked a cheroot. Isherwood's *Lions and Shadows* was published at the same time. In it Upward, as Allen Chalmers, was a major figure. It dealt in part with the creation of Mortmere, a contribution to British modernism and a significant part of literary history. In *Journey to the Border* the central character's movement leftwards was a familiar theme in British writing in the 1930s. In Upward's case it included his conversion to Communism. Virginia Woolf was pleased with the reception of the books, noting in her diary: 'Our last Leonard & Virginia season is perhaps our most brilliant: all the weeklies I think single out Isherwood, Upward, & even Libby Benedict [author of *The Refugees*] for the highest places. Yes: if there is success in this world, the Hogarth Press has I suppose won what success it could. And money this year will fairly snow us under'.[60]

Journey to the Border draws on his teaching experience after receiving his degree from Cambridge, when he served as a tutor for private families, particularly his time at Lockerbie. It takes place on one day beginning at a grand country house when the unnamed narrator wishes not to accompany his nouveau riche employer, Mr Parkin, and his son, the tutor's pupil, to the races but he finds himself weakly going along. At the racetrack he has experiences which represent the various 'borders' that he might cross to a different life. Drawing on Upward's earlier Mortmere writings these have elements of the fantastic and are probably taking place in the tutor's

CHAPTER 6: BEING A COMMUNIST AND A WRITER

mind. Some verge towards madness while others are more realistic, standing for the struggle throughout Upward's life between his political world of social realism and the world of the imagination reflected in fantasy. He conceives his text as revolutionary yet also thinks of it in Arnoldian/Forsterian terms. As he wrote about the novel in his notebook in January 1936 with rather the air of a New Year's resolution:

> The prime aim of writing is to say something that ought to be said . . . I cannot write unless I believe that it is duty to write. What am I here for? To help the revolution to the best of my ability . . . To show for the middle class intellectual there is no way out except communism . . . Shall I write a bad book for the workers or a good one for the middle class? And my present trouble is that I am still not absolutely convinced that the second course is the right one. I know it is but I don't yet feel it . . . [The Border Line] is genuinely, organically revolutionary, not just verbally revolutionary . . . My object shd be to convert the middle class to communism or at least to bring them closer to communism. What is a 'good' book? Roughly, one that sees life steadily and whole. And to see life steadily & whole at present means to see it moving towards revolution.[61]

He also wished the book to be an honest history of himself as he travelled towards Communism. He had a dream of being much more involved with the working class than he could ever achieve. He may eventually have come to know some working-class individuals in his party cell. He was not a union organizer. He did not engage in revolutionary action. Yet he hoped that his writing would advance

CHAPTER 6: BEING A COMMUNIST AND A WRITER

the revolutionary cause.

Being a tutor in a country house represented a willingness to conform to the system. Will the tutor be able to break free? Can he be more than a lackey to the world of capitalism? The narrator fantasizes the dominant villain as the local M.F.H. Upward assumed that his readers would understand that this stood for Master of Foxhounds, the head of the local hunt. The M.F.H. is an owner of mines. 'He's got no ability, and yet he's a millionaire. The fact that he isn't capable of doing his own thieving makes him even less excusable. He poses as an amiable country gentleman, and lets his paid agents do the dirty work of collecting his rents and squeezing profits out of his mines ... His father stole a fortune from the miners ... The only people who really provide anything are the miners themselves'. Later on in the book the M.F.H. in fantasy morphs into a Fascist leader, perhaps in some sense echoing that the leader of the British Fascists was a baronet, Sir Oswald Mosley, a member of the gentry who was wealthy because his family was lucky enough to own land in Manchester.

The tutor's employer's friend, MacCreath, offers the tutor a better job. This turns out to be a fantasy. He does issue an invitation to a dance that evening, as one of his daughters is fond of the tutor. The tutor fantasizes a conversation with her at the racetrack. He proposes that they take off and travel. 'Come to Reykjavik ... Anywhere. Ecuador. London. Now. Just as we are ... Without even a toothbrush'. He also believes that he has converted her to socialism and that she is now more active than he is, selling pamphlets to the workers down at the docks. She accuses him of inaction. 'The strange thing about you is that you see quite clearly what is wrong

CHAPTER 6: BEING A COMMUNIST AND A WRITER

with the system under which we are living... But you take no action. You are content to hate and despise your life'. He claims that he will take the job her father has offered to procure for him and work for the cause of the workers at the same time. But she refutes his position. 'You will never be free in your mind and heart so long as all your actions, your real life, are still wholly in the service of the rich'. The next possibility that the tutor considers is going out to the empire for a job, Nigeria or South Africa. The endless frontiers of the empire.

Another possibility would be to join the Fascists led by the M.F.H. As one of the characters says to him: 'After the Election we decided to form our first Storm detachment down here. Now we've got three detachments. We take our orders from G.H.Q. in London. The party is developing at the rate of about ten thousand new members per week'. The next frontier the tutor considers is the psychological. The problem is that one doesn't live according to one's desires. This was a point of view heavily influenced by Auden and adopted by him for a while when he was in Berlin, an amalgam of the ideas of Freud and Homer Lane, as expounded by Auden's friend John Layard.

> Disease is a result of disobedience to the inner law of our own nature, which works by telling us what we want to do and has no use for 'don'ts'. From childhood up we are taught that our natural desires are evil, that we must control them, deny them room to grow. But they will not be denied. Twisted, clogged with moralizings, driven back from all normal avenues of development, they nevertheless find a way of asserting them-

selves, appear in disguise, take on unexpected and abnormal forms ... There is hope for the sufferer. If only he will abandon Conscious Control ... There is only one sin ... and that is disobedience to our desires.

The next possible border to cross would be through sex and travel. The tutor meets a girl he had fallen for on one meeting in Cambridge some years before. They consider running off together immediately to 'Anywhere. Everywhere. Honolulu. London. Now. Just as we are. Cape Wrath. Better still – Reykjavik'. (Upward seems to enjoy echoing Auden and MacNeice's trip to Iceland.) These encounters are fantasies.

A growing sense in the text is that if he doesn't make the right decision he will go insane. Upward sees this as the border of his title. 'Between sanity and insanity there is a sort of no-man's land. The opposing forces in the deep trenches on either side wear conspicuous uniforms and can be easily distinguished from one another, but no responsible psychologist would be prepared to state categorically to which side belonged an individual crawling in the intervening mud among shell-holes and wire-snags. Your condition could be best described, in clinical languages, as "on the border"'. The tutor must learn that his problems cannot be solved in the heart or the mind but in the external world. In the dialogue with himself the tutor says: 'You would have achieved something, however little, for the cause. Your life would not have been altogether wasted and worthless, as it would have been if you made no effort at all to help the movement'. Having come to this conclusion, he fortuitously meets a worker at the racetrack and discovers an opportunity to

CHAPTER 6: BEING A COMMUNIST AND A WRITER

Kathy, Edward and Hilda Upward, Jean Ross and daughter Sarah, Scotland, 1951

assist in unionizing his factory, establishing contact by simply walking into one of the meetings. He would commit himself, and political action would be more important to him than his personal life.

Perhaps the eternal dilemma for any life, perhaps but not necessarily more acute for the artist, is what is more important, what one does, art, or what one is, life. Throughout his life Upward vacillated, as recorded in his numerous notebooks; should his first commitment be to politics in order to try to make a better world, or should it be to what was so important to him, his life as a writer? Would that ultimately allow him to make the more significant political contribution? In order to try to achieve both, which should he devote himself to? Would the commitment to making a better world sustain his art or would it be the other way round? This journey to the border in the book would seem to argue in favour of politics first. Were art and life two different countries with a frontier, or one

CHAPTER 6: BEING A COMMUNIST AND A WRITER

world? In the novel he partially puts the dilemma in terms of love. 'Love could never come first, could never be sufficient in itself. The fight for the cause must always come first. Afterwards there might or might not be love, but he would never find it if he went out deliberately hunting for it. Nevertheless, he must not turn his back on it, like a monk'. What he attempted to do in the novel, and succeeded not totally but to a considerable degree, was to achieve what would generally be regarded as a contradiction: imaginative socialist realism. His wish was to write in a simple style that at the same time would be fantastic. His main aim in his writing was to create a work of art.

The commitment is low-key, as befits an English novel, and the tutor declares his independence by telling his employer that he won't be returning that night, not to go to a dance as his employer first thought but to go into the town and establish contact with the local workers' movement. He has now committed himself to be with the working class. But he recognizes that he still needs employment so he hasn't left his position. 'What the workers would require him to do for the movement he did not know. They would certainly not advise him to run away from his job as a tutor ... He would at least have come down to earth, out of the cloud of his cowardly fantasies'.[62]

The book also demonstrated that Upward was a master of prose, that the hours that he devoted to his writing paid off. For instance, here is a long quotation from *Journey to the Border* about a steamroller!

The tutor had time to look carefully at the steam-roller. He looked carefully because it reminded him of something. After his shock he saw it at first as something dangerous, but he soon realized that it was not a danger – it was a power. It was simple and bold and powerful, crested in front with a rampant brass unicorn, thumping with its pistons like a thumping heart. The echoing of its roller over the stones was like the hollow sounds of skates on ice. It was bold with the gala boldness of engines stared at by children from a nursery window – big traction engines dragging gipsy caravans to a fair, engines with wire guards over their funnels and with funnels protruding through their long decorated roofs, engines with their long roofs supported by gilded pillars and with dynamos in front of their boilers for making lights on roundabouts in the evening. It was bold with a reminiscent boldness. It was bold with the naïve boldness of a child who sticks out his stomach and makes piston movements with his arms in imitation of a big locomotive. It was bold, too, with a mature efficient boldness, with the boldness of its austere-looking driver. It was simple with a generous mechanical simplicity, with the simplicity of its whirling governor and of its ponderous flywheel, of its burnished steering-wheel, and of the wheel at the back for lowering and raising its steel road-breaking teeth. It was powerful with the chuffing indifferent power of a train carrying away a boy to a school which he hates and fears but which he knows nothing can save him from. It was powerful with the gay sun-glittering power of a motor-coach in which a middle-class young man sets out for an unfrequented part of the country where he thinks he is going to live the just life, like Socrates. It was powerful with a steaming sighing power, a power not of despair but of compassion and understanding, as though someone were saying gently to the tutor: 'Remember your past. Look how you have betrayed yourself, wasted yourself, you poor blunderer. How you have brought disaster upon yourself, trying to go your own way. But from now on you will go my way, will be iron, be new'. It was powerful, more powerful, far, far more powerful with the power of a great mountain, which no apathy, no forgetfulness, no wishing can ever destroy. It was the victory of the new vision. Its boldness, its simplicity, its power, were what the tutor had wanted to see, had struggled to see, and now they were here before him, outside him, wholly independent of his wanting and struggling. Now he could cease to want and to struggle and the steam-roller would still be there, animating him from outside with its boldness and simplicity and power. The new vision was here and it was solid and real and it could not fade. It was here, it was everywhere. He hardly needed to look elsewhere to prove its ubiquity. He was certain of it. His eyes were full of tears. He had triumphed.[63]

He had travelled to the border. The novel is, I believe, one of successful resolution. Yet it also marked, sadly, the beginning of a long period of artistic sterility. Upward would barely write again, with a few exceptions, until the early 1950s after he had left the party in 1948. There was the war and the moving about with the school that that entailed. He did continue his party work but what he was most interested in was his art.

His novel received an interesting set of reviews. On 12 March

1938 V. S. Pritchett wrote about it with three other novels (by Libby Benedict, Upton Sinclair and Osbert Sitwell) in the *New Statesman*. He found it something more than 'another conducted-tour over the well-worn macadam of New Country'. The tutor is 'a Left-wing prig yet a very likeable fellow ... The book is a brilliant, acute and most refreshing study of a widespread contemporary state of mind. Mr Upward has, moreover, the art of saying important and serious things with lightness, economy and wit'. Pritchett was less enthusiastic about the book in an essay he wrote in the *Fortnightly Review* in June. There he felt that new left-wing novels had replaced the traditional aspect of English novels – the countryside as the location of all that was good – by the proletariat. 'By inverted snobbery, they now long to get into the proletariat as they used to long to get into the country', as Upward was doing in his novel which he here misnamed, interestingly, as *Over the Border*. He wrote that Upward made 'his fussy little intellectual hero realize that the famous New Country over the Border, the promised land and its accompanying fight for freedom and so on, is as yet nothing but a day-dream. Even more, a private nightmare or war game. It is merely a state of mind ... I doubt whether any political novel of the first order will be written until the period of faith passes and the disillusion of the crusaders sets in'. Ironically Harold Brighouse in the *Manchester Guardian* criticizes the novel in class terms, not to Upward's credit, seeing him as something of a snob in his view of his nouveau riche employer. Upward was bred as a gentleman after all. 'I could sympathise the better with this fellow were he less conscious that he is, and that Parkin is not, a gentleman ... The tutor decides finally to live down his morbid fancies in active work for the Labour movement, and

CHAPTER 6: BEING A COMMUNIST AND A WRITER

what the workers thought of their recruit is not stated. The manner is immensely superior to the matter. There are phrases that elate'. Arnold Palmer in the *Yorkshire Post* was unhappy with the ending. 'So many modern novels end in this way that one is tempted to wonder if some enterprising Communist has set up a central bureau for the supply of Final Fifty Pages to Writers of First Novels. But if . . . the concluding pages of his book are ignored, what remains is as far as possible from being a standardized product. His intelligence – quick, flashing, illuminating – is matched by a style of exceptional ease and distinction'. The poet Edwin Muir in the *Listener*, reviewing it with three other novels, including Samuel Beckett's *Murphy*, was very enthusiastic, finding it the best of his group and devoting half of his review to it. He also splendidly captures what the novel is about.

> The first book in this list is so extraordinary in its quality, has such concentrated seriousness, and does so effectively what it sets out to do, that it makes the other three, in spite of their good qualities, appear less serious than they ought to be. Technically, *Journey to the Border* is brilliant, and the problem it deals with enormously difficult; the precise statement of a fanciful and yet quite common view of the world, or rather the statement of that view in terms of fantasy; the development of its consequences, which brings the hero to the border of madness (hence the title); the crisis; and the final approximation, both reluctant and grateful, to a view of things as they are. Mr Upward describes all this with a continuous concentration, a continuous invention of clairvoyant incident, which satisfy one's mind and imagination at the same time. The gradual

emergence out of this fantasy into the actual world – the most difficult part of the theme – is perhaps not so successful as the rest, and contains one or two absurd touches; but it shows such insight into the evasions and false hopes of the mind, such a comprehensive knowledge of the hero's problem, that it justifies itself.

The novelist Forrest Reid in the *Spectator* was far less enthusiastic. 'The moral seems to be that the teaching of small boys is degrading when not combined with militant socialism. It did not convince me, nor can I imagine that in any position this tutor would prove a reliable person. Nevertheless, Mr Upward can write'. There was a very brief review in the *Daily Worker*, intriguingly of both it and Isherwood's *Lions and Shadows*, presumably unaware that Upward under another name is a major figure in that book. The reviewer, Ralph Wright, doesn't seem to take it in that although the tutor is avoiding madness, he is moving towards Communism. In conclusion, he writes: 'Both [books] are honest attempts to find what you might call the intellectual's way out. And both their authors, if they don't quite see what they ought to do, at least are united in knowing what they detest'. In the *Times Literary Supplement* in a group of one-paragraph reviews of seven 'Notable First Novels' by now forgotten novelists (other than Upward), the anonymous reviewer states, giving Upward's novel first place, that 'although we may not agree with Mr Upward's analysis of the contemporary scene nor the solution which he advocates, "Journey to the Border" is, as a first novel, a great achievement, both in the skill of its construction and the accomplishment of its style'.

CHAPTER 6: BEING A COMMUNIST AND A WRITER

In June there was an extremely negative review in *Scrutiny* by R. G. Cox, in typically dyspeptic but rather impressive Leavisite terms, of both Upward's novel as well as another surrealistic novel from the Auden group: Rex Warner's *The Wild Goose Chase*. The concluding paragraph of the review powerfully reminds one of the class aspects of the Auden group and how these gentlemanly revolutionaries might be resented.

> Neither of these writers can plead the excuse of extreme youth, and yet their emotional and intellectual immaturity has been allowed to pass without comment: no reviewer to my knowledge has made the slightest protest against the intellectual dishonesty and moral vulgarity of *The Wild Goose Chase* or the naïve muddle-headedness of *Journey to the Border*. On the contrary, both books have been praised for their literary as well as their propagandist merit. The decline of critical standards has brought us, it is clear, to a point where the regular critics cannot be relied on to make the simplest and most obvious judgments of taste and morality. Of course, the groups which these authors represent and by whom they are hailed as important writers appear to control most of the reviewing in literary periodicals: they are also, which is more important, practically the only modern literary movement. This only makes it more depressing to see that if you wear the right colours and know the right people you need observe no higher standards than those of the best-selling thriller and middle-brow novel with a purpose. Mr Day Lewis, it will be remembered, is on the selection committee of the Book Society. If a revolution leaves the

Public School communists in privileged positions (as they seem sure it will) and follows the lines of their writings, it is impossible that the triumphant new culture of the classless society should be anything more than our present intellectual and moral chaos writ large. At least we know what to expect.[64]

John Lehmann provided a strong and no doubt biased summing-up of the significance of the novel in his pamphlet *New Writing in England* published the following year, citing the book both as something new but as in a definite English tradition.

> This 'novel' must be considered as one of the most original works of any young writer of Upward's generation, and indeed as something new in English literature. There have been many remarkable fables and fantasies written in English, from Swift's *Gulliver's Travels* to William Morris' *News from Nowhere* and Lewis Carroll's *Alice in Wonderland*, but there has been, I think, none which made Upward's precise use of the distortion of reality characteristic of dreams and hallucinations – the quality of the Mortmere world – to illustrate the steps in a very closely worked-out argument, a philosophical argument that ends in a revolutionary conclusion. There are passages which recall the methods used by Swift in his social satire, by William Morris in his imaginative projection of how revolution came to England, and by Lewis Carroll in his fantasy world where the subconscious plays havoc with the processes and relations of the normal world; but Upward makes all these methods his own and integrates them in his argument.[65]

There was a further unsuccessful effort to publish it in the United States: Dutton declined although it thought it was brilliant even if too much of a tract.[66] It did receive some notice in the United States, rather improbably in *Vogue*, sometime later. There in the issue of 15 August 1939, shortly before the war broke out, Auden and Isherwood wrote a piece, 'Young British Writers – on the Way Up'. They felt that the 'times of crisis' of that moment were not a favourable time for novelists, yet good work was being done. They very briefly discussed George Orwell, Ralph Bates, Arthur Calder-Marshall, Henry Green, Graham Greene, William Plomer, James Stern (a short story writer), Rex Warner and Edward Upward. Comparing Upward to Rex Warner, they stated that *Journey to the Border* was 'far more exciting, though less technically successful . . . [it is] one of the most important things of its kind published in England since 1918 . . . This story becomes, in a most amusing and graphic manner, an analysis of all possible religious and philosophical theories . . . It is impossible not to feel, when we read this book, that we are in the presence of a master of English fiction. It is interesting to note that the lives of Warner and Upward have much in common. Both are schoolmasters, living quietly and unsensationally in the routine of their jobs. Both are happily married. Neither has done much travelling . . . Neither has had any very dramatic adventures. Both Warner and Upward have approached the Left Wing Movement theoretically, through a study of Marxism'.[67] They seemed to ignore Upward's work as an active Communist.

'The Leaning Tower' was a talk that Virginia Woolf gave to the Workers' Educational Association in Brighton in April 1940. Along with her 'Letter to a Young Poet' of 1932 addressed to John Lehmann it was part of her debate with the writers of Upward's generation. In her essay she argues that peace and prosperity shaped the British writers of the nineteenth century, that they looked at a world from their secure towers. This lasted until 1914. 'They had leisure; they had security'. Except for Dickens and Lawrence these writers were on towers of stucco – their middle-class birth – and of gold – their education. But then after the war the situation changed. She identifies the writers that she has in mind exactly as Upward's circle although she does not mention him: Auden, Day Lewis, MacNeice, Isherwood, Spender. As was true of most earlier writers they came from the middle class and had the same private education, the point made by R. G. Cox in *Scrutiny* but written in a more sympathetic way. 'They are tower dwellers like their predecessors, the sons of well-to-do parents, who could afford to send them to public schools and universities'. Yet the view from the tower after the First World War was so different, changed by revolutions, Communism, Fascism. The towers themselves were leaning. She argues that being on a leaning tower, a tower leaning to the left, makes these writers much more self-conscious of their class. She feels that hence it is harder for them to create characters and also that the angle of vision makes them angry at their society. Much as they might wish to, they cannot divest themselves of their class formation. 'And thus, trapped by their education, pinned down by their capital, they remained on top of their leaning tower, and their state of mind as we see it reflected in their poems and plays and novels is full of discord and bitterness, full of confusion and of compromise'.[68] They would like to come off their tower and join the mass of humankind but are unable to do so.

She feels that these writers lack creative power to write about others but they could, in her view, write creatively and truthfully about themselves. She is hopeful about the literature that might come about in the world without towers, without class, but that world does not yet exist. The essay ends on rather a tangential and odd note, urging her readers and her listeners to the original talk to read freely from books taken from the library, which she seems to suggest will help to eliminate the world of class. She published her essay in the *Folios of New Writing,* edited by John Lehmann, dated Autumn 1940 and issued by the Hogarth Press.

In the Spring 1941 *Folios of New Writing* there were four brief replies to her essay by those whom she had attacked, with the exception of B. L. Coombes who was in fact a working-class writer. The other authors were Louis MacNeice who in particular was in her sights as well as John Lehmann, now again her employee, and Upward. The replies of course were rather overshadowed by her suicide the previous March. 'The Leaning Tower' was one of her very last compositions. Only two further pieces were published before her death, one short essay on Ellen Terry and a review of a book about Mrs Thrale although she was also at work on her last novel, *Between the Acts.*

Coombes in 'Below the Tower' makes the case for the capabilities of the working-class writers and urges the middle-class leaning-tower writers to climb down to their level before the tower collapses and gives them no choice. On the ground level they could teach working-class writers what they need to know. Louis MacNeice wrote the next response. He was the most specifically attacked author in Woolf's essay with quite a few quotations from his *Autumn*

Journal, 'feeble as poetry, but interesting as autobiography'. He is on the leaning tower and can't get off, which explains, she asserts, the destructiveness and emptiness of his writings. MacNeice disputes her conception that the writers of the nineteenth century accepted the status quo and also that discontent with the status quo among MacNeice's generation restricts their ability to be successful. He does see flaws in the writings of those in his circle, disliking the polemical poetry of Rex Warner, the social satires of Day Lewis, and Auden and Isherwood's *On the Frontier*. He remarks that Edward Upward 'ruined his novel, *Journey to the Border*, with his use of the Deus ex Machina – i.e. "the Workers" – at the end'. But whatever their faults MacNeice sees these writers, particularly Auden and Spender, as bringing new hope and new spirit to English writing. He doesn't respond to her particular criticisms of his poetry but concludes that 'we were right to advocate social reconstruction and we were even right – in our more lyrical work – to give personal expression to our feelings of anxiety, horror and despair'.[69] John Lehmann participated as the editor who published the original essay but also the person who knew Woolf best. He argues that she was more sympathetic to the writings of these young men of the 1930s than might appear and felt that they wrote well when they wrote about themselves but not when they wrote about the outer world. As he points out, she was a socialist but was also intensely self-conscious about her own class position. He ends his very brief 'A Postscript' stating how interested and anxious she was to bring into print new young authors and to encourage their work. And indeed it was true that she did publish the authors she was attacking in 'The Leaning Tower'.

Upward's reply, 'The Falling Tower', was the first of the group and he argued strongly for the necessity to be a Marxist as he had pointed out in the essay he had published in *The Mind in Chains* in 1937. He stated that the writers of his group were right to attack the bourgeois world, even though that world has given them some economic security. Such a point of view is a necessity in order to be a significant writer. He does accept that the 'leaning tower' writers are not great and that their work 'was filled with confusion and compromise'. He does not feel that the writer needs, in order to be a proper socialist, to throw away bourgeois advantages. As he points out, neither Marx, Engels nor Lenin did so. 'It is true that in order to write like socialists they would have had to *be* socialists and to work with other socialists, but this does not mean that they would have had to spend all their time in committee meetings or door-to-door canvassing or in composing propaganda leaflets. They could have taken part in ordinary political work and they could have written poems and novels as well. Their inherited money gave them – or those of them who possessed inherited money – the time and the freedom both for political work and for imaginative writing'. It reminds one of the 'golden islands' of E. M. Forster's *Howards End*. Although very much from the solid middle class, the Auden group on the whole did not have private incomes. He ends his brief essay by stating that the tower will fall and that socialist writers will be the better after the tower, the economic system, has collapsed. In his concluding lines he defends the Auden circle. 'There is much in the poetry of Auden and of Spender which is fit to stand beside the great poetry of the past. The "leaning tower" writers are abler and more serious than most of their detractors. No better work than theirs appeared in England in the 'thirties. They may produce their best work in the 'forties'.[70]

Lehmann went on to edit a third version of *New Writing* called *Penguin New Writing*, an immensely popular paperback among wartime readers. In no. 14, July–September 1942, the first two pieces were by Upward and Isherwood. Along with a short Blitz story by Henry Green these pieces formed the first section of the publication, labelled 'Report on To-day'. Lehmann wrote in his foreword that there was now a division in thought between the Yogi and the Commissar, using Arthur Koestler's phrase. As he commented: 'The former [Isherwood's] [leans] towards an out-and-out pacifism and concentration on inner problems, the latter [Upward's] towards revolutionary action and complete domination by one group within the state in the interests of social change. This divergence is all the more interesting when it occurs among writers who, in an earlier phase, were closely associated; and it is because it can be traced in new contributions from Christopher Isherwood and Edward Upward, two writers who played a large part in forming the literary consciousness of the 'thirties, that they have been placed side by side in the forefront of the present issue'.[71] Theirs were the first two pieces in the publication, Isherwood's 'The Day at La Verne' being about a meditation group in California while Upward's very short short story 'New Order' pointing out the necessity of resistance to invasion and occupation. It is unclear whether the story takes place in an unknown country occupied by the Germans or in Britain itself. The last sentence reads, 'You, few at first, rebels, saboteurs, guerrillas, you yourselves are the guarantee that others over the whole world will strike with you to destroy the oppressors'.[72]

'New Order' was as it turned out his last new publication until his novel *In the Thirties* came out in 1962. In 1949 a version of his unpublished story 'The Railway Accident' appeared in the American annual anthology *New Directions* with a short introductory note by Isherwood. It was a long silence. In the years between he devoted many pages in his notebooks to his commitment to being a writer, how extremely important it was to him. Yet he was unable to fulfil that obligation, indeed compulsion. There was the dislocation of the school moving to Lancashire during the war. According to John Lehmann his creativity was stifled by his being encased in the 'iron maiden' of Marxism. There was the trauma of his leaving the Communist Party in 1948 because he thought it was abandoning the principles of Marxist Leninism. With the publication of *Journey to the Border* in 1938 and other literary activities, his party activities, his marriage, his children, the 1930s were a rich and productive period. Yet it was as if his writing was paralyzed by the two conflicting forces. He was drawn to imagination and fantasy. Yet he felt that if he could write in a plainer style he would be more likely to reach the working-class reader. In a sense it was, which he would have hated, a somewhat patronizing attitude, writing 'down' so the working-class reader might be able to read him. Rather he should have written as he wished, and hoped for the best. In the twenty years between 1942 and 1962 he was less politically active, although he became quite involved in the Campaign for Nuclear Disarmament after leaving the party. He published less than other members of the Auden circle. He was nevertheless a highly significant influence in shaping the dominant literary trend – its style and content – of the 1930s.

Chapter 7: The Years Between

THE DIVISION OF interests, Isherwood in religion and Upward in war and resistance, can be taken to mark an end to the dominant literary movement of the 1930s. The members of the Auden group now went their separate ways. Not that it was ever a coherent group but it had shared in varying degrees common political attitudes – that English society and the state were corrupt, perhaps doomed, and that radical change was necessary. At the same time these writers demonstrated, in the English tradition, a somewhat ironical approach as well as elements of fantasy. This was to a degree indebted to the influence of the undergraduate literary experiments of Upward and Isherwood, the world of Mortmere. Virtually all of the members of the group moved away from their flirtations with Communism. In the case of Spender, Day Lewis and Lehmann this had led them to join the party. Day Lewis became quite an active member. (Of course it is a nice irony that it was he of the group who would become Poet Laureate. What an English story.) Upward was certainly the most devout party member. This was one reason that he was less productive and less well known. In many senses party work came first, and he also had to fulfil his obligations as a teacher. It must be emphasized that these men – and it was exclusively male never functioned as a group. Upward did become a fairly close friend of Spender's but always had doubts about him. His period of close friendship with Auden was comparatively brief. Despite their short-lived rift in 1939, his friendship with Isherwood, beginning when they were public school boys at Repton, was the closest relationship within the Auden circle with the possible exception of the personal and literary connections between Auden and Isherwood.

Isherwood had written to Olive Mangeot after going with Auden to the United States in 1939 that he had become both a pacifist and a follower of Vedanta. She showed his letter to Upward. He then wrote to Isherwood a long letter attacking his pacifism. 'I have seen your letter to Olive. Shocked isn't the word for what I felt when I read it . . . I wish I could convey what I want to write by grimaces and inaudibilities instead of by crude statements from a distance. In brief, I feel much as we once imagined one of us would feel if the other turned Roman Catholic . . . I never expected you to become a Marxist . . . Pacifism is almost the most pernicious theory you could have chosen . . . You know that I loathe violence and shall make a very bad revolutionary, but I recognise that this is a weakness and I don't try to justify it'.[1] In reply on 6 August Isherwood wrote: 'I have made a mess of my leftism. Laziness, dilettantism and cowardice have prevented me from doing the only possible thing: becoming a rank-and-file worker, as you did . . . So I don't belong to any movement . . . So what remains for me but pacifism, of some kind? . . . Yes, believe it or not, your unlucky Starn has set his feet on the bottom of this crazy goat-track which is to lead over the peaks of the never-never mountains . . . If only I could see you. I could make you accept my position, at any rate on a Mortmere basis'.[2] He felt that his only choice was to be a pacifist and to follow the way of Vedanta, under the leadership of Gerald Heard, the British philosopher now living in the United States.

CHAPTER 7: THE YEARS BETWEEN

In reply Upward wrote a loving letter on 24 August.

> Your letter would have melted a heart of stone. [But] you are still looking for a way to reform the world, even if only by changing people's hearts. But there is only one way to reform the world, and that is by first of all changing material conditions . . . I still have and always will have a foot in Mortmere. But Mortmere did not try to reform the world. That was its strength. It was wholehearted, not a murky compromise between the real and the ideal. It rejected the real world outright and created a more satisfying imaginary one . . . I wish with all my heart that you and Wystan may continue to "escape". It is important that you should survive.[3]

He also wrote in his notebook the same day, 'I forgive him all'.[4] Despite the cordiality of the second letter it is striking and significant that there was now a six-and-a-half-year gap in their correspondence. Despite papering over their disagreements there was clearly a profound break. The 1930s were over.

Throughout the long course of their friendship the division between Upward and Isherwood suggested by their contributions to *Penguin New Writing* was its most serious rift. It was probably a crisis in Upward's own aesthetics. Virtually uninfluenced by developments on the continent, his writing had begun as an English form of surrealism. His other considerable later literary as well as political commitment was to Marxist Leninism. These two aesthetics were somewhat difficult to reconcile and were one explanation for his long literary silence. (The surrealistic movement both in France and

CHAPTER 7: THE YEARS BETWEEN

Britain did try itself to reconcile surrealism and leftism with limited success. The party line on surrealism was that it was a fake revolution.) Upward ultimately wrote himself out of the situation in the third volume of his trilogy, *No Home but the Struggle*. After that he could move on in his short stories. There he could effectively combine his two literary impulses.

Upward was loyal to the party line at the time of the outbreak of the Second World War on 3 September 1939. The position of the party, because of the Nazi-Soviet Pact, was that it was an imperialist war and Communists should take no part in it. There is no indication that Upward was uncomfortable with this. The war years went fairly smoothly politically for Upward once the Soviet Union had been invaded and joined the Allies. But when the war was over and the question of the shape of the new world came to be raised, politics became an awkward subject for Upward and his wife. Political cooperation to win the war was all very well but what would happen in the post-war world? The party line in Britain before the outbreak of the Cold War was to continue wartime cooperation and to support the creation of a welfare state in league with the Labour Party. The party alternated in its attitude towards Labour. In the years before Upward joined, the policy of 'Class against Class' had meant that Labour was seen as 'social-Fascist'. But in the time of the United Front when Russia and Britain were allies Labour was viewed favourably by the party. The Labour Party itself, despite some efforts from those on its left, such as Stafford Cripps, had little inclination to affiliate in any way with the Communists. At the same time, after the war the party was trying to come closer to Labour. It was also concerned with purifying itself, of getting rid of 'The Rotten Elements', the deviators, the title and subject of Upward's second novel in his trilogy. Ironically it might be the most 'Communist' of his books as it is written in the flattest, most 'socialist realist' prose of any of his fiction.

Upward was a member of the Communist Party during its heroic age in Britain. In the 1930s it represented for many a viable solution to the political and economic woes of the nation, an alternative to the oppression of the working class. At the time of the Spanish Civil War, unlike the Labour Party it took a firm stand on behalf of the Loyalists and the primary role in recruiting for the International Brigade. Upward could genuinely feel that he was taking part in bringing about a better world. But he did then go along at the time of the Nazi-Soviet Pact in August 1939 with the party line that the war was an imperialist one and hence shouldn't be supported. He might have been relieved when the Soviet Union was invaded in 1941 and Russia was an ally. Finally the twists of the party line were too much for him when the party decided to try to cooperate with Labour after the end of the war. It abandoned, he thought, the idea of literal revolution, with the likelihood of violence, which he felt was an essential part of the Marxist-Leninist take on the world. In these years after the war he became increasingly uneasy about Stalinism. Some years later, in 1957, after the full revelation of Stalin's actions, he both strongly stated his disillusionment and then also characteristically modified his position. 'The crimes of the USSR have at least destroyed the illusion that communist politicians might be morally of a different type from other politicians. With a very few if any exceptions, politicians always have been, and are, and always will be, criminals of the vilest kind

... Do I really believe all this? Not quite'.[5] He was in effect critical of two aspects of the party: its moderation in terms of what it was doing in Britain and its excesses in what he saw as the Soviet Union's growing imperialism. He increasingly felt that he should leave the party and become what he called 'a loyal fellow traveller'.[6] Yet in many ways he kept hankering for the party as it had been. He was depressed at what he saw as its decay after the war. The party cooperated with Labour in the general election of 1945, running only twenty-one candidates, two of whom were elected. After the war the party unsuccessfully applied for affiliation with the Labour Party. Upward certainly did not have a positive picture of the Labour Party's leadership. 'The colourless Attlee, the spiteful Morrison, the philistine Bevin, the holy Cripps'.[7] He became increasingly disillusioned with the party and what he saw as its mistaken wish to cooperate with Labour. It was an abandonment of Marxism. He began seriously to consider resigning and indeed the second volume of his trilogy is devoted to that painful step. No doubt the most traumatic event of the period was his leaving the party in 1948. Yet he never lost his radical political commitment and would continue to be politically active, mostly at a local level and primarily with the Campaign for Nuclear Disarmament. By the mid-to-late 1950s he was quite disillusioned with politics and belief systems in general. He saw the events in Hungary in 1956 as the result of Stalinist 'errors and crimes'. 'I don't think, no matter what changes in a liberal direction may happen in the USSR, I could ever again "believe in" any political system. Communism is all right in theory but in practice it has proven to be as inhumane as Christianity or capitalism ... The crimes of the USSR have at last destroyed the illusion that communist politicians might be of a morally different type from other politicians ... A return to communism. Impossible. I no longer know what communism is. But turning to religion? Impossible while I remain sane. By a belief in art? Yes, that's the only way'.⁸

Although he did not publish again until 1962, he actually started to write again, the first part of his trilogy *The Spiral Ascent*, on 5 September 1950. 'This morning I've written the first sentence of my novel ... To-morrow I write the first paragraph'. Then on 24 December: 'The first sentence is all right. But can I go on from that? ... [his ellipses] No'. To indicate the extraordinary slowness of his writing, seven years later he wrote on 22 June 1957: 'Two years ago to-day, after chapel, I rewrote or finished rewriting the first paragraph of the first chapter of this novel, proving to myself that I still had the skill to write the whole bk well eventually'. And then in October, 'Have spent several hours on one or two sentences, but I've got them right at last'. And the following February: 'Woke last night worrying about a sentence in ch 3 ... This sort of thing must stop'.⁹ It would be funny if it weren't so sad. He thought he would finish a first version of the novel in 1957 but then spent three years revising it!

He continued teaching until 1961. Yet he saw his writing as his primary commitment. He reported on his progress on *In the Thirties* to Isherwood. If there had been an estrangement between them it was over by 1947 when Isherwood visited England for the first time since he had left in January 1939. On 9 March Isherwood had lunch and dinner with the Upwards in Dulwich. It is worth quoting his description of the occasion at length. In his reconstructed diary Isherwood refers to himself in the third person:

What Christopher valued in both Edward and Hilda was their simplicity; Hilda was certainly intelligent, Edward had one of the subtlest, clearest, most perceptive minds that Christopher had ever come in contact with. But what made Edward different from most of the other people whom Christopher would have described as intelligent was that Edward lacked a certain fashionable urban sophistication; down in their drab little home on Turney Road in Dulwich, he and Hilda seemed quite out of the swim, like country cousins ... The Upwards' political life was also an expression of their simplicity. They didn't advertise their activities, didn't use left-wing jargon, didn't make a show of righteous indignation or enthusiasm, they just went ahead with dull routine jobs, attending meetings, selling the *Daily Worker*, etc . . . Christopher lost awareness of everything but their relationship, which hadn't changed in any important respect since Cambridge. What their relationship was and had always been about was the writing of books.[10]

Their support of one another was crucial. As Upward wrote to Isherwood in August 1962 when *In the Thirties* was published, 'I shall never be able to tell you – the language of Mortmere is inadequate – what you've done for my morale throughout my adult life & before'.[11]

Over the years Upward had reported to Isherwood on the writing of his novel and the problems that he encountered. As he was starting out working on it he had written: 'As for the novel, the worse it goes – and it could hardly go worse than at present – the more optimistic I unaccountably feel . . . My trouble is that I have been trying to write something as different as possible from Mortmere, something austerely originating in actuality (i.e. in the trivial experiences of my own life), but no matter how I wangle it and try to unify the quite interesting separate incidents I can't soberly see it as anything but a string of rather static sketches. Probably my only hope is to start from the abstract, to invent a *story* no matter how fantastically Mortmereish provided it's exciting, and then to adapt it to what actually happened'.[12] Three years later he wrote to him at the time of his nervous breakdown: 'It may be that this crisis was what was needed to break the bonds of the last fifteen years. I have freed myself from the Political Life, and instead of trying to get back somehow to the Poetic Life which I dream we lived at Freshwater and which I have been trying to get back to ever since the war, I now propose to live the Philosophic Ordinary Life ... I am very lucky to have Hilda. Marrying her was one of the few really sensible things I've done in my life'.[13]

Isherwood was encouraging but was not actually totally honest with him. As he noted in his diary: 'Am I being frank with *him* about his novel? Well – ninety percent. I think and hope it will work out – what I fear is a suburban, thin wanness and dullness, a grey Dulwich lighting. But I know I have really succeeded in encouraging him. And that, surely, is good'.[14] As they had always done he and Isherwood sent one another their works in progress. Upward was self-aware, commenting to Isherwood in 1956 that 'there are certain vital problems to be solved – such as how not to be boring when dealing with political material'.[15] He came to the conclusion that part of the point was to convey that politics could be tedious. 'I have become reconciled to its being flat and commonplace in its language and I comfort myself with the thought that at least I've got it down on paper, however badly. Better write badly than not at all is my motto at present. Even if it turns out to be quite unpublishable it will have had an auto-therapeutic value. I have given up trying to make something really good out of it'.[16] That same year, 1958, he wrote to Isherwood about the trajectory of the series and what he saw as the position of his alter ego in the novel, Alan Sebrill, and ultimately himself.

> He will admit, as handsomely as I can make him, that he has been dead wrong about Stalin and the Soviet trials and concentration camps and all the rest of the Soviet crimes, and he will blame himself above all for the wilful blindness & wicked obstinacy which prevented him from trusting men like Gide and allowed him to trust politicians. But he will not cease to disbelieve in original sin, nor will he exchange a discredited political faith for a discredited religious one. He will remain some sort of humanist – with a horror of all blind faiths. He will continue to see communism as something that will eventually spread all over the world and that – like Christianity – will have its bad and its not so bad periods. But he will never again be politically active. He will see himself as primarily a poet. Having escaped from being a communist he won't make the mistake of becoming an anti-communist. The final message of novel 3 is the rather obvious one that a poet in his poetry should not try to serve other than poetical ends, and that poetry is not just a kind of game but something that humanity needs . . . If he had it to live it again he wouldn't join the Party but he wouldn't be

neutral in the struggle between fascism & communism, would still be on the communist side. However his main aim would be to be a poet'.[17]

Perhaps he had achieved a reconciliation between art and life. In 1955 a reissue of Isherwood's *All the Conspirators* had reminded him of the glorious promise of youth when they had been working together on their writing at Freshwater. 'Lately when I have been in a state of gloomy confusion I have become aware of you standing tangibly just out of eyeshot behind my shoulder and reminding me clearly of Freshwater and of what we were born for'.[18]

He was also deliberately changing his style of writing to flatten it out and abandon the earlier elements of fantasy. He wrote about this change in 1979: 'Although the style ... cannot properly be called socialist realist, it is deliberately anti-modernist – that is to say it is a plain style, and as lucid as I can make it. It tries to avoid literary allusiveness, and all types of ambiguity ... I admit that at times I regret not having been able to continue writing in the richer style I was capable of in the nineteen thirties. But I think the loss has been compensated for by a gain in strength and artistic wholeness in my later work'.[19]

He was also in touch with Stephen Spender about the manuscript of *In the Thirties*. Although they now differed politically he was on good terms with him and had invited him down to Alleyn's to speak. He had written him a long letter in 1951 when Spender published his autobiography, *World within World*, in which Upward appeared as Allen Chalmers. In this was the classic and much quoted statement about his importance for the canonical writers of the

1930s. 'Just as Auden seemed to us the highest peak within the range of our humble vision from the Oxford valleys, for Auden there was another peak, namely Isherwood, whilst for Isherwood there was a still further peak, Chalmers'.[20] Upward liked the book and was grateful that he appeared under a pseudonym as he feared that in the atmosphere of McCarthyism at the time he might have otherwise been in political trouble, particularly as the school was now being partially supported by the London County Council. He disagreed but not all that strongly with some of the ways that he was presented in the book. Although he admitted that perhaps he didn't take the Soviet purge trials as seriously as he should, he still thought it was likely that those who were executed were guilty. But some years later he changed his mind on the basis of Stalin's persecution of the Jewish doctors. On 27 June 1956 he wrote to Spender 'to admit to you how wrong I was and how right you have been about the Soviet trials . . . Now after the Kruschev [sic] speech, I would like to believe that though I have been a dupe I have been an honest one. I have tasted the horrors of Faith and from now on shall try to be a rationalist'. It was four years later that he sent his manuscript of *In the Thirties* to Spender. Spender responded but his criticisms do not survive. He apparently legitimately assumed that Alan Sebrill's views were the same as Upward's. In reply Upward wrote:

> I don't see why a book which reveals a stupid political attitude on the author's part need therefore be artistically bad, any more than a book which reveals an intelligent political attitude need be artistically good. It happens that my attitude does differ radically from my hero's: if it had been similar to his I

couldn't have begun to write the book ... In so far as my trilogy has a message at all it is an indirect one and to the effect that the poet ought never to allow politics (communist or anti-communist) to dominate his poetry ... I haven't really any doubt – I wish I had – that your objections to my book are artistic and that what you are criticising is not the author's ideological attitude but the dullness & unimaginativeness with which he expresses it. I am all too well aware how flat the political passages are compared with those in "Engaged in Writing" [Spender's novella about a cultural congress in Venice] for instance.

Rather in contradiction of his earlier statement Upward wrote to him three years later when unsuccessfully submitting a chapter from the book for publication in *Encounter*, the journal that Spender coedited, that 'the purpose of the novel as a whole is to try to reproduce faithfully – and without protesting to the reader that I am now a reformed character – some of the feelings and ideas I had in the 'thirties'.[21] There is no doubt that the trilogy was designed to reconcile his political and his artistic lives, but this is marked by a continual veering between the two. It represented the working-out of a dialectic: entering politics, leaving politics, returning to art enriched by political experience. The driving force of *In the Thirties* is Sebrill's desire to join the Communist Party, though a member of the bourgeoisie. The leap of religious faith was that only through being a Communist could he be a poetic writer. 'If he lived his external life rightly, kept unfailingly in touch with the Party and worked for it, there would be no need to worry about his soul or his poetry'.[22]

As he remarked in an interview in 1964, 'At the beginning of *In the Thirties* the hero comes to Communism as a kind of religious conversion, and this represents my own attitude. I came to it not so much through consciousness of the political and economic situation as through despair'.[23]

Having finally finished his book the next challenge was to get it published. He submitted it to the Hogarth Press. Leonard Woolf turned it down, put off mostly by not liking its central story of joining the party. He wrote: 'The pace is much too slow and there is, I feel, much too much internal questioning about Communist principles. If you told the story of how the young man entered the party and then eventually left, which after all is the theme, the book might be extremely interesting and readable, but in its present form it is too long drawn out'.[24] McGibbon & Kee declined the book as did Gollancz, sending it back without even a rejection slip. He continued to send the manuscript out unsuccessfully. An extract from the first chapter was published in the *London Magazine* in 1961. On the basis of that, Charles Monteith of Faber & Faber expressed interest but concluded on reading it that the characters were too much mouthpieces for political points of view and never came to life. Upward commented: 'Capitalism will never publish me. I must therefore make my peace with Communism, which will never publish me either'.[25] In his view it wasn't fundamentally a political book but rather one that used politics as its material. It was about a young middle-class man who is trying firmly to anchor his aesthetics by becoming a Communist. He was seriously considering simply creating fifty duplicated copies of the text, which he found he could do for £121. But in September 1961 he received an inquiry from

James Michie of Heinemann about the book. He had been alerted to it by Michael Croft. He knew and was intrigued by the Mortmere stories and he had a brother who was a member of the party. On 17 October Upward had lunch with Michie who told him he wished to publish the book. He was particularly happy that he was able to tell his father, who was mortally ill, that it had been accepted. His father was pleased, saying that the announcement called for a cigar and a double whiskey. He died before the book came out. Upward thought that might well be for the best as his father might not have liked certain parts of the text.

In some ways the novel is a longer version of *Journey to the Border*. It tells the story of a young man, Alan Sebrill, becoming a member of the Communist Party and of his doubts about being accepted, as he is a member of the middle class. This is the political life that is necessary, he thinks, in order to lead a valid artistic life. The novel is also a Communist love story. Upward/Sebrill, even if there isn't an exact equivalence between author and character, is such a divided man, driven by his politics to seek a working-class (although she really isn't) Communist bride yet rebelling against the idea. By marrying Hilda/Elsie, he felt he was marrying into the party. The book traces Alan's movement towards political action but also his efforts to be a writer. It begins at Freshwater with Sebrill and Richard Marple, based on Isherwood, writing. The book contains vivid accounts of school life as well as of a Fascist rally and ends with a nature walk. On it Sebrill is hopeful that radical politics would psychologically support the life of writing.

In August 1962 Upward wrote to Olive Mangeot with family news: his son Christopher was engaged to a Cambridge graduate, his

In the Thirties, *first published in 1962 and reissued in this paperback edition in 1978*

daughter Kathy had a boyfriend and 'I am expecting stinking reviews of my book from left, right and centre'. In September he wrote to her: 'The D.W. [Daily Worker] hasn't reviewed it. I expected a stinker from them but perhaps they have decided just to ignore the book. I have had a lot of other reviews, nearly fifty so far, half of them hostile and half favourable. The Establishment critics didn't like the book, as you can imagine'.[26] It was reviewed in the main Sunday broadsheets. The day before publication on 12 August Francis Hope gave it a negative review in the *Observer*, yet recognizing Upward's position.

> A quick glance through Mr Upward's novel will confirm the worst suspicions raised by its title: – 'I've realised lately that the time has arrived for me to show definitely that I'm against the plus-foured poshocracy, and for the cockneys and the lower orders' . . . Oh, God do we have to go through this again? Mr Upward, the *eminence grise* of the decade, was in a position to throw new light on it. Instead he has produced a book which, apart from some keenly observed minutiae, might have been put together by anyone from a few of Auden's minor poems, Isherwood's 'Lions and Shadows' . . . and a copy of 'The God That Failed'.

The same day in the *Sunday Telegraph* the philosopher Anthony Quinton, although he called it one of 'the two best new books this week' and mentioned the 'strange and memorable' *Journey to the Border*, condemned the book for its deliberate lack of literary qualities. The following Sunday in the *Sunday Times* the novelist Olivia Manning included it with three other works of fiction, although she gave it pride of place. She was also negative about the book. 'The present volume seems less a novel than a fictionalised memoir. Except for an incident here and there . . . wit, characterisation in depth, the evocation of place, progression by reporting of events – are missing . . . What we are given is a sincere and painstaking exploration of the mentality of those Left-wing idealists who, despising their own bourgeois origins, vested virtue in the workers with whom they sought to identify themselves'. Andrew Leslie on 17 August in the *Guardian* wrote a favourable review. 'Here, through the development of the young poet-hero, Alan Sebrill, we recapture the attempt of the quintessential Auden-Spender-Cornford character, the Upwards and Isherwoods, to find a proper basis of the good life. Away from *rentier* guilt, the poshocracy, public school upbringing, Georgian lyricism – and up and over that literary watershed towards hard thinking, tough writing, social concern, the workers (but what accent to use in talking to them?) and communism, friend of poetry, champion of the doomed'. Stuart Hampshire's review in the *New Statesman* is positive about what others found the defects of the work. 'This is a novel that lacks all of the novelist's ordinary craft, and it is written without any exuberance of imagination. Like *Marius the Epicurean*, it is the record of the pursuit of a moral ideal – the ideal of "the poetic life" – through phases of disillusionment or disappointment. The title is exact. The story is a picture of the Thirties, if we understand "the Thirties" to stand simply for the intellectual moods and ambitions of a very small group of young and very gifted writers'. Malcolm Bradbury gave it a favourable review in *Punch*.

There were two intriguing, reserved but sympathetic reviews

CHAPTER 7: THE YEARS BETWEEN

by John Mortimer in the *Spectator* and Randall Swingler in the *Times Literary Supplement*, although Swingler's was anonymous. Both caught the dilemma that Upward faced in attempting to be a poetic middle-class Communist. Mortimer comments on the atmosphere of a boys' club run by a public school in Upward's approach to the workers, diffident as he might be about being accepted.

> That mixture of tremulous excitement and revulsion with which the intellectuals then approached the working class . . . School was, in fact, the great experience from which the writers found it hard to recover . . . There are rare moments when the book lights up with a strange, surrealist glow which has nothing whatever to do with Party rambles . . . . Perhaps the truth about the Thirties writers was the trouble they had reconciling a very private talent with a strong public conscience. By nature they were withdrawn in a world of private schools, private jokes, nicknames and obscure if cunning poetry. Nothing could be less calculated to appeal to the Masses.

Swingler had been an active Communist until he left the party in 1952, having been the book review editor of the *Daily Worker* and an editor of *Left Review*. He was best known as a poet. He places the novel firmly in the context of Upward being the great friend of Isherwood, his *il miglior fabbro*. Indeed, as he points out, the novel starts out at the moment in *Lions and Shadows* when Upward and Isherwood are at Freshwater. Then, after a not very serious consideration of suicide, Alan Sebrill takes off to London to become a Communist. Swingler wonders whether in fact the solemnity and seriousness of the book might be some sort of parody. But he concludes that 'it is a great credit to the author that he has been able to recollect and reproduce this characteristic mental tone, though it does not make comfortable reading'. He admires him for depicting the activities of the ordinary member of the party rather than being, as Swingler himself was, part of the Writers' Group within the party. 'But the picture is obscured and distorted' by Alan's sense of guilt at having been born in the middle class and also an awareness that it will end with his leaving the party. He also found the book without humour. His review occasioned a riposte from John Lehmann, implying that the anonymous reviewer, unlike himself, had not lived through the period. (Although of course Swingler had.) Lehmann wrote: 'To me the book is full of the most subtle irony and humour. I find the way in which the hero's continually reviving desire for the free "poetic life" is always steamrollered by the Marxist cant of the other side of his mind exquisitely ironic'. Lehmann may have been seeing what he wished to see. The reviewer replied that he did consider whether the book was intended to be comic but concluded that it was rather meant to be sad and serious.

Finally – what are friends for? – Isherwood in *Time and Tide* declared the book a masterpiece. He mentioned that it began with Alan and Richard (based on Isherwood himself) meeting on the Isle of Wight, with Richard behaving badly and taking off in pursuit of a love affair. Isherwood writes about Richard, 'Perhaps he will appear more sympathetically in a later volume'. The review is actually rather lacklustre, devoted to a plot summary culminating in the 'religious' sense of conversion to Communism. Alan finds bliss in his work for the party. In June Spender wrote a short review in *Encounter* com-

CHAPTER 7: THE YEARS BETWEEN

Edward in the garden of 3 Hill Street, September 1962

plaining about the book being dismissed as a humourless account of becoming a Communist. He felt that the irony and the quality of the writing were not sufficiently appreciated. He concluded, 'What Mr Upward is really involved with is the contrast between imaginative truth and materialist analysis – and with the question of whether poetic imagination has something after all more important to say about modern society even than politics'.[27] Despite Upward's difficulty in having the novel published, it had certainly received a fair amount of attention. He had returned to the literary life. Now he needed to complete the trilogy. Upward wrote an interesting thank-you to Spender reporting that he was having trouble with his second volume and that 'it may take me another two years at the present rate of progress'. He was self-aware of his problem in writing. 'I wish I could write easily instead of painfully. I have filled thirty-three

CHAPTER 7: THE YEARS BETWEEN

The Upwards at the wedding of Christopher Upward and Janet Hutcheon, 1963

thick notebooks in my time with writing about what I wanted to write'.[28]

The second volume in the trilogy, *The Rotten Elements*, was published in 1969 and had as its main subject his leaving the Communist Party. But as usual the subtext was about his life as a writer and the relationship of political events to the world of art. Also, as usual the writing was painfully slow. He himself found the style of the book bleak and dull. His mood was volatile, as recorded in his notebook in January 1962: 'Despondent & afraid. The future seems a total blank ... Wish I were dead. How much better it wd have been if I'd committed suicide at Cambridge forty years ago'. And then his immediate next entry: 'Back to work – or at least thinking about

The Rotten Elements, *first published in 1969 and reissued in this paperback edition in 1979*

work – thank goodness . . . Despondency is due to expecting too much of my writing'. Towards the end of the month he wrote: 'How fortunate I am to have my writing to return to. How it lifts me up out of all that's dispiriting in ordinary life. At least, that's how I feel about it this morning'. In March he commented: 'I want to express the sorrow of a generation who thought they had found the answer in the P[arty] and then discovered that the P had gone wrong. But they remain convinced, more or less consciously, that only a revival of the P can save the world. But how does poetry fit into this? The b[oo]k is about the tragedy of the P's decline from marxism'.[29] For Upward the political struggle had to be resolved in order for him to move on as a writer. He still believed that being a Marxist would help him be a good writer but it was no longer possible to be a Marxist writer within the party. He finished the manuscript in early 1968 convinced that Heinemann wouldn't publish it. But it did the next year along with a collection of most of his fiction to date, *The Railway Accident and Other Stories*. That collection contained an article on his work by W. H. Sellers, reprinted from the *Dalhousie Review* of 1963; 'The Railway Accident' with Isherwood's introduction; and the text of *Journey to the Border*. Sellers placed him in the context of *the* British writers of the 1930s: the Auden group. Indeed it was a bonanza year in Upward publications as Heinemann persuaded Penguin to issue a paperback of *In the Thirties*. The normally pessimistic Upward could hardly complain and took some pleasure in the situation, remarking about the proofs, 'Both books are good, very good'. Nevertheless he wrote: 'But whether they'll survive except as historical curiosities I doubt. I don't suppose for a moment they'll reach the people I want them to reach – I mean the students'.[30] The collection was reissued again in 1972 with the cover art being a famous painting by René Magritte, *Time Transfixed*, of a train coming out of a fireplace. It was priced at forty pence and ultimately sold more than ten thousand copies. For a second reissue Penguin wished to have an introduction by Valentine Cunningham, which Upward rejected, and then one by Humphrey Carpenter, which he said was impossible as well. Nevertheless Carpenter wrote one, which Upward found 'appalling' and would rather the book not come out than it be used.[31] It finally appeared again, a reprint of the first edition, in 1988, with the same introduction by Sellers but with the addition of a map of Mortmere.

The Rotten Elements deals with the inner fighting within the Communist Party after the war, unlikely to be of wide interest. Indeed the novel did not sell well, although it was reissued as a paperback in 1979. As he wrote in his notebooks, its subtitle, 'A Novel of Fact', was 'because one of its aims is to give an historically accurate picture of policies and attitudes in the British Communist Party during the late 1940s. "Rotten Elements" is a phrase that was sometimes used in the party to refer to members who deviated seriously from the correct party line'.[32] He did not wish to write a heroic novel but rather to capture the ordinary life of a member of the party. Paradoxically, at the same time he thought of it as the poem he announced as finished at the end of the third volume in the trilogy, *No Home but the Struggle*. Frank Kermode praised his style and skill in this novel, arguing that his aim was a socialist simplicity.[33]

What of the novel itself? It begins with Alan Sebrill giving a series of lectures to members of his branch about Lenin, concerned that the British party is deviating from the Leninist line, under instructions from Moscow. The novel is more poetic than Upward

No Home but the Struggle, *first published in 1977 and reissued in this paperback edition in 1979*

himself claimed, as Alan contemplates the field outside his house, its horses and the memories it brings back of his childhood and of first love. As in the notebooks, the author ricochets between the political life and the poetic one. How was the poetical life possible when not only had he to be a teacher but there were the demands of the party? 'Committee meetings, mass meetings, group meetings, Branch meetings, Borough meetings, District meetings, union meetings, jumble sales, ticket sales, leaflet distribution'. Elsie and Alan are determined to take up their doubts with the leadership of the party but have an unsatisfactory conversation with a member of the executive. At a borough meeting Elsie, its secretary, needs to explain why she was declining to sell the party leader's book on going forward in cooperation with the Labour Party. At this point she resigns as secretary. Alan is concerned how these developments will relate to his attempt to write poetry. He would go further in criticizing the party but he hesitates when he suspects that the member of the branch who is assisting him is very likely to be a police spy. At a meeting of the branch Alan and Elsie are called upon to justify their disagreement with the party line that there should be cooperation with the Labour Party. For their pains they are accused of being in the pay of the Yugoslav embassy, of being Titoists. On coming home, Elsie tears up her party card. Alan asks, 'But how can you bear to live outside the Party?' Unlike his wife he cannot see how he could continue the political fight outside of the party, even though now he would have more time for his poetry. 'From tomorrow on he must, in his free time, give himself utterly to solving the problem of how to write poetry for communism. This would be his political work. And also in a sense it would be his Party work. "Even though I shall no longer be in the Party", he thought, "as a poet I shall still be able to serve it"'.[34] He does leave the party but there is no personal moment as dramatic as his wife's. He now feels that he is again ready to write poetry. But as usual he is overcome with despair at his inability to write the poem he wished to write, leading to the nervous breakdown of his year's sabbatical. The only solution seems to be to return to his ordinary life as a schoolteacher. Alan is able to return to poetry but without politics, as he is disillusioned by the revelations after Stalin's death. The book ends with him recommitted to poetry.

How was the book received? It was frequently reviewed together with his collection *The Railway Accident and Other Stories*. Francis Hope, who had reviewed *In the Thirties* unfavourably in the *Observer*, now wrote about the two books in the *New Statesman*, placing Upward firmly in the context of the Auden group, giving him the role of The Marxist. Hope regarded the writing in *Journey to the Border* as being as bad as what was to be found in Soviet literature. He again is highly critical. 'Every impulse to create is met by a counter-impulse of despair'. But unlike Doris Lessing, Upward, Hope feels, does not make anything creative out of the situation. Philip Toynbee, the novelist, who identified himself as a former Communist, was more sympathetic yet still highly critical in the *Observer*.

> During the Pink Decade Upward was a mysterious figure of enormous prestige . . . Let me say at once that I found 'The Rotten Elements' even more fascinating than 'In the Thirties': I don't see how anyone of my age, class and political background could fail to be enthralled by these gruesome pieces of family

Edward, November 1969

history. It is sad to have to add that this trilogy seems to me to be totally misconceived, a profoundly unsatisfactory work which is not saved from its heavy faults by the rare flashes of that submerged Upward who won so much admiration years ago . . . Indeed I cannot conclude this review without saying that there is, in these books, a strange kind of pervasive decency, a sort of holy sweetness, which is not without its exasperating charms.

In the *Sunday Telegraph* John Lehmann not surprisingly gave a very enthusiastic review to both *The Rotten Elements* and *The Railway Accident and Other Stories*, writing of the title story as 'the most brilliant piece of surrealist prose to have been written in English (if you don't count the Alice stories)'. The novel is praised for its clarity and precision. He views this novel as being the story of Upward being released from the torture by the 'iron maiden of Marxism'. Julian Symons in the *Sunday Times* both salutes and regrets Upward's abandonment of fantasy on behalf of seriousness. Samuel Hynes in his review in the *Times Literary Supplement* emphasizes as Upward's great contribution the 'realistic nightmare', a dominant idea in the writing of the 1930s. Hynes finds the present book 'dimmed by dialectics' but he hopes that now, free from the party, Upward can return to the world of imagination. Martin Seymour-Smith in the *Spectator* celebrates the achievement of 'The Railway Accident' and bemoans the tediousness of *The Rotten Elements*. Ian Hamilton in the *Listener* takes the same position, the promise of *The Railway Accident* destroyed by the party, both in the joining and the leaving of it. Robert Nye in *The Times* was more sympathetic. He found the novel 'simply and scrupulously *true*, a truth wrung from the most unpromising and difficult material by complete response to detail and a calm attentive style that never permits itself to show off or write up'. The novel is effective but it is undercut by Upward's desire to write in a plain style and to repress his imagination.[35]

The new line as enunciated by the party leader, Harry Pollitt, in his *Looking Ahead* of 1947 argued that socialism in Britain could be achieved by parliamentary means. From 1945 on the party line in Britain was almost embarrassingly subservient to the ruling Labour Party and its emphasis on increased production in the years after the war. The party did abandon this position in 1947 but without moving further to the left. This culminated in 1951 with the publication of *The British Road to Socialism* which turned out to be parliamentary even though the document attacked the Labour Party. In terms of tactics it was at least in Britain largely ineffectual but it was what had been ordered by Stalin. This was despite the fact that the Labour Party was an enemy of the Soviet Union during the Cold War and attacked the role of Communists in the trade unions. In the 1951 election ten Communists ran to be members of Parliament. None was elected and all lost their deposits, that is, they received so few votes that they had to forfeit the money they had put up to run, a policy to eliminate frivolous candidates. The two sitting Communist members lost their seats as well and no Communist would be a member of Parliament before the party was dissolved in 1991. On the other hand it was a period in which Communists were becoming increasingly influential in trade unions although at the same time there was intense opposition to them within the unions. The Upwards opposed

CHAPTER 7: THE YEARS BETWEEN

the party's policy from the left; they were regarded as left-wing deviationists and as Titoists. This was the central story of the novel. In terms of his own development its significance was to free his imagination. But first he had to write out the story. *In the Thirties* was the thesis of joining the party. *The Rotten Elements* was the anti-thesis of leaving it. His break with the party was in 1948, a significant year in the history of the Cold War: the Communist coup d'état in Czechoslovakia, the expulsion of Tito from the Cominform and the beginning of the eleven-month Soviet blockade of Berlin.

Those who were opposed to the party moving to the right were bolstered by the publication in the Communist weekly, *World News and Views,* of a letter from the Australian Communist Party criticizing *Looking Ahead*. It totally rejected the view that a Labour government could in any way be a transition to socialism. Rather it was a means to preserve the imperialist state. It depicts the British Communist Party as the enemy of the workers in its opposition to strikes. This was the precipitating event in *The Rotten Elements*. The Upwards' position was closer to the Cominform's Cold War stance than that of the British Communist policy. But in the eyes of the British party the Upwards were deviationists. A file on the dispute between the Upwards and the party is preserved in the archives held at the People's History Museum in Manchester. For no apparent reason MI5 took a great interest in this dispute or perhaps it was just because the letters about it were in the copies of the thousands of documents it had of an important party member. As recorded in *The Rotten Elements,* Alan and Elsie Sebrill had supported the Australian party's statements. The British party took with the greatest seriousness any disagreement with its line. According to the notes in the party file on the incident, the Upwards had typed out twelve copies of the Australian statement and wrote to Australia for more. They were then distributed to various people, presumably members of the party, in Cheltenham, Oxford, Bristol and London. It was also noted that the Upwards were 'Party members of 20 years standing, but started to express opposition to Party policy about 18 months before the above incident'. (The length of membership was slightly erroneous. Hilda had joined in 1930; Edward tentatively in 1932 and definitely in 1934.) Hilda was secretary to their branch while Edward was a loyal member fulfilling the ordinary obligations of selling the *Daily Worker*, distributing leaflets and going to demonstrations. It is unknown what the party regarded as their earlier subversive activity.

The Upwards' questioning of the party line on the Australian position was causing great concern and was seen as deeply disruptive of party unity. On 21 September Monte Shapiro, the head of the Dulwich branch, wrote to the executive committee of the party expressing his feeling that something needed to be done. 'The Dulwich Village Branch recently sent you a letter asking whether you intended to publish the reply recently published by the Australian C.P. to our Party's reply to their criticisms'. There were rumours that the executive committee was split on these issues. Shapiro wrote: 'I feel that the circulation of these rumours can do untold harm to the Party, and that it has already succeeded in sowing doubts and confusions in the minds of members of our Branch, at least . . . My main reason for writing this letter is my belief that no rumour which can in any way weaken the confidence of comrades in the Party should be allowed to circulate unchallenged'. On 29 September Dennis

Goodwin, the district organizer for the party, wrote to Shapiro to ask who were the comrades who raised the question of the Australian letter and requested its distribution. His tone is very similar to that used by the MI5 officials when requesting information: 'Will you please treat this as a confidential matter and a matter of some urgency'. The next day Tom Gibson, the secretary of the Camberwell Borough Communist Party, reported that the Upwards had been responsible for 'diversionary discussions amongst certain of our members' about the Australian letter. 'The Upwards continue to raise this question in their branch, Dulwich Village, and have succeeded in sowing a certain amount of confusion in the minds of certain comrades'. Gibson felt that the Upwards were misleading one loyal member in particular who had read the letter at a meeting of the Dulwich branch. 'I would point out that Comrade Youle is a first class industrial comrade, absolutely devoted to the Party, but has a fixation on the Upwards who are essentially middle class'. On 15 October the Upwards (and two others) were summoned to a meeting on 25 October to discuss their distribution of the Australian letter. Goodwin wrote to Tom Gibson that 'the purpose of the meeting is not to castigate the comrades but to satisfy ourselves on where they stand, to give them some opportunity of discussing the issue with us and to give a few words of warning if necessary on where this sort of thing can lead to'. They were to meet with John Mahon who was a member of the party's political committee as well as being the London district secretary. On 16 October the Upwards accepted the invitation to the meeting, writing, 'As the second Australian letter will be one of the subjects under discussion, we assume that every member of the Committee will be provided with a copy of that letter well in advance of the meeting. We should be glad if you could assure us that this will be done'. This assurance was not given. There are notes in Upward's papers of what he and Hilda said or intended to say. They both believed that capitalism needed to be destroyed before a socialist state could be built. Yet at the same time he had in his notes, *'I trust that it will be quite clear that I am not suggesting that there should be a revolution now or in the near future'*. He did feel, however, 'that Britain should certainly have a revolution eventually and that the post-war Welfare state was far from satisfactory. "I am convinced that we are living not in a new & progressive Britain, not in a people's Britain, not in 'our' Britain, but in a monopoly-capitalists' Britain, an imperialists' Britain, a reactionary and pro-fascist Britain which is doing its damnedest to destroy every decent progressive movement all over the world"'.[36] In neither the government's nor the party's files is there a description of the meeting.

Upward gives his version of the meeting in *The Rotten Elements*. In it, Elsie delivers an attack on the policy of the party to cooperate with Labour, which took the form of supporting its drive for increased production in factories. The local party secretary, Gibson, called Sammy Hollingworth in the novel, accuses her of sectarianism and infantile leftism as well as operating on the instructions of the Yugoslav embassy. Alan and Elsie conclude that the leaders of the party have 'become out-and-out political tricksters, as bad as the worst of the bourgeois politicians and much cruder than most of those'.[37] It is when she comes home from this meeting that Elsie tears up her party card.

Upward's life was full of hesitations and doubts. He found it much harder than his wife to break with the party, although both remained firmly on the far left. On 28 October Jean Shapiro, the secretary of the Dulwich Village Branch of the party, wrote to Goodwin that Upward had telephoned her to say that both he and Hilda intended – quoting him, to 'drop out of politics altogether' – to hand in their party cards and to resign from the British-Soviet Society. Yet two days later on 30 October she wrote to him about a visit she had made to see Upward. 'The position now is that he himself does not wish to leave the Party, but that Hilda has destroyed her card and sent it to me. He further agrees that, subject to the approval of the Party, he will continue to work in the British-Soviet Society'. But finally at the end of December he took decisive action. Shapiro had asked him to a branch meeting to discuss his position but he declined to come, stating to her, according to her letter to John Mahon on 30 December, that he thought that if he came to a meeting he would then be expelled officially, which he wished to avoid. He had decided not to take out a 1949 party card. She enclosed a copy of the letter from him dated 28 December where he wrote: 'I am very sorry that after sixteen years' membership of the Party I am now asking you to accept my resignation . . . Cde Mahon made it clear to me that if I engage in further discussion of the second Australian letter I shall be expelled from the Party. As I am not prepared to give an undertaking to be silent about the Australian letters, and as I do not want to be expelled from the Party, I am taking the only alternative course of offering my resignation'. The last document to be found in both files on this contretemps is a letter Shapiro sent to Sid French, presumably in the party's central office, on 31 January 1949 pointing out that officially Upward had not resigned but rather had not renewed his membership for 1949. Jean Shapiro also felt that someone from the central office should come to the branch 'to explain the reasons for the censure of Cde Upward, because some of the comrades felt there were lessons to be learnt for any possible future occasion when any of us might find ourselves in disagreement with Party policy'.[38] On 2 March 1949 Shapiro wrote to Upward to accept what amounted to his resignation.[39]

Despite leaving the party Upward continued still to believe in the truth of Communism, that ultimately the class struggle would bring about a better society. He never abandoned those convictions but he never fully explained why a revolution would enable him to be the poet he wished to be. He did not waver from his belief in the necessity of the intertwining of poetry and politics. It was almost as if he were hearkening back to the nonconformist conscience of his grandparents in his sense of obligation to be politically active when it really wasn't his true nature. As he rather startlingly remarked in an interview in 1976: 'There's hardly anything I less wanted to do than to be active as far as direct political activity goes. It isn't my cup of tea in a way, and yet I felt that I had to'.[40] Isherwood initially had the impression that Upward was giving up politics entirely rather than just the party. 'Hilda and I have both gone right out of party politics. We should have been kicked out if we hadn't gone. But as a result I find that I am able to write once again'.[41] In reply Isherwood wrote: 'I can't help feeling glad about the ending of your political activities. Just as I imagine you were glad when I stopped living with the Vedanta people'.[42] Upward didn't actually stop being politically active but certainly wasn't to the extent that had been true when he was a member of the party. And he still regarded himself as a Marxist Leninist.

Leaving the party proved to be eventually an essential act to free him to write again. It took him a long time to recover from the trauma of his departure. He recognized how similar it was to losing one's faith: Communism had been his religion. As he said in an interview in 1978: 'It's difficult for anyone nowadays to realise what it meant; to be disloyal to the Party was to be disloyal to the future, to everything. I suppose people in religious movements have felt that same kind of pressure...The compulsion was internal: the very isolation of the Party, the hostility towards it, strengthened our loyalty to it. Its hold was based on our own beliefs, outside was darkness again'.[43] He had as usual great difficulty in writing, which was what he most wanted to do. He worried about his prose sentence by sentence. He stated in his notebooks that he was about to tackle a paragraph or that he was satisfied with one sentence but that he must give the next one colour and character. He wanted to limit his political activity. As he wrote in his notebook in 1953: 'I know that I can never, and do not want to, go back to the old life of constant political activity. I feel that physically and temperamentally I am unfit for it. To be in the party means to be a leader, and I haven't got the qualities of a leader. At most I could be a follower or a fellow-traveller'.[44] He had been its loyal member but had not played a particularly prominent role. Rather he fulfilled a party member's traditional obligations. He had extended a bit beyond this by being on the editorial board and writing for *Ploughshare*. He also from time to time gave talks here and there, such as one on modern poetry to a staff discussion society at his school, emphasizing that poetry must connect with the real world. He gave talks on Marxism and literature. In his notes for such a talk he underlined that *'for the*

CHAPTER 7: THE YEARS BETWEEN

Marxist the greatest books are those that are truest to life. Those which give the fullest and deepest picture of life as a whole'. At the same time in another talk he emphasized that the first necessity as a writer and reader was to be in love with words, with rhythms and with stories.[45] He also served as a tutor for the National Council of Labour Colleges, giving some courses by mail.

The third volume of his trilogy, the synthesis, was *No Home but the Struggle*. In his notebook he wrote on 14 September 1967 that he was 'getting ever nearer to the first para[graph]' and in the next volume he reported that he had started writing on 22 June 1968.[46] His working title for the work was the 'NPL', the New Poetical Life. Upward wrote to Isherwood in 1968 that 'volume three shows him [Alan Sebrill] trying to live the new poetic life by returning to the place which he especially associates with the old poetic life and by remembering that life. As his memories get nearer to the point where the old poetic life collapsed so simultaneously his current new poetic life is nearing collapse also, and the book ends with his turning to a new political life – not to the Party again but to a life in which the political struggle becomes primary for him and poetry becomes his best means of carrying it on'. He was writing his life story in reverse order. This volume dealt with the years before the 1930s when he was growing up a rebel. He felt it was then that he was, as he wrote in a notebook in 1969, committing himself to 'art for the sake of the fight – this must be my motto. Better a well-written art-work (with a Marxist message) about a bourgeois childhood than badly written pseudo art-work (with a Marxist message) about the working-class struggle'.[47] Years later he is still struggling with the book, writing to Isherwood in September 1974: 'Another fearful feeling I have is that the book as a whole is neither an autobiography nor a work of art. I don't know what it is. Perhaps I have overplayed the simplicity gambit and the writing is just flat'. In November he commented: 'Why does one write at all? The only answer I can find which doesn't bring doubts with it is in order to be oneself'. Then finally on 29 July 1975 he wrote to Isherwood that he had finished the third volume. At some point he sent the manuscript to him and in September 1975 wrote how much his approval meant to him. As at Cambridge they were still one another's 'first reader'. 'Your praise does me more good than I can say. Most of the time nowadays I think of myself as a naturally rotten writer who is only able to produce anything tolerable by taking almost infinite pains, but every now and again, as when I get letters like your last two, the Black Monk comes down in a whirlwind from the sky and says to me quietly "You're a genius after all"'.[48]

The Rotten Elements had received widespread though mixed critical attention. The initial printing of 2,200 copies sold out. In 1972 Penguin issued a second paperback edition. Nevertheless Heinemann was unenthusiastic about publishing the concluding volume and in October 1975 turned it down. It seemed as if Upward wouldn't be able to have it published at all. He felt that he was being ignored and discriminated against because of his having been a member of the Communist Party. But Stephen Spender came to his rescue. Upward told Isherwood the story in a letter in July 1976.

> Stephen wrote an article in the New Statesman in the course of which he said that it was a scandal that I couldn't find a

publisher, and as a result of this I had a letter from Roy Fuller who is now in charge of the Arts Council's Literature Panel, saying that the Council would be likely to guarantee a publisher against loss who would publish my Vol 3. This was decisive with Heinemann. I think also they had been made to feel somewhat ashamed of themselves, both by Stephen's article and by a letter next week in the NS from Neville Braybrooke which endorsed what Stephen had said and also mentioned that it was Heinemann who had published the previous two volumes of the trilogy.[49]

Upward wrote Spender a letter of thanks saying that he had heard from Fuller and that Spender's piece was crucial in making Heinemann reverse its decision. 'This seems very hopeful, and it comes just as I was resigning myself to the prospect of never again being able to get any of my work published. How nice it was to meet you again after all these years'.[50] Upward himself was willing to contribute £2,000 toward publication costs but it never came to that. In fact he received a £250 advance.

Heinemann decided to reissue the first two together with the third in an omnibus volume as *The Spiral Ascent*, a pun on his name but also suggesting the dialectical nature of the three books. At the time there was a growth of interest in the Auden group. As mentioned, in 1976 from 25 June to 7 November there was an exhibition at the National Portrait Gallery of 'Young Writers of the 1930s centring on Auden, Day Lewis, MacNeice, Isherwood and Spender. But in the exhibition itself Upward was featured along with quite a few other writers such as Orwell, Julian Bell and John Cornford as well as some older writers such as Leonard and Virginia Woolf and Edith Sitwell. The press notice made a sweeping claim for the group: 'This generation brought English literature into closer contact with social and political upheaval than it had been since the French Revolution fired the imagination of the Romantic poets'. Upward was a major lender to the exhibition, contributing his map of Mortmere as well as other Mortmere material. Included was the letter Auden wrote to Upward with its line, 'I shall never know how much in these poems [*Poems*, 1930] is filched from you via Christopher'.[51] Some visitors complained that the exhibition reinforced the stereotype of the period, that concentrating on this core group narrowed the definition of who were the young writers of the 1930s.

What was the third volume about? He kept changing his mind: was it about his failure to be a poet or was it about his now being able to be a poet, as the ending of the book seemed to suggest? The last line refers to an unseen completed poem. Is this the ideal or has life, for better or worse, superseded art? A fulfilment that may have happened? This is suggested by a possible title for the trilogy: 'A Man Who Became Himself'.[52] He aimed in the trilogy for a plain style influenced by his reading of Bunyan, Defoe, Cowper, William Hale White, Robert Tressell, George Gissing and perhaps surprisingly, William Wordsworth's *The Prelude*. This echoed the claim made for the Auden group in the exhibition in the comparison with the Romantics: the disillusionment with the Russian Revolution paralleled Wordsworth's disillusionment with the French Revolution.[53] In terms of its writing, Upward deliberately turned away from a modernist style. Though he had left the party, he was – many would say too much so – still loyal to its literary values. He wished to make his work accessible to the working class.

More than the first two volumes of the trilogy the third deals with the period of his formation, the portrait of the artist as a boy and a young man. It opens with the beginning of Alan Sebrill's retirement in 1961 when he will be living permanently in the house his grandfather acquired in Sandown on the Isle of Wight. The identification between Sebrill and the author is even stronger in the third volume, as unlike the first two it is written in the first person. He has long left the party but now is politically active with the Campaign for Nuclear Disarmament. The book is a counterpoint between the recent past when his main commitment is to his writing, and his growing up and education at prep school, public school and university. The novel is a rich discussion of the making of a writer. The point of view is intriguingly unclear in all three volumes. Is the author looking back on himself with a certain amount of ironic detachment or presenting himself in a more immediate way? All three books are the story of an English middle-class man caught up in and committed to being a Communist or, in the third volume, a former Communist. In the tradition of English writing, it is very much the story of an individual and his shaping. As Rodney Koeneke has written, 'Even in "The Rotten Elements" the split with the Party comes across as a set of broken relationships rather than a slate of ideological deviations. This seemed very "English" to me, and one of Upward's most winning qualities. His crippling self-doubt and self-consciousness, which can be most aggravating in his ongoing struggles to finish a poem, also seemed like a national (or at least a class) trait, as well. But then, maybe it's as an anthology of class and generational traits that Upward shows at his best'.[54]

CHAPTER 7: THE YEARS BETWEEN

As usual Upward's newest book, published together for economic reasons as a trilogy with one new part, received a fair amount of attention in the press. Upward exaggerated the degree to which he was ignored. Although he was not as prominent as others associated with Auden, his books were reviewed in most of the major publications, the sort of attention most authors would die for. He had several interviews on television and in newspapers. Admittedly the reviews were mixed. Among the first was one by Angus Wilson in the *Observer* on 24 July. He provides a summary of the plot of the three novels which clearly he found simplistic and somewhat at odds with what he felt must be Upward's own sophistication as in the 'Auden-Isherwood high-jokeyness of his punning play upon his own name in the title'. Wilson, despite being on the left himself, ultimately found Upward's romanticism about Communism repugnant, considering how much death and destruction it had caused in the world. The next day Raymond Williams reviewed the book in the *Observer*'s sister paper, the *Guardian*. It is a rather abstract piece saying practically nothing about the trilogy itself other than seeing it as an alternative to the standard account of the life of a 1930s' poet. Michael Ratcliffe reviewed it the next day in *The Times*, pointing out that Isherwood when they met at Repton had described Upward in *Lions and Shadows* as 'a natural anarchist, a born romantic revolutionary'. He felt Upward was trying to tame through his doctrinaire Marxism the imaginative poet given to fantasy, who he was by nature. Ratcliffe clearly felt that Upward had succeeded far too well and had wilfully made his writing boring and tedious.

The next day Christopher Isherwood reviewed the book in the *New Statesman*. One might regard this as too cosy but their close friendship was no secret. The previous April Upward had reviewed Isherwood's *Christopher and His Kind*. While very favourable it was primarily merely an account of the book. Claire Tomalin, at that point literary editor of the *New Statesman*, had asked Upward to review *Christopher and His Kind*. In his notebook in January 1977 Upward remarked, 'I suppose I shall have to try, but I hate the idea'. He seemed to have a hate for the *New Statesman*, writing two days later: 'Filled with agitation and rage ... But I think my duty to CI demands that I should write the review rather than leave it to a CIA spook like [name omitted]. And yet what is the value of my opinion in this disgusting country where I am little more than an internal exile with no comrades?' In his notebook the assignment led him to reflect very honestly on his great friend's recent writing.

> What do I really think of his post-war writing? Well, partly because of my own ageing, I can't respond to it with the same enthusiasm as I did to Lions & Shadows or to The Nowaks. But Kathleen & Frank moved me very deeply ... There is an unseemliness in my praising him ... We were all of us failures, all the 'young writers of the 'thirties', in our different ways, but I was a worse failure than the others ... With the exception perhaps of Louis MacNeice CI was the least politically-minded writer of that group who have come to be regarded as most representative of the 1930s.[55]

Both he and Isherwood saw his homosexuality as his revolt against England, parallel in many ways to Upward's revolt via Communism. Both were partially triggered by what they hated in their world, the world that had shaped them as English gentlemen. Isherwood fought that world through his homosexuality; Upward through his Communism. Another driving force for both of them was their desire to be writers. Isherwood went to Berlin and then to the United States and could only come to terms with his own country after the Second World War when it was far less powerful. Rather movingly, Upward writes about himself in the review of Isherwood in the third person. He comments about the moment on the ship to America when Isherwood abandons his fight against Fascism through becoming a pacifist. 'Though he must have been aware that his closest heterosexual friend, Edward Upward, who had always approved of his homosexuality, would bitterly disapprove of his abandonment of left-wing politics, he must also have felt that their friendship, founded on the indestructible world of imagination they had shared at Cambridge and on their continuing interest in each other's writing, would survive'. Isherwood's review of *The Spiral Ascent* treats it as similar to his own book, but in this case the autobiography is somewhat fictionalized. His review is primarily a summation of the three novels and the relationship, both hostile and supportive, between Upward's two great themes: the political life and the poetical life. Isherwood loyally concludes that the book is a masterpiece. '*The Spiral Ascent* (I do hate that title, though) is one of the most truly original books in modern literature'. Upward wrote Isherwood an enthusiastic letter of thanks in which he commented on the reception the book had received.

> What an utterly marvellous review by you in the N.S. It filled me with an extraordinary happiness as though I had suddenly

become fifty years younger and we were talking together at Marine Villa in Freshwater. It was especially cheering because of the unfavourableness of all the other reviewers so far . . . There was a neutral one in The Guardian by Raymond Williams which I had to read several times before I could discover what it was about. However even the unfavourable reviews have given a lot of space to me and have been peevishly respectful . . . I have not yet solved the problem of what I'm going to write next. I hope I don't take another twenty years to solve it. But I'm pretty sure I shan't be driven into a nervous breakdown this time – or if I am it won't be by my writing but by the world.[56]

Isobel Murray in the *Financial Times* in writing about the five novels published that week gave the lead and more than half of her space to the book. Yet she was strongly negative, citing the total lack of irony and humour. 'It is, however, a painfully honest book, and while I cannot but see it as a total literary failure it may provide useful documentary material for the political historian and psychologist'. Tim Heald in the *Daily Telegraph* was unenthusiastic about it as he was about the other four novels he reviewed, including Joan Didion's *A Book of Common Prayer*. Samuel Hynes who had anonymously, as the paper's policy had been, written about Upward before in the *Times Literary Supplement* now wrote a signed review. He pointed out that Upward was an exception to so many writers in the 1930s who flirted with Communism but then reverted to being 'individualistic literary liberals'. For Upward the conflict between art and life may have been dialectical but for Hynes it had meant the stifling of Upward's imagination, a decline from the 'brilliant but imperfect' *Journey to the Border*. The problem for Upward according to Hynes was how to write political novels that will be works of art. In the third and new part Upward was attempting to be a 'Marxist Proust' recovering the significant moments in his past. Hynes sees the trilogy as part of a tetralogy including *Journey*. 'All four dwell on that one problem, the conflict in one man of two powerful and incompatible wills – the will to be an artist, which is individualist, heterodox, and subversive, and the will to be a political man, which is collective, orthodox, and conformist'. Hynes ends his review with faint praise. 'It has a convincing honesty about it that is a saving grace, and that makes the whole sequence one long – too long, many readers will say – cautionary tale of the expense of poetic spirit in a waste of Party life'. Despite its reservations Upward was pleased with the review which certainly took his work seriously. He wrote to Hynes on 8 August. 'I think my work should be seen in the light of the Puritan tradition – from Bunyan to Mark Rutherford . . . I do not regard myself as a socialist realist writer. While I was in the Party I did attempt to become one, but I was unable to produce anything satisfactory to myself in this style . . . A more modern writer who has influenced me in writing this trilogy is Robert Tressell . . . His novel [*The Ragged Trousered Philanthropists*] is the only great English socialist novel I have read'. He went on to say, 'The "long Poem" which Alan Sebrill finishes at the end of *No Home but the Struggle* is of course *The Rotten Elements* in real life'. The subtitle of that novel is 'A Novel of Fact' and is the most 'socialist realist' and least poetical of his writings. He concluded, '*No Home but the Struggle* is in reality the first product of the "new political life"'. It is indeed the most imaginative volume in the trilogy.⁵⁷

On 14 August in the *Sunday Telegraph*, Neville Braybrooke, Upward's friend and fellow resident of the Isle of Wight, favourably reviewed the trilogy, pointing out that it had taken twenty years to write and that it was a work of 'epic proportions and certain to become a classic'. On 2 September the trilogy was also favourably reviewed, although with some criticisms of its style, by Kevin Cully in the left-wing publication *Tribune*. The Communist novelist John Sommerfield wrote a rather neutral review in the *London Magazine* but in common with other reviewers found the style problematic, although he tried to justify it. 'Upward is far too intelligent and talented to be boring except on purpose'. One feels that Sommerfield wished to like the book more than he did. He concludes his review: Sebrill 'remains a talented and honest man who has nothing to lose but his self-imposed mental chains. But he is committed to them for life'. On 1 December in the *Morning Star*, the successor paper to the *Daily Worker*, there was perhaps surprisingly a positive review.⁵⁸ The book did fairly well. There was an edition of 1,500 copies in July and then in October there was a second impression of 750 copies.

In 1978 and 1979 Quartet Books published separate paperback editions of 3,400 copies of the three volumes. The completion of the trilogy marked an important stage in his career. Though he may have thought of writing further novels, he now returned to his earlier interests and became a writer of short stories. To a degree that he might have disputed, he was known and established and remained a significant literary figure for the next forty years of his life.

Chapter 8: Free at Last

IT WAS HARD FOR Upward to handle his freedom. He was no longer imprisoned by the 'wrong line' that in his view the party had taken. He was as likely to have difficulty writing when he had no further commitments. In *The Spiral Ascent* he had written out his past. Some felt that he had, particularly in *The Rotten Elements*, deliberately and sadly suppressed his imagination. He was now free from the party. It had never asked him to be more than a loyal local member and had not involved him in the movement's larger literary life, other than with *Ploughshare*. Perhaps in retrospect he felt some regret that he had not played a more prominent role. He had lost his infatuation with Stalin, vividly symbolized at one moment of crisis years before by his chanting his name as an incantation, as one might pray to the Virgin Mary. The trial and persecution of Jewish doctors in Russia just before Stalin's death had alerted him that something was rotten in the Soviet state. He still regarded himself as a Marxist Leninist and was impressed with what Mao was doing in China. He did have a period of revulsion and divested himself of Lenin's works, only later to replace them. In the 1930s he had believed that writers were in a better situation in the Soviet Union than in the West but he later came to realize that that was far from true. In *The Spiral Ascent* he had certainly achieved an accurate account of what it was like to be a middle-class member of the Communist Party. Nevertheless he felt it was a necessary step in his political

CHAPTER 8: FREE AT LAST

development. Others might well see it as a high price to have paid.

After the trauma of leaving the party he couldn't bear for a while the idea of any political involvement. He and Hilda maintained a keen interest in current events both in the world and in Britain. He did return to some political activism, however, stimulated by a broadcast talk he heard by Isaac Deutscher, the independent Marxist thinker. Upward belonged to a local organization, Unisoc, an eclectic group of socialists. Starting in the later 1950s he devoted his primary political energy to the Campaign for Nuclear Disarmament (CND). It was a worthy and important cause on the left of the political spectrum. On the other hand, it was somewhat ironic for him to become so active in it. Most of its supporters were members of the Labour Party and middle class, two groups that by being a Communist he hoped he would avoid. Indeed, he left the party because he felt it was too accommodating to the Labour Party and possibly to the middle class as well. His and Hilda's interest in politics was less intense than it had been in the past. He was present at the CND's first major public meeting in Central Hall in London on 17 February 1958. Five thousand attended and a thousand were turned away. Among others, Michael Foot, J. B. Priestley, Bertrand Russell, A. J. P. Taylor and Alex Comfort were the original leaders.[1] Approximately forty to fifty thousand supported the movement by 1959. It had come into being in the autumn of 1957 with the intensification of the arms race and the real possibility that nuclear weapons might be used if the Cold War transformed into a hot one. A decade after leaving the party Upward felt that he could be politically involved again. But as before when he was in the party, he limited himself mostly to the local level. In May 1962 he joined a CND

CHAPTER 8: FREE AT LAST

march on the island from Newport to Cowes. He did not aspire to join its more radical wing, the 'Committee of 100', with its commitment to civil disobedience nor did he go on any of the Aldermaston marches although his children did. He still managed to maintain his fragile belief in Communism but with more and more qualifications. He wrote in his notebook in 1962: 'The Soviet breach of the H test moratorium came just in time to prevent me from believing in the Soviet Union once again. Of course I know that the capitalist powers are more to blame . . . "My Party right or wrong" can never be my attitude . . . The future – if there is a future – is with communism, I know. But does that mean that one must ignore the crimes – crimes against the future – that communism is committing now? I must believe in communism but hope little of it. My hopes must be set on writing'. Twenty years later he noted that 'CND can never mean for me what the Party once did, can never replace the Party. I still see M-L [Marxist Leninism] as the only hope for the world'.[2] He kept his hand in with some political activity but it was far less intense than it had been in the past. The CND campaign locally did wane by the mid-1960s when he went to a meeting in Newport attended by five and then another with ten present. He did go to successful demonstrations in London. He somewhat deluded himself that CND was a movement out of which a revolution might arise, that it was a serious challenge to the capitalist state. He was also active in protests against the Vietnam war. In November 1967 he was involved with CND chapter's laying an anti-Vietnam war wreath on the First World War Cenotaph in Newport. By the mid-1960s CND was no longer a significant political force although it did have something of a resurgence in the 1980s when he recorded local meetings of forty to sixty and there were five hundred members on the island. He wrote to Isherwood in 1981: 'Yesterday I laid flowers on a local war memorial, the last thing I've ever imagined I would do, but it was for Hiroshima day. And in two days' time on Nagasaki day we are having a big picnic on Boniface down above Ventnor near the bolt-hole or underground H.Q. which the V.I.P.s of the Island plan to retire to in the event of nuclear war'.[3] There was a campaign to make the island a nuclear-free zone. Hilda kept up a stream of letters to the local press.

From his retirement in 1961 until he moved to Pontefract in Yorkshire in March 2004 he would live in his grandfather's house in Sandown on the Isle of Wight. He inherited its leasehold from his father and then paid a further £250 to convert it into a freehold. It was divided into two separate attached houses in 1959 so that his brother Mer could live there as well, which he did until a few years before his death in 1999. Upward jokingly referred to it as 'the ancestral house of Usher'.[4] On the other hand, he could say about it, 'I have come home. There is no other house I have so often longed for as this one'.[5] He wrote in the mornings, trying to start by ten. He would frequently take walks along the cliff top towards Shanklin and then back along the beach. He had local friends including the distinguished poet and translator David Gascoyne. Gascoyne was the president of the Isle of Wight Poetry Society, and Upward became its vice president. Rather improbably they visited Queen Victoria's Osborne House together and from time to time would have pub lunches and go on Sunday excursions. Gascoyne was chronically depressed and Upward was one of the few people he saw. Upward introduced a reading of Gascoyne's, remarking in advance, 'I shall feel much more at home there than I shd do if I

CHAPTER 8: FREE AT LAST

Hilda and Edward Upward photographed by Jeremy Wynne, late 1983

were chairing a political meeting'.[6] They had both quit the Communist Party in 1948. Though they were both regarded as being in some sense surrealists, they actually did not have that much in common. They maintained a casual and not very deep friendship. He was also friendly with the writers Neville and June Braybrooke, she as a novelist under the name of Isobel English. His children, with their children, came on regular visits as did his sister Yolande. They had a fairly active social life with a circle of friends. He corresponded with close friends such as J. M. Cohen, the critic and translator whom he had come to know at Alleyn's, and increasingly with scholars and graduate students in Britain, Germany, Italy and the United States who were interested in his work. He loved the island and regarded it as the most beautiful place on earth.

He thought he might continue writing novels but in fact after

CHAPTER 8: FREE AT LAST

CND social, Tudor Rose Restaurant, Shanklin, 1984 (Joan Ruddock, chair of CND, with Hilda and Edward)

The Spiral Ascent he devoted himself in the remaining years of his long life to the short story. The publication of his next book was in 1987, *The Night Walk and Other Stories*. It consisted of nine stories and nine very short 'Political Prose Pieces', the latter written between 1976 and 1979. Eleven of the eighteen had previously been published in periodicals. Isherwood had died in January 1986 and Upward dedicated the book to his memory, 'my friend for sixty-five years'. In 1953, the year of Upward's breakdown when it seemed he might give up writing, Isherwood wrote a powerful letter to Hilda underlining the importance of their relationship. 'It seems to me terrible that E. must give up what was such a vital part of his life. I feel this not only because I love him but because I'm only a writer myself because of him. At the beginning he taught me everything and I've always felt that his talent is far greater than mine, even if he hasn't used it as

CHAPTER 8: FREE AT LAST

much'. He would accept Upward's negative judgements, agreeing with him that his novel *The World in the Evening* was a failure. He wrote to him frankly about *Cabaret* which made him so much money. 'As for Cabaret I try to keep as far from it as possible. It's an ill bird that fouls the nest where the golden eggs are laid. Especially when the nest is anyhow made entirely of sawdust and shit'.[7] They would see one another when Isherwood was in England, Upward writing about one visit, 'I felt desolated after he had gone'.[8] In 1961 they did a talk together on the BBC Third Programme. In March 1970 Upward came up to London in order to see Isherwood, who remarked about him at the time: 'One always has a tremendous sense of his vocation as a writer. *Nothing* else matters to him. (This actually isn't true; he is devoted to Hilda and the children.)' At a later point Isherwood added to this entry: 'To me he seems to have fears of rejection by publishers on political grounds and fears of prosecution on grounds of libel which verge on paranoia. Perhaps this is a result of the kind of life he has led – always feeling himself to be an illegal underground worker. But, without his life, Edward wouldn't now have his own personal myth'. Some years later, listening to a tape of Upward reading, he remarked about him: 'What is wonderful about this style of his is its reticence. He tells you everything in his own time. He isn't one bit worried about your possibly getting impatient. His deliberation is remorseless. He builds the structure of matchsticks with maddening patience. But it gets built, and what's more, the matchsticks are magnetic. They can't be blown over – no, not by a hurricane'.[9]

There was something of a tapering off of their relationship in Isherwood's last years, Upward writing about him in 1983: 'CI won't answer my letters. But I shall not reproach him even in my mind. If it weren't for him none of my books would have been published. I shall never forget what he has meant to me, what he meant to me when we were young'.[10] Isherwood was suffering from prostate cancer which Edward may not have known. This may well have made correspondence less congenial to Isherwood. He too felt that the relationship was not quite as strong as it had been even though they continued to send one another what they had written.

The Night Walk and Other Stories is dominated by Auden. Upward tended to be an obsessive thinker and his imagination was haunted by the break in their relationship. Auden himself, who had dismissed Upward after what he thought was his inconsiderate treatment of Isherwood at the time they went to America, probably rarely thought about Upward. In 1947 Upward wrote about The Downs school in Malvern where Auden taught: 'Every yard here is holy ground. In any other age he wd have been one of the greatest. Now he is an American. Why has he left this country, more beautiful than any on earth? Because of the corruption of our middle-class, in which he shared'. He remarked in 1963 on reading Auden's collection of essays *The Dyer's Hand*: 'Such a variety of feelings & memories it roused in me. What a sparkling intelligence . . . Wystan's later poems are not as good as his critical writings. Even he, by far the most talented of our generation, cannot successfully create now. But he has lived the life he wanted to live'. The following year he recorded a dream he had about Auden in which he told him truthfully how much he admired his early work and untruthfully his later poetry as well. In the dream Auden replied, '"And I admire everything you write". Though I didn't believe this, tears (of pleasure or of nostalgia) came into my eyes'. He was more negative in 1967, perhaps feeling guilty for selling for £230 his copy of Auden's poems printed by Stephen Spender at Oxford in 1928. He justified it by his fear that when he died it might be thrown out with the notebook with which it was kept. Auden had given him an inscribed copy and also had made manuscript corrections in it. 'Feel a pang at parting with it, however. He is the only one of our 'thirties lot who is likely to be remembered at all, though his reputation will probably be no higher than that of a secondary Victorian poet'. But he felt so badly about selling the book that he asked Alan Clodd to whom he had sold it to return it. It is now in the British Library with Upward's complete archive.

He wrote at the time of Auden's death in 1973: 'I shall never be able to get over his having died without my having made any move to break the 35 years' silence between us . . . This grief is likely to be with me for the rest of my life. Nothing can console it. It goes deeper even than the loss of the Party. He could have been one of the greatest among the English poets. There is this consolation only – that he is no longer the Lost Leader but is poignantly alive for me again as he used to be when he was my friend in the 1930s'. The issue continued to obsess him. In 1976 he wrote: 'The ambivalence of my feelings about him. On the one hand the exaltation which his use of words aroused in us, the words of the earlier poems (which were socially progressive poems). On the other hand his later views which damaged the poems . . . One of the reasons why I mourned him was that I mourned the decline of all our generation'. Whatever his doubts about Auden and whatever others might say about how coherent a group they were, Upward identified with them. In his notebook in 1993 he wrote: 'I am the oldest and, with the exception of Stephen

Spender, the only surviving member of the group of writers who were young in the 1930s and who are sometimes referred to as the Auden Generation. I am still writing'.[11] He indicated the dilemma he felt about Auden in a letter he wrote to Spender in 1981. 'There is so much that still needs saying about all that he has meant for writers of his generation. Larger than any of us he represents us all. But I get in a muddle whenever I try to think about him'.[12] Almost immediately after Auden's death Upward wished to write about him. His essay about him for the *Socialist Worker* (a rather incongruous venue) was rejected. He thought it was better than the one he wrote for *Adam International* published in 1974 and later issued as a chapbook, *Remembering the Earlier Auden*, in 1998. His most important piece about their relationship is his story 'At the Ferry Inn', in *The Night Walk and Other Stories*. He wrote it in 1984 and it was published initially in 1985 in the *London Magazine*. There were also two other items in the collection that were concerned with Auden. Failing to resolve his feelings about Auden was a recurrent problem for Upward. He thought of him, rightly, as the giant of the group but yet he felt he had failed to fulfil his promise.

The first piece in the collection that deals with Auden is 'The Poet Who Died'. It is very short, written between 1976 and 1979. In it he mourns the poet who appears more in his dreams than any other figure. Upward deeply resented Auden calling the 1930s 'a low dishonest decade' and what he thought was his support of the Vietnam war. Auden in fact did not do so but nevertheless he disapproved of what he felt was the knee-jerk and unconsidered reaction of literary figures against the war. Upward felt unhappy at what he regarded as Auden's disowning his past. 'I could not disassociate him from himself as the young poet who for me and for other poets of his generation had been the only potential giant among us'. In 'The Procession', initially published in the *Guardian* in May 1980, Auden is changed into a painter. The Upward character, also a painter, is watching his own funeral from a balcony. He is engaged in conversation by someone who knows his work and points out that he began as a more imaginative painter whom some called surrealist. Upward gives the common criticism of his writings in what the character Everard Axtell says to him: 'Why didn't you develop that style farther instead of going on to produce the flat and unallusive naturalistic stuff you've confined yourself to for the last twenty-five years – utterly without undertones or overtones or warmth or atmosphere or wit, bare of all feelings except the most commonplace and dubious political ones?' Then the Auden figure appears, J. R. Sedgely, 'whom I revered more than any other painter of the twentieth century'.

Undoubtedly the most powerful coping with Auden's death was his story 'At the Ferry Inn'. It tells of a meeting after forty years of the Auden and Upward characters on the Isle of Wight. Upward makes the Auden character look quite young and in contrast to his famously craggy face describes 'his cheeks plump and smooth-skinned as ever'. Walter/Auden begins by praising Arnold/Upward's new book, clearly *The Rotten Elements*. There are references to the poetry of Auden in the story, 'the clever hopes' of the 1930s. Though Arnold is disillusioned with Stalin he still defends 'Leninist Marxism'. Walter responds that he had pointed out that poets didn't save a single Jew from the gas chamber, that they know no more about politics than dustmen. Walter then leaves for the men's room and

Upward deeply regrets not having told him how much he admires his poetry. "'If I had not been his friend and known him as a living poet", Arnold thought, "I would never have known how marvellous human life at its best can be'". Walter does not return but rather has left the inn and taken the next ferry. Arnold goes to the quay and sees him on the ship. Walter waves to him in a friendly way. Arnold was 'sure now that whatever unguessable reason Walter had had for so abruptly leaving him it didn't mean that the ending of their long estrangement had been illusory'.[13] As he said in 1998: 'The ferry is not just a plain real ferry, it is also Charon's ferry. The man was dead, that's it'.[14] Nevertheless one feels that Upward's sense that he had not reached any real closure in his relationship with Auden is still powerfully there.

He wrote to Alan Ross, the editor of the *London Magazine*, about an earlier last sentence of the story: 'It's intended to be ironic. The reader is supposed to realise that Walter is in fact dead and that there has been no reconciliation between him and Arnold and that their meeting is no more than a wistful dream of Arnold's'. Upward was self-aware that he might drive the editors of the publications where his stories appeared somewhat demented. He sent in innumerable revisions, sometimes twice a day. Ross or one of his colleagues noted on the top of one such letter, 'This will be the first of many'. He delayed his writings by endless revisions which went on even after publication. Six years after it had appeared, he sent Spender a copy of *The Night Walk and Other Stories* with the corrections, alterations and emendations he had made to the text. In a letter on 10 April 1991 to Ross, Upward remarked, 'I'm afraid you must be all accustomed to this sort of behaviour by me', and then the next day, 'I promise not to make any further corrections'.[15]

Some years later, in 1995, Upward contributed a short piece about one of Auden's most famous poems, 'In Praise of Limestone', with four others in a volume of material by and about Auden. Unlike his colleagues in that group he used the unrevised 1948 version of the poem. It is mostly a straightforward piece comparing Auden with Gerard Manley Hopkins. He does quote some lines from Auden's 'A Communist to Others' and from his own story 'The Poet Who Died', recording his distress at Auden's death and evoking the Isle of Wight. The last paragraph of the piece reads: 'I have always believed that Auden will be lastingly remembered, but I do not think he is as great a poet as he might have been. I regret that I must end these thoughts by saying that I regard "In Praise of Limestone" as an uneven poem'.[16]

Among the other stories in *The Night Walk*, the first, 'Her Day', was about his mother's funeral. It is rather elegiac and expresses none of the criticisms that he had had of his mother's social pretentiousness in the past. In his notebooks after her death he would mark her birthday on 18 August. Contrary to the story, there was in fact a service in the local Anglican church and not just a burial in the churchyard. He wrote in his notebook in November 1990, 'I looked at the steeple of Christchurch where the short funeral service for my mother was held, and I wished I had been kinder to her when she was alive'.[17] The stories are very brief and dwell on single incidents – a difficult pupil, an encounter on the Isle of Wight. They have some political implications drawing on his CND experiences. In 'The Interview', one of the longer stories, initially published in the *London Magazine*, a member of CND interviews a Cabinet minister who might order an atomic attack. He informs her that the movement wouldn't succeed as it didn't have the support of the working class and that his main purpose was to maintain the power of the English ruling class. The title story, 'The Night Walk', returns to the world of Mortmere. It takes place in a world where Britain has been invaded and is ruled by an authoritarian regime. The protagonist has fought in a seemingly endless litany of good causes: CND, against the Vietnam war and chemical and biological warfare, the use of British troops in Northern Ireland, racism in Britain, apartheid in South Africa, the exclusion of Palestinians from their own land, the pollution of the environment – and so on – up to the campaign to prevent American nuclear missiles from being installed in Britain. In the course of the story the protagonist meets a radical prostitute, two thuggish secret policemen who claim to have been pupils of his, a minister of the government (the client of the prostitute). He also attends a secret Communist cell meeting. The story ends at his house; it is not clear whether the events were a dream or reality. The conclusion seems to be that although his innumerable efforts to achieve a better world had failed, it was still a worthy struggle.

How was the book received? As usual it had a fair amount of attention. It was published on 23 February 1987. Among the most prominent reviews was one by D. J. Taylor in the *Independent* that referred to him as a member of 'a group of writers who ganged up and captured a decade'. There was a favourable review in the *Financial Times* as well as a good one and an interview in the *Guardian*. In March Valentine Cunningham panned the collection in the *Observer* as overly self-righteous Marxism although rather surprisingly he praised as magisterial the trilogy, which he misnames amusingly as 'The Upward Spiral' (perhaps it was a deliberate joke). Alexander Snowden in *Tribune* compared Upward to Wordsworth: 'The plainness is as much a matter of conscious artistic choice as was Wordsworth's, and like Wordsworth, Upward uses it to convey the simple essence of basic, common, "ordinary" human experiences, like fear and age and loneliness'. His friend Neville Braybrooke reviewed it in the Catholic publication the *Tablet*, calling *The Spiral Ascent* 'one of the great autobiographical novels of the century' and continuing with measured praise for the collection of stories. A favourable review in the Communist *Morning Star* commended his continued commitment to Marxist politics (it doesn't mention that he had left the party) in contrast to other members of the 'Auden generation'. In December Katherine Bucknell, on her way to becoming an eminent scholar of Auden and Isherwood, wrote in the *Times Literary Supplement* about the Auden theme in so many of the stories. Yet her favourite story in the collection was the rather sad one, 'The White Pinafored Black Cat'.[18]

That same year in March, Stephen Spender published a long and important essay on Upward in the *London Magazine*, using *The Night Walk* as its occasion. He begins by noting Upward's special combination of close observation and visionary imagination, commenting that 'his whole life indeed goes into his art, and his art is an expression of his politics. No writer today has suffered more than Upward from the charge that having started off as a writer of uninhibited fantasy he put his genius into a strait-jacket of Marxist ideology'. The essay is rather odd as while it mostly praises Upward's writings it ends rather negatively, pointing out that his continued allegiance to Marxist Leninism severely limits his work. Spender does reassert

Upward's position as an important writer. In the June issue Upward wrote a letter in reply claiming, legitimately, that he is far more sympathetic to bourgeois characters than Spender states.[19] As Upward wrote to his son in 1988: 'I'm never surprised by anything Sir Stephen writes about me – it's as likely to be dismissive as laudatory, but I'm grateful when it is laudatory. The mystery is – why is he so two-faced?'[20]

After this publication Upward became again a rather forgotten figure for the next six years. He had achieved a certain prominence in the 1930s publishing in what became its emblematic collections: *New Country* and *New Writing*. He was a major figure in setting what would be the tone and style of the 1930s, that mixture of imagination, verging towards fantasy, combined with realism. He had resurfaced from 1962 to 1977 with his trilogy and a collection of his 1930s' writing. In 1987 he received some attention from the publication of his more recent stories. In 1990 he published a short story 'The Theft' in an anthology in support of the African National Congress with a foreword by Nelson Mandela. Other writers included were Joyce Carol Oates, Raymond Williams, Nadine Gordimer, Wole Soyinka and Margaret Atwood. It is a rather menacing surrealistic story.[21] In 1991 his opinion was solicited for a volume on the Gulf War by Cecil Woolf and Jean Moorcroft Wilson but it was not published until 2004. In it he succinctly stated what he felt should happen and what he thought wouldn't. 'This war may mark a turning point after which the exploited peoples of the world, in the homelands of imperialism as well as in the impoverished countries, will begin to understand that united action by them against the imperialists is more important than national loyalty. I see little of

CHAPTER 8: FREE AT LAST

Edward at his word-processor, photographed by Ian Pert for the Southern Evening Echo, *10 September 1993*

this yet, but there seems no other way of preventing the polluting competitiveness of the imperialists from destroying the human race'.[22]

On the eve of his ninetieth birthday he was rediscovered yet again and this precipitated an active interest in him virtually until the end of his life in 2009. Peter Parker, the biographer of J. R. Ackerley but not yet the biographer of Isherwood, interviewed him for the *Independent Magazine* on 4 September in a piece provocatively subtitled 'The Fourth Man', alluding to him not as a Communist spy but as possibly the fourth most important of the 1930s' writers, after Auden, Isherwood and Spender. The interview summed up where he was so far in his writing life, mentioning that Spender had treated

CHAPTER 8: FREE AT LAST

Mer and Edward at 3 Hill Street, Sandown, 16 September 1993, photographed by Keith Langridge

him as a religious writer. 'The religion happens to be Communism and people don't understand that sort of religion. Upward is a kind of purist, but he is also a visionary'. Upward felt that he was dogged by the notorious essay he wrote about Marxism and literature which he now somewhat disowned: 'I think the essay's pretty awful. I tried to rewrite it later, but it was basically wrong, I think, in its approach. What I was trying to do – what hadn't been done at that time – was to establish some sort of connection between Marxism and literary values'. Parker went on to comment, 'Isherwood's description of *The Railway Accident* as a "nightmare about the English" might serve to define Upward's entire work'. Although Upward was not optimistic about having more of his work published, he concludes the

CHAPTER 8: FREE AT LAST

interview with a remark he had made before. 'My motto is: you may not get published if you write but you certainly won't if you don't'. In the *Times Literary Supplement* of 15 September Spender wrote a short piece, 'Upward at Ninety'. It had Spender's characteristic tone of immodest modesty. 'Of the writers of the 1930s "Oxbridge" generation of Auden, Isherwood, Day Lewis, MacNeice and myself he is the one whose life has been most in keeping with his principles and ideals, the most deserving, as such, of being honoured'.[23] Upward wrote to Spender to thank him for the piece but mentioned that Marx was not his 'God'; rather the universe was. He also informed him that the *London Magazine* would be publishing his story 'An Unmentionable Man'. Contrary to what Spender was actually doing, the figure based on him in that story is berated for never mentioning Upward.[24]

As always he was writing away but had been unable at this point to find a publisher for a book of his short stories. In 1987 Stephen Stuart-Smith had become director of Enitharmon Press and was alerted to Upward by Peter Parker's piece. He would become Upward's publisher and bountiful encourager for the rest of his life. Upward was continually and with painful slowness writing stories and despairing of how little recognition they would receive. But in 1994, the year after his ninetieth birthday, there was quite an upsurge in his publications. On 24 October three books by him were published: *An Unmentionable Man,* with six previously unpublished stories; a revised edition of *Journey to the Border;* and with Christopher Isherwood as co-author, *The Mortmere Stories.* For that Katherine Bucknell wrote an introduction and Stephen Stuart-Smith a note on the text. *An Unmentionable Man* had an introduction by the eminent

CHAPTER 8: FREE AT LAST

literary critic Frank Kermode, who also wrote a preface for the bibliography of Upward's works published in 2000. The introduction captures the contrasting qualities of Upward's writings, a dreamlike tone precisely stated, a mixture of fantasy, autobiography and realism. Most of the stories appear to be dreams by a man who has been mugged and is in the emergency ward. In the first he meets on a foreign island a former close friend of the 1930s, based on Stephen Spender. The narrator is rather rude to the latter, asking why in all he has so far written about the 1930s he has never mentioned him. Playing on guilt, the Spender character replies that he had been writing on the Spanish Civil War in which the narrator, called Stephen, did not take part. He then meets a young man with whom he has dinner and who takes him to an art studio of a group called The Excrementalists who make art out of their own shit. This rather echoes the lavatorial themes of the Mortmere stories. Although he admires the subversive view of the painters, he doesn't actually like the paintings themselves. The dream ends with him back in the hospital, not recovered, but his wife is there and in answer to the doctor's question as to why he went out on the dangerous streets and was mugged she replies, 'It must have been due to one of those attacks of fury that sometimes came over him about the way his writing was being ignored, and whenever they came he just had to go out and pace the streets'.

The next three stories consist of dreams Stephen Highwood, the Upward character, has while still in a coma: in a club meeting a publisher, in a city involved in a civil war, and on a cruise ship. They are all rather Mortmereish but now the central character is an elderly fiction writer who has kept loyal to his political principles. The atmosphere of the stories is rather sinister and macabre. The two last stories in the collection are quite contrasting. The first, 'Fred and Lil', is a sweet account of the retirement of a couple to the countryside. The last, 'With Alan to the Fair', turns out to be another dream of a rather unpleasant visit to a fair where his alter ego, Alan Sebrill, meets a former lover, Lara, based on his first love affair. The narrator refers to her getting in touch with him years later and chiding him for not responding. Their conversation is rather bitter, commenting on Lara having slept with both him and Douglas whom she married. She accuses Alan of behaving similarly, clearly referring to Upward's affair with Olive Mangeot. Alan responds: 'I had had a friendly *faute de mieux* affair with an older woman who wanted to get her own back on a husband who was being unfaithful to her, but I gave it up after I met you. Except once, after several evenings when you had set out to excite me to the limit and then to refuse me'. In the story he visits a large tent labelled 'Oxbridge' full of sports displays. There is also a literary section in the tent where he meets a writer, Aubrey Marshall, who has written a book attacking Sebrill's writings as 'grossly overrated', claiming that his poems 'would never have been heard of but for the boosting they got from my Public School pals'. Upward may have been thinking of Valentine Cunningham, who had written about him negatively in *British Writers of the Thirties* published in 1988. Alan accuses him of 'the prolific production of flashily written unscholarly books', to which Marshall replies, 'How much longer do you intend to stand here mouthing out your senilely imbecile insults'. Alan says, 'I tend to be neglected because most of my poems are political and, worse still, my political views are contrary to those that are dominant in this country now'.[25] He believes his work

CHAPTER 8: FREE AT LAST

is neglected because of his politics, a central theme in Upward's thinking.

Except for 'Fred and Lil' all of the stories in this collection were infused with Mortmereish elements. In 1952 Upward had destroyed most of the Mortmere stories he had written, feeling that their surrealistic grimness and jokey semi-obscenity were no longer acceptable in a post-concentration-camp world. Yet the stories demonstrate Upward's fundamental commitment in his writings, except in *The Spiral Ascent*, to the interplay of fantasy and reality. In *The Mortmere Stories* Upward and Isherwood wrote jointly 'The Settings and the Characters', the introductory section of the book, including a map of Mortmere. Also surviving were four fragments by him as well as 'The Railway Accident' and an abandoned and incomplete 'The Return to Mortmere' that he wrote in 1943. His short story 'The Railway Accident', written in 1928 and the culminating Mortmere tale, many regard as his finest work. He wrote it before he moved steadily to the left and became so politically involved. While at Cambridge and for a time thereafter he had little interest in politics. His writings after his conversion to Communism have many admirers as well as detractors. Would they have been better if he had not been a Communist? It is an unanswerable question. And yet it was one that he was continually asking himself.

Also issued on 24 October 1994 was a revised version of *Journey to the Border* with a brief introduction by Stephen Spender. He placed Upward in the tradition of Samuel Butler and H. G. Wells but writing under the influence of Joyce. He points out that although Upward was anxious to join the workers, in fact he only depicts the middle class. Upward wrote Spender a letter of thanks saying: 'I think it is

CHAPTER 8: FREE AT LAST

Sir Stephen Spender in 1992, photographed by Robert Mort

absolutely marvellous and I am tremendously grateful to you for it. No one else could have done it anything like as well and as understandingly as you have'. He wrote how pleased he was that Spender had written the introduction, particularly at the time that he was preoccupied with preventing the publication in England of David Leavitt's *While England Sleeps,* which drew in an unfavourable way upon Spender's involvement in the Spanish Civil War. In another earlier letter, thanking Spender for his ninetieth birthday piece about him in the *Times Literary Supplement,* Upward mentioned that he had been asked to review *While England Sleeps* for the *Guardian* and had been sent an advance copy to read. He wrote that 'quite apart from its blatant thefts from your and Christopher's writings I found its monotonously repetitive detailed descriptions of acts of buggery merely mercenary. The book was obviously written for no other purpose than to sell. So I declined to review it. Perhaps I ought to have written a vitriolic attack on it'.[26]

The changes that he made in the new text of *Journey to the Border* were not very dramatic. There were minor revisions in the first two parts and then in the third section he recast a dialogue between the tutor's two selves as well as the conversation with the worker, making it in his view more plausible. In both versions the tutor commits himself to working against his employer, a member of the bourgeoisie. As in the earlier text there is no indication that he is going to leave his job unless fired. Upward became a Communist as ever since Repton he had loathed English society for its unfairness, its class structure, its mistreatment of the working class. Now in his life and in his fiction he was committing himself to the working class, reconfirmed in the republication of *Journey to the Border*.

The British Library gave a reception for him to mark the publication of the books and also to celebrate its acquisition of his papers; some were on display at the event. The three books received a fair amount of attention in the press. Upward was irritated that despite his writing to them neither Repton nor Corpus nor Alleyn's took any notice that at the age of ninety-one he had published so much. 'The only thing that will buoy me up is the belief that the peoples of the world will destroy imperialism before it destroys us all'.[27] Anthony Curtis wrote a praising notice of the appearance of the three texts in, of all places, the *Weekend Financial Times*. Neville Braybrooke in the *Tablet* quoted an eleventh-century pope, a line known to Upward: 'I have loved righteousness and hated iniquity; therefore I die in exile', and Upward's own version from his eighties: 'I have loved Marx and Lenin and hated capitalism, therefore I have become

CHAPTER 8: FREE AT LAST

a non-person in the country of my birth'. The piece is mostly a favourable brief account of the three books. Dave Beecham in the *Socialist Review* commended his seeking after truth in fiction. As he perceptively pointed out, there is a considerable tension in the course of Upward's writing between his natural proclivity to fantasy and the party's belief in socialist realism. In *Journey to the Border* Upward 'conveys a political message through an account of the inner working of the mind in a language which is more like painting or film than writing. Upward's new collection of short stories, *An Unmentionable Man*, uses this style to great effect but also demonstrates his special ability to mix realism and the fantastic'. Ian Hamilton in the *London Review of Books* found it all a bit smug-sour, Upward moaning about his neglect at the same time that three books by him were coming out.

Hamilton questioned a fundamental premise of much of Upward's work, that he was ignored because of his politics. One is not actually aware of the literary establishment consciously or unconsciously deciding to ignore him because he was a Communist. As Upward liked to say from time to time, 'Just because I'm paranoid it doesn't mean they're not out to get me'. With some difficulty he did manage to publish much of what he wrote. His writings are intriguing, interesting and important. He led a significant literary life. He occupied an almost mythological position as the great almost-guru figure behind the most significant writers of the 1930s, as in Spender's oft-quoted lines about him as the great looming figure behind Auden and Isherwood. The statement probably exaggerated the degree that Auden was influenced by him both through Isherwood and directly. Or in John Lehmann's version: 'I heard with the tremor of excitement that an entomologist feels at the news of an unknown butterfly sighted in the depths of the forest, that behind Auden and Spender and Isherwood stood the even more legendary figure of an unknown writer, Edward Upward'.[28]

Edward Mendelson, the doyen of Auden studies, wrote a definitive review of the three books in the *Times Literary Supplement*. He copes with the two Upwards: the political plain stylist and the fantasist, both the product of 'a single impulse: an imaginative writer's puritan horror of his own imagination'. The recent stories are written in 'Upward's unique perfected style, impassioned and drab, that gives ordinary events a hallucinatory strangeness and renders dreams as if they were entirely ordinary, subject to the same ethical and political judgments appropriate to the daylight world'. In Mendelson's view 'the neglect that Upward endured earlier was caused less by the severity of his politics than by the austerity of his middle style'. He concludes that in these latest short stories Upward now has a third style 'that liberates his private vision while putting it in service to a public cause'. Upward was moving towards a synthesis of life and art.[29]

It is fair to say that for Upward 1994 was a year of some triumph. In contrast 1995 was a time of great grief as Hilda Upward died that year. It cannot be emphasized enough how happy a marriage it had been and how their political activity was a partnership. Ever since 1977 there had been the family sadness when his son Christopher told his parents that he had multiple sclerosis. He was having an excellent academic career as a linguist, having done well at his father's old college at Cambridge and later joined the German faculty at Aston University in Birmingham. His main fields of interest were German (he translated letters between Marx and Engels) and spelling, and he became editor of the *Journal of Simplified Spelling*. He was the co-author of *The History of English Spelling* published posthumously in 2011. In 1963 he married Janet Hutcheon. She had been at Newnham at the same time that he was at Corpus and both belonged to the Labour Club. But they did not actually meet until after graduation when they were on a teacher training course in Bristol. In his notebook for 2 September 1977 Upward wrote: 'Oh Christopher my son, my son, oh my son Christopher. But I must think of him with love not with sorrow. I must love him not grieve over him. Only my love for him can overcome my grief for him'. And on 17 April 1982 he wrote: 'If only it could be me instead of him . . . My brother 55 years ago, and now my son whom H & I love so much. I must return to writing, the only consolation'.[30]

Christopher died in 2002, seven years before his father. As for all those who live long, and Upward lived a spectacularly long time, life becomes punctuated with the deaths of not only contemporaries but those younger than oneself. He remembered his parents with increasing affection, writing in his notebook on his father's birthday, nineteen years after his death, 'He, and M[other], did so much want me to be a writer, and now I am, at their expense. But I loved them, for all that, and I hope this comes out in the book [*No Home but the Struggle*]'. His younger brother Mer died on 11 July 1999. Living in separate homes in the same building, they would see one another practically every day, frequently for a drink before dinner. Hilda's death in 1995 was particularly devastating. The marriage might well have been originally something of a political act. Certainly she was not from the same social sphere as himself. His parents disapproved

CHAPTER 8: FREE AT LAST

Edward photographed by Granville Davies, 1995

but were reconciled to a degree when the children came. She was the better-organized party member, more articulate at meetings and the secretary of the local branch. He was less likely to participate in the cell discussions. He felt he was the middle-class interloper while she wasn't. It was an extremely successful marriage and Upward became more and more in love with her as the years progressed. He was buoyed up by her love and loved her devotedly in return. She had a series of debilitating illnesses in the early 1960s. Hilda being ill

CHAPTER 8: FREE AT LAST

meant that life might be grim. It also would be bad for his writing which was what he most wanted to do now that he was retired. As usual, one day he would say that his writing was the most important thing in his life and some weeks later it was the political struggle. He wrote on 23 April 1964: *'The step forward I have made already this morning at 10:17 is the recognition that the fight still comes first'*. And he would state, admittedly thirteen years later, also underlined, *'There can be only one reason for writing and that is primarily for myself'*.[31] At the same time he wanted ordinary people to read him and was disappointed that his books did not sell better. Throughout, Hilda was a positive constant and the reason that he wanted to stay alive. When she recovered her health in the 1960s it made him happier than he had ever been except for the months that he had spent at Rouen.

He was devastated by Hilda's death on 14 March 1995. He recorded her last days and his feelings in his notebook. On 17 February: 'My poor darling Hilda has not got long to live. I know that she is ready to go, will even be glad to go . . . She recognizes me and knows how much I love her and shows how much she loves me . . . How can I bear to live without her?' The day before her death he promised her that he would continue writing. On 18 March he wrote: 'My poor poor darling little Hilda . . . I would not go to the mortuary or "chapel of rest" the next day to see her lying cosmeticised there. But I went with the others to see her biodegradable coffin lowered into the grave . . . As we turned to walk away I burst out into uncontrollable weeping. The dreadful finality of it all. My wish now is to be lying dead beside my darling in the grave in the space that is reserved for me there . . . My grief will last until the end of my life, which I hope will come soon'. He wrote the next day, 'My grief for her will last for the rest of my life, but I must not let it prevent me from carrying on the political fight in my imaginative writing'. And a few days later: '"Shall we ever be in bed together again?" my darling asked me. I can answer her now: "Yes, we shall, when I lie beside you in the space reserved for me in your grave under the beech tree in the green cemetery"'.

At the same time he was very practical as Hilda and he had agreed that if she predeceased him he would find another woman, but wouldn't marry her as he didn't want to diminish his children's inheritance. Some time later he even advertised in the local press. By August he was involved with two women with whom he wanted to sleep and was thrilled that he did so with Margaret. At that point he felt he might be in love with her and she said she was in love with him. Born in 1947, so considerably younger than he, she had been married and divorced and had a son. He was quite realistic about the situation, assessing it in perhaps an excessively clear-eyed way on 2 December. 'I am very fond of M and I know now that she loves me, but are we going to be able to live together? . . . I know that she cd live without me. But cd I learn to live alone'. Then at the end of the month he wrote:

> This is going to be a real diary, at least for today. What do I really think of M? That it would have been better for me if I had never met her? Only if I'd met someone more in tune with me, a widow who had been happily married, nearer to me in age and sexually attracted to me as well as being interested in reading and in me as a writer. There's no doubt that M is sexually attracted by me as I am by her. She has many merits. She

is a good carpenter, practically minded, competent organiser, a corrector of bad habits in me, though inclined to be too bossy.

But she refused to go to bed with him when his children were in the house. He went on: 'Could I learn to live alone? I think I could, even though I would feel the loss of her very deeply... I cd try to find another woman'. Their affair followed a somewhat rocky course. In January he felt that they were in love with one another. But all seemed to be over by July 1996 when he wrote about Hilda, 'the only woman I have really loved & been loved by'.[32] In fact the connection with Margaret lasted until December 2003.

The publisher Enitharmon's interest in him and his compulsion to write gave him a new lease on his career. In 1996 he published in a limited edition a short memoir of Isherwood celebrating their close friendship. In 1997 *The Scenic Railway* appeared, consisting of five stories, three previously published in the *London Magazine*. The other two had been written in 1995 and 1996. He composed a blurb for the book. 'Any reader at all familiar with the writing of EU will be likely to feel that no one else could have written these stories. These five stories, written in a direct and unambiguous imaginative style which can at times be humorous as well as uninhibitedly serious'. Although the characters in the stories are different, he felt that the five were a 'connected whole'.[33] The first, the title story, is a fantasy. The narrator is taking a group of disabled adults to a funfair which includes a trip on a scenic railway. (For about seven years Upward had provided transport once a week through the Red Cross for disabled people.) The railway passes scenery that depicts the famous Christmas truce of the First World War, then a farm field in

CHAPTER 8: FREE AT LAST

With Stephen Stuart-Smith at Freshwater, 4 September 1999

Ukraine from Upward's 1932 trip to Russia as well as scenes involving British fighters in the Spanish Civil War. Leslie, the narrator, later finds himself in his home town passing the house of his first love, to whom he sent a copy of Rupert Brooke's poems. He then goes to his own house, apparently in a sort of dream, and has tea with his parents. It becomes clear that the narrator is dead. The second story, 'Investigation after Midnight', is primarily a nightmare about old age. The third, 'People Hate Me', deals with a man who becomes hateful because he was treated badly at his prep school. All the stories deal with the elderly; the fourth, 'The World Revolution', again appears to be in a dream state involving love and political action, while the last, 'Emily and Oswin', concerns a poet who was trying to write poems 'which though they would most of them continue to be political would never be other than implicitly so.' Emily, a widow,

CHAPTER 8: FREE AT LAST

Revisiting Marine Villa, Freshwater, 4 September 1999

reads about the poet Oswin living in a retirement home in Sussex. She drives there and they go together to Rouen (where Upward had been so happy in the period between Repton and Cambridge) and become lovers. Oswin looks for a lodging house where his brother had told him 'he was happier than he had ever been before'.[34] It is called Le Vert Logis, the name of the house where Upward had stayed in Rouen. For some reason Oswin is unwilling to tell Emily he is looking for this *pension*. Most of the stories have a certain serenity; they deal with coming to terms with writing, poetry, old age and death. Boyd Tonkin in the *Independent* began his review with a remark about 'The Railway Accident', not in the collection. 'In the mid-1920s a legendary young writer wrote the most uncannily brilliant slice of surrealistic fiction ever to appear in English ... As Upward neared extreme old age, the magician and the militant have edged towards a truce ... As a painter of hallucinatory dreamscapes – a kind of prose Magritte – Upward at his finest still has no peer'. Elisabeth Mahoney in the *London Magazine* dwelt on how the stories oscillated between dream and reality.[35]

Another collection, *The Coming Day and Other Stories*, was published in 2000. The title story was a novella followed by a sequence of six unconnected short stories but bearing the collective title *The Suspect* which is also the title of the last story of the group. The stories generally deal with an older man coming to terms with being on his own, having lost his spouse. They are a mixture of dream and reality, with some political content. They certainly reflect Upward's own personal situation, including a continuation of his sexual life. The last story tells of a seemingly younger man, Edgar, who is arbitrarily arrested and then released. To a degree the story circles back to its author's very beginning as he returns to his home town and walks past where his home had been, now replaced by a large block of flats, though strangely the block seemed to show an affinity architecturally with what it had supplanted. He reminisces about his two brothers, Vernie and Vaughan, the latter who at the age of eighteen had become mentally ill, echoing the story of Upward's brother, Laurence. He remembers with fondness his kindergarten as he passes its house, which has now become an old people's home but with the same name, Queensfield Lodge. The story ends with his going to another town where he participates in some sort of strike

CHAPTER 8: FREE AT LAST

Cartoon by Nicola Jennings published in the Guardian, *8 April 2000*

Edward Upward

action. 'At last he became sure that there could be no home for him except in that [political] struggle'.[36] He is captured by the neo-Fascists. About to be liberated by neo-Communists, he is shot.

In 2000 Alan Walker compiled an extremely helpful bibliography of his work. In 2003, on 9 September, to mark his one hundredth birthday, there was a large party at the Parkbury Hotel in Sandown as well as one at Stephen Stuart-Smith's house in London on May Day some months earlier. Among others who attended that party were Margaret Drabble, Michael Holroyd, Frank Kermode (who gave the toast), Peter Parker and Jill Balcon, the actress and widow of C. Day Lewis. Enitharmon published a pamphlet, *The Real*

CHAPTER 8: FREE AT LAST

Signing the sheets for the limited edition of A Renegade in Springtime, *2003*

Edward Upward, by Alan Walker and a collection of twelve previously printed stories, *A Renegade in Springtime*, which was dedicated to the memory of Upward's son Christopher. It began with his most famous story, 'The Railway Accident', and concluded with 'The Scenic Railway', a more elegiac tale in contrast to the violence and surrealism of 'The Railway Accident'. Walker in his introduction emphasized both the poetical and surrealistic qualities of Upward's writings while at the same time observing that they were closely linked to his political beliefs. Francis King referred to this collection as a little masterpiece. Upward's last story, 'Cromelin Brown', was not published but was broadcast on the BBC in 2003. There was even a notice about him in *Tatler*, the society journal. His one hundredth birthday was listed on the court page of *The Times*, along with Hugh Grant, Shirley Summerskill and Raine, the Countess

CHAPTER 8: FREE AT LAST

With Sir Frank Kermode and Dannie Abse at the launch party for A Renegade in Springtime, *1 May 2003*

Spencer, Princess Diana's stepmother. There was a one-day symposium on him at Jesus College, Cambridge, organized by the Jesus Fellow and Upward scholar Rod Mengham. In 2004 a German translation of *Journey to the Border* was published with an introduction by Elfriede Jelinek, the recipient of the 2004 Nobel Prize in Literature, as well as a thesis on him in German. He was written about elsewhere in essays and dissertations in Britain, Italy and the United States.

The following year, 2004, he left his beloved Isle of Wight for Pontefract in Yorkshire where his daughter Kathy Allinson and her husband Jeff lived. Shortly afterwards he moved into Carleton Court, a care home. The most dramatic event in his last years was in 2005, three weeks before his one hundred and second birthday, when he was elected a Fellow of the Royal Society of Literature and awarded

CHAPTER 8: FREE AT LAST

Edward on his 100th birthday, with Jeff Allinson, Kathy Allinson and Janet Upward, 9 September 2003

its Benson Medal for a lifetime's contributions to literature. As he wasn't strong enough to go to London to receive it, it was bestowed upon him at Carleton Court on 19 August. Maggie Gee, the novelist and chair of the society, travelled to Yorkshire with the roll book of the society which he signed as a new member. He had a choice of doing so with either Byron's pen or Dickens' quill. He chose the former. There had been only thirty-six recipients of the Benson Medal since its establishment in 1916. Among its more illustrious recipients were Lytton Strachey, Edmund Blunden, J. R. R. Tolkien, Philip Larkin and Nadine Gordimer.

Upward was a genial and charming man but it is too easy to forget his inner turmoil, his hatred of his own bourgeois society and his belief that it needed to be destroyed, by force if necessary, in

CHAPTER 8: FREE AT LAST

Edward at his 100th birthday party, photographed by Antony Upward

order to create a socialist and more egalitarian world. He dedicated much of his life to that purpose, outraged by what he considered the inequities of his own society. He had mixed feelings about recognition from society. There had been some fear that he might decline Fellowship of the Royal Society of Literature because of it having 'Royal' in its title. At the time of his one hundredth birthday he was worried that he might receive a congratulatory card from the Queen. If he had, he felt that his obligation as a republican was to inform her that she had been misinformed. Yet he might have felt some regret at not receiving one. He did receive one on his one hundred and fifth birthday, the family having alerted the Palace, and he seemed pleased. Other 1930s' writers had accepted the Establishment's embrace. Upward still kept his distance even though he enjoyed the recognition that his work received.

CHAPTER 8: FREE AT LAST

Edward at 3 Hill Street, 2004

He died on 13 February 2009 in his one hundred and sixth year. Full obituaries appeared in the quality press. He has had the accolade of having his life recorded by Peter Parker in the *Dictionary of National Biography*. He is buried next to Hilda at the Springwood Woodland Cemetery at Newchurch on the Isle of Wight. He is a subject of continuing academic interest, mostly as a figure of the 1930s. Young scholars would come to see him and write about him in their dissertations. Quite a few articles were published about him in scholarly journals. He is discussed in the innumerable books written about British writers of the 1930s. In 2012 Mario Faraone published a book-length study about him in Italian. Years before in 1986 the eminent scholar Franco Moretti had devoted some pages to him in

CHAPTER 8: FREE AT LAST

Edward Upward and Maggie Gee at the presentation of the Benson Medal, Pontefract, August 2005, photographed by Peter Parker

his study in Italian of the British 1930s' writers. He is a recurring figure in Auden studies. In 2013 the brilliant young German scholar Benjamin Kohlmann edited a collection of essays on Upward, *Edward Upward and Left-Wing Literary Culture in Britain,* and devoted a chapter to him in his 2014 *Committed Styles: Modernism, Politics, and Left-Wing Literature in the 1930s.* He is not neglected. He was the last link with the canonical young British writers of the 1930s. He was called, with a nod to the spies, somewhat younger than he at Cambridge, the fourth man to Auden, Isherwood, and Spender. His literary achievement was less than theirs and his political commitment was greater. Like them, he was an Englishman of the middle class, educated at a prep school and a public school. Yet more than they he was a

CHAPTER 8: FREE AT LAST

Signing the register of Fellows of the Royal Society of Literature with Byron's pen, photographed by Marco Livingstone

profound critic of his society, a rebel from within. He was in the tradition of those English radicals who were rebels, such as William Morris and E. P. Thompson, whose class background and education helped endow them with the skills and knowledge that enabled them to dedicate themselves to the attempt totally to transform their society. Being English gentlemen endowed them with the authority to fight the society that had trained them. Their backgrounds gave them strengths but may have also imposed limitations. They were enemies of the class to which they belonged.

So much of Upward's life can be seen as an attempt to reconcile

CHAPTER 8: FREE AT LAST

his literary and political activities, to bring together art and life. He saw writing as political defiance, as his way of asserting himself against his society. He recognized the importance of political action and certainly was a committed Communist. He could say in 1992 when being interviewed by Peter Parker: 'I'm not the type of person who wants to be political . . . In fact, I still, like Christopher Isherwood, both of us at Cambridge, we despised politicians, thought them a lot of insincere crooks'. A common view of him was that his commitment to Marxism diminished the quality of his writings. But Marxism gave Upward's writings their moral focus and their power. It anchored his great gift for fantasy. For him dialectical materialism was a reflection of reality.

In many ways he had a happy life although he did suffer from intense inner torments. He had a very successful marriage, two fine children – Christopher, a linguist, and Kathy, who had gone to Manchester University and gave private tuition in German and French – and four grandsons. In a rather traditional way he bemoaned the fact that none of them were interested in going to Oxford or Cambridge. 'I can't help being a little sorry that none of the grandsons wd consider the idea of going to Oxbridge. But Ian will do well anywhere. And the other three will too. How different they all are in character & how likeable they all are'.[37] One of Kathy's sons, David Allinson, maintains a website about him. Upward preserved his legacy, selling his notebooks and manuscripts for £45,500 to the British Library in 1988. The bookseller Bertram Rota had valued them at £65,000.[38]

He could never make up his mind whether his writing or his political activity were more important for him – but on the whole his writing triumphed. Yet he never abandoned his hope that it would help the political struggle. He kept worrying about what he should write and he found writing so difficult, spending a year for instance on his short story 'The Scenic Railway'. Should he return to poetry? Should he return to Mortmere? Had he wasted his life? Was it his fault or the fault of capitalist society?

In the 1930s he had hoped for considerable literary achievements but when he realized that wouldn't happen he turned to the political struggle as a way of avoiding despair. His writing needed to fit into his Marxist analysis. He came to feel that he had overstated the case in his notorious essay, 'Sketch for a Marxist Interpretation of Literature'. Yet he did maintain his opinion that the very best writer needed to be a Marxist in order correctly to understand society. As he said in 1998, 'It isn't that Marxism is the truth, but the truth is Marxist'. Talent was essential but beyond that 'the good writer must recognise the truth of the world. He can't be a great writer if he can't see the world as it is . . . In society politics in the deepest sense is more important than art. But, on the other hand, in the work of art, art must be more important than politics'.[39] He did not aim for socialist realism, which he preferred to call social realism, in his writings, with the possible exception of the first two parts of *The Spiral Ascent*. He felt that through some use of fantasy he could better penetrate the world as it truly is. He wrote a significant body of work and he was an intriguing and powerful figure. As the novelist Margaret Drabble said of him: 'He stuck to his strong convictions. But that has given his later work a sort of haunted integrity. It has a very strange note of elegy and persistence, hopelessness and hope all mixed up in a very poignant way'.[40] He has remained in literary consciousness not only for his own work but as a member of the Auden circle and as a great friend and influence upon Christopher Isherwood. At the same time, paradoxically, Upward became very well known for being forgotten. He had a distinctive voice of his own, a combination of realism and fantasy that gave considerable power to much of his work, particularly *Journey to the Border*, 'The Railway Accident' and many of his later stories. His was a considerable literary contribution. He wished to translate the abstract into a concrete dream, frequently a nightmare, about the English. He was deeply steeped in English literature. He was shaped by his society and rebelled against it. His writings and his life were significant in themselves and for illuminating English life and artistic achievements for much of the twentieth century.

Notes

Archival Sources

BL   British Library, London
CI   Christopher Isherwood Papers, Huntington Library, San Marino, California
EA   Enitharmon Archive, Brotherton Collection, University of Leeds Library, Leeds
NA   National Archives, Kew, London

Chapter 1: Family and Childhood

1. Mario Faraone, interview with Edward Upward, July–August 1998, *L'isola e il treno* (Rome, 2012), p. 388.
2. Christopher Hitchens, 'The Captive Mind', *Atlantic* (May 2009), p. 100.
3. Samuel Hynes, 'Dimmed by Dialectics', *Times Literary Supplement* (31 July 1969), p. 849.
4. Samuel Hynes, 'Between Poetry and Party', *Times Literary Supplement* (5 August 1977), p. 953.
5. EA, Edward Upward, 'Autobiography of a Nonagenarian', Folder 2000.
6. I don't know exactly why St Aubins was selected as the name of the house, but it was probably in honour of Edward's grandfather's first wife, Caroline, who came from Jersey. It is a version of the name of the sixth-century saint Albinus of Angers, particularly revered in France, Germany, Poland and England. The town of St Aubin, a variant of the name, is on Jersey and the parish church bears the same name. Perhaps Caroline was from there. (Coincidentally and irrelevantly, but nevertheless intriguingly, St Aubyn is the family name of Lord St Levan of St Michael's Mount. A member of that family is the novelist Edward St Aubyn. Although there is no indication that Upward read his novels, he might have enjoyed their surrealistic qualities and their depiction of the decadence of the English upper classes.)
7. This is his career as outlined in the records of Sidney Sussex, Cambridge. Upward in his autobiographical notes records that Mer taught after Radley at Bryanston and Ottershaw. EA, autobiographical notes, Box 6B, 1999-2000.
8. Information about early history of the family from Christopher Upward, 'Edward Upward: Family and Forbers [sic]'. (Christopher, a distinguished linguist, believed that English should be spelt without unnecessary letters.) MSS dated 21 March 1991, courtesy Janet Upward. Also, Francis Odell to Peter

NOTES

Stansky (20 September 2013); and Peter Parker, interview with Edward Upward, 3 July 1993, courtesy Peter Parker.
9. Information from Matthew Vaughn, 'Allen Upward', *The Modernist Journals Project*, http://modjourn.org/render.php?view=mjp_object&id=mjp. 2005.01.061, accessed 6 February 2013. On Upward and Pound, see Humphrey Carpenter, *Serious Character: The Life of Ezra Pound* (Boston, 1988), p. 218, and letter to Dorothy Pound, no source given, p. 218; and Donald Davie, *Ezra Pound* (New York, 1976).
10. Edward Upward, *No Home but the Struggle* (London, 1977), p. 63.
11. BL Add MS 89002/1/7630, August 1997–9 February 2002, 3 April, 11 April 2001. The notebooks were sold to the British Library in 1988 but were not to come there until after Upward's death. Other archival material arrived sooner. As he wrote to Stephen Spender: 'I could have sold the archive to Tulsa for more than the B.L. could afford, but I thought it was time one of The Thirties writers left something to the B.L. They have nothing of Christopher's at all, and they hadn't a copy of Auden's 1928 poems before they got mine. Now they have all C.I's surviving Mortmere writings and a large number of his letters to me, and the typescripts of some of his books'. Stephen Spender Papers, Bodleian Library, Oxford, 20 May 1988.
12. BL Add MS 89002/1/1, September 1924–September 1927, 5 December 1925.
13. BL Add MS 89002/1/14, April 1946–April 1947, 6 April 1947.
14. Peter Parker, interview with Edward Upward, 3 July 1993, courtesy Peter Parker.
15. BL Add MS 89002/1/25, September 1957–June 1958, 14 December, 4 January, 26 April; Add MS 89002/1/32, December 1962–April 1963, 26 February 1963; Add MS 89002/1/ 37, June 1964–November 1964.
16. BL Add MS 89002/1/17, August 1949–May 1952, 21–31 December 1951.
17. EA, Upward to Alan Walker, 30 April 2000.
18. Upward, *No Home*, p. 64.
19. Peter Parker, interview with Edward Upward, 3 July 1993, courtesy Peter Parker.
20. BL Add MS 89002/1/46, October 1969–May 1970, 17 January 1970.
21. BL Add MS 72689.

Chapter 2: Repton

1. Quoted in Ernest Griffin (a pupil of Upward's at Alleyn's in Dulwich), 'Conversation with Edward Upward', *Modernist Studies* 2.2 (1976), pp. 19–20.
2. BL Add MS 89002/1/76, August 1997–February 2002, 26 January 2002.

3. Edward Upward, *No Home but the Struggle* (London, 1979), pp. 116–17.
4. EA, interview with Edward Upward, *Tatler* (May 2003).
5. Peter Parker, interview with Edward Upward, 3 July 1993, courtesy Peter Parker.
6. Mario Faraone, interview with Edward Upward, July–August 1998, *L'isola e il treno* (Rome, 2012), p. 419.
7. BL Add MS 72690, DD.
8. BL Add MS 72690, AA.
9. Calling him Upward here raises the question what to call him in this book. Edward seems too informal, Upward perhaps a little too formal. I have referred to him as Edward in his childhood to make it clear which Upward I am writing about, but from here on I will refer to him as Upward.
10. Interview with Edward Upward, *The Reptonian* (Michaelmas 1994), p. 27.
11. Ibid.
12. See Brian Finney, 'Laily, Mortmere and All That', *Twentieth Century Literature* 22.3 (October 1976), pp. 286–302.
13. See Owen Chadwick, *Michael Ramsey* (Oxford, 1990).
14. Donald Sturrock, *Storyteller: The Life of Roald Dahl* (London, 2010), p. 54.
15. Interview with Edward Upward, *The Reptonian* (1994), p. 27.
16. Interview, 10 August 1993.
17. EA, interview, 8 December 1969, 765–87.
18. Upward, *No Home*, pp. 129, 155.
19. Ruth Dudley Edwards, *Victor Gollancz* (London, 1987), p. 108.
20. Victor Gollancz and David Somervell, *Political Education at a Public School* (London, 1918), p. 1.
21. Victor Gollancz, *More for Timothy* (London, 1953), p. 266.
22. Interview with Edward Upward, *The Reptonian* (1994), p. 27.
23. Upward, *No Home*, p. 153.
24. BL Add MS 89002/1/47, May 1970–December 1970, 5 September 1970, 17 December 1970.
25. Stuart Hampshire, 'In the Thirties', *New Statesman* (17 August 1962), p. 204. Also Alan Powers, 'In the Thirties', unidentified source. Clippings courtesy Janet Upward.
26. Interview with Edward Upward, *The Reptonian* (1994), p. 27.
27. The questionable intellectual wisdom of this technique forms an important theme in Alan Bennett's *The History Boys*.
28. Christopher Isherwood, *Lions and Shadows* (London, 1938), pp. 18–19.
29. Upward, *No Home*, p. 157.
30. BL Add MS 72690.
31. BL Add MS 89002/2/5, Thorn to Upward, 14 August 1962; and CI 2508, 17

NOTES

August 1962.
32. BL Add MS 72688, 22 August 1962.
33. CI 2536, 9 February 1973.
34. BL Add MS 89002/1/68, June 1986–August 1987, 26 July 1987.
35. Upward, *No Home*, p. 126.
36. *Books from the Library of Edward Upward* (London, 2006), p. 18. Catalogue compiled by Charles Cox.
37. BL Add MS 72689, I, N.
38. BL Add MS 72690, V.
39. Isherwood, *Lions and Shadows*, pp. 17–18.
40. Interview with Edward Upward, *The Reptonian* (1994), p. 27.
41. *The Reptonian* (March 1920), pp. 299–300; (May 1920), p. 332; (October 1920), p. 389; (December 1920), p. 3; (June 1921), pp. 78–80; (July 1921), p. 102. 'Gloom' was reprinted in Neville Braybrooke, ed., *Seeds in the Wind: Juvenilia from W. B. Yeats to Ted Hughes* (London, 1989), p. 123.
42. Alan Walker, *Edward Upward: A Bibliography 1920–2000* (London, 2000), pp. 59–60. An invaluable text.
43. Peter Parker, interview with Edward Upward, 3 July 1993, courtesy Peter Parker.
44. Meic Stephens, 'Vernon Watkins', *Oxford Dictionary of National Biography*.
45. CI 2289, 9 November 1922; 2291, 6 December 1922.
46. BL Add MS 72689, X.
47. CI 2288, 15 February 1922.
48. BL Add MS 72692, ff. 4, 45, 127, 135.
49. Alan Munton and Alan Young, 'Edward Upward: A Conversation', *PN Review* 7.5 (1 January 1980), p. 42.

Chapter 3: Cambridge

1. BL Add MS 89002/1/8, December 1938–August 1939, 5 January 1939.
2. See *Books from the Library of Edward Upward* (London, 2006), p. 10.
3. BL Add MS 72689, JJ. Courtesy Benjamin Kohlmann.
4. Christopher Isherwood, *Lions and Shadows* (London, 1938), pp. 173–74.
5. CI 2295, 19 March 1923.
6. Peter Parker, interview with Edward Upward, 3 July 1993, courtesy Peter Parker.
7. EA, Stephen Stuart-Smith, interview with Edward Upward, 4 August 1999, Box 1999–2000.
8. The possible grades were First with Distinction, First, Second (2-1, 2-2), Third.

9. Isherwood, *Lions and Shadows*, p. 135; interview with Edward Upward, *The Reptonian* (Michaelmas 1994), p. 27.
10. Isherwood, *Lions and Shadows*, p. 71.
11. Peter Parker, *Isherwood: A Life* (London, 2004), p. 288.
12. Edward Upward, *No Home but the Struggle* (London, 1979), p. 167.
13. BL Add MS 89002/1/1, September 1924–September 1927, 23, 27 September and 4, 9, 30 October 1924; 5 December 1925; 25 July 1925.
14. Courtesy Janet Upward. To Christopher, 17 December 1994.
15. CI 2468, 11 May 1950; 2332, ?1924.
16. BL Add MS 72668, 2.
17. BL Add MS 89002/1/1, 14 September 1924–25 September 1927, 16 October 1924.
18. Isherwood, *Lions and Shadows*, pp. 121–22.
19. BL Add MS 89002/1/1, 21 October 1924.
20. Upward, *No Home*, pp. 189–90.
21. BL Add MS 42690 X, 4.
22. BL Add MS 89001/1/2, June 1926–October 1931, ?September 1931.
23. BL Add MS 89002/1/22, June 1955–February 1956, 22 July; 89002/1/23, March 1956–April 1957, 22 December 1956.
24. M. E. Bury and E. J. Winter, eds., *Corpus within Living Memory* (London, 2003), pp. 23–29.
25. Quoted in Parker, *Isherwood*, p. 91.
26. Peter Parker, interview with Edward Upward, 3 July 1993, courtesy Peter Parker.
27. Isherwood, *Lions and Shadows*, pp. 114–17.
28. BL Add MS 89002/1/1, 8 October 1924.
29. CI 2362.
30. Upward, *No Home*, p. 178.
31. Isherwood, *Lions and Shadows*, p. 75.
32. BL Add MS 72688, 3, 22 March 1923.
33. BL Add MS 89002/1/1, 10 February 1925. The surviving stories have been published: Christopher Isherwood and Edward Upward, *The Mortmere Stories* (London, 1994).
34. CI 2342, 12–13 March 1926.
35. CI 2303, 5 April 1924.
36. Isherwood and Upward, *Mortmere Stories*, p. 31.
37. CI 2472, 4 February 1953.
38. BL Add MS 89002/1/, January 1953–April 1954, 5 February 1953.
39. BL Add MS 89002/1/34, June 1963–November 1963, 29 October 1963.
40. Peter Parker, interview with Edward Upward, 10 August 1993, courtesy Peter

NOTES

Parker.
41. BL Add MS 89002/1/59, August 1987–September 1988, 24 January 1988.
42. Peter Parker, interview with Edward Upward, 10 August 1993, courtesy Peter Parker.
43. Edward Upward, 'Remembering Mortmere', *London Magazine* n.s. 27.11 (February 1988), pp. 54–59.
44. Isherwood and Upward, *Mortmere Stories*, p. 167. Ellipses in original.
45. Isherwood, *Lions and Shadows*, p. 273.
46. CI 2291, 6 December 1922.
47. See Benjamin Kohlmann, 'Christopher Isherwood and Edward Upward', in *The American Isherwood* (Minneapolis, 2015), pp. 199–214; Parker, *Isherwood*, p. 75.
48. CI 2460, 18 January 1949.
49. Upward to Jenny Uglow, 20 October 1984, 918079, Hogarth Press Archives, University of Reading, Reading, UK.
50. Christopher Isherwood, 'Foreword', *New Directions* 11 (New York, 1949), pp. 84–85.
51. BL Add MS 89002/1/64, December 1983–October 1983, undated loose page.
52. BL Add MS 89002/1/39, July 1965–December 1965, 26 July 1965.
53. Isherwood and Upward, *Mortmere Stories*, pp. 150–51.
54. BL Add MS 89002/1/3, January 1931–January 1934, 6 January 1934.

Chapter 4: Out in the World

1. BL Add MS 89002/1/1, September 1924–September 1927, 1, 2 March 1926.
2. Christopher Isherwood, 'Foreword', *All the Conspirators* (New York, 1958), n.p.
3. Ibid.
4. CI 2444, 2 September 1934.
5. BL Add MS 89002/4/2.
6. Ibid., 26 January 1928.
7. BL Add MS 89002/3/15, James R.C. Greenlees, 10 June 1930.
8. CI 2401, 20 February 1930; 2424, ?1931.
9. CI 2407, 18 October 1930.
10. BL Add MS 89002/1/3, January 1931–January 1934, 27 November 1931.
11. BL Add MS 89002/3/15, H.W. Marsden, 18 May 1931.
12. CI 2411, n.d.
13. Information and quotations, Peter Parker, interview with Edward Upward, 10 August 1993, courtesy Peter Parker. In a letter to Isherwood he referred to Stowe as 'the pinchbeck Eton'. CI 2441, 19 February ?1932.
14. BL Add MS 89002/1/18, May 1952–December 1952, 15 May 1952.

15. CI 2358, n.d. ?1926.
16. BL Add MS 89002/1/52, December 1972–August 1973, 28 July 1973.
17. BL Add MS 89002/1/3, January 1931–January 1934, 25 August 1931.
18. CI 2349, 13 June 1926.
19. CI 2321, 2400, n.d.
20. Inventory of Upward's library, compiled by Katherine Allinson.
21. CI 2438, ?1932; 2440, ?1933.
22. CI 2441, 19 February ?1933; 2442, n.d.
23. BL Add MS 89002/1/3, January 1931–January 1934.
24. BL Add MS 89002/2/1, undated letters.
25. Letter 25 October 1962, loosely inserted in BL Add MS 89002/1/31, July 1962–December 1962.
26. CI 2431, 31 October 1932.
27. CI 2433, 31 December 1932.
28. Christopher Upward, 'Edward Upward: Family and Forbers [sic]'. MSS dated 21 March 1991, courtesy Janet Upward.
29. BL Add MS 72701, f. 259r MSS notation 26 June 1995.
30. CI 2446, 23 December 1934.
31. CI 2448, 10 February 1935.
32. BL Add MS 89002/1/4, January 1934–May 1935, 23 March 1935.
33. CI 2450, 20 May 1936.
34. BL 89002/1/5, May 1935–November 1936, 17 April 1936, draft of letter to Hilda.
35. EA 1 August 1936, quoted in Alan Walker, 'Edward Upward in the 1930s', Box 6B.
36. CI 2451, 7 December 1936.
37. BL Add MS 89002/1/5, May 1935–November 1936, 20 May; 7, 8 June; 28 July; 1, 7, 8 August 1936.
38. BL Add MS 89002/1/34, June 1963–November 1963, 10 August 1963.
39. BL Add MS 89002/1/6, November 1936–February 1938, 21 January 1938.
40. BL Add MS 89002/1/5, May 1935–November 1936, 25 August 1936.
41. BL Add MS 89002/1/36, April 1964–June 1964, 26 May 1964.
42. Edward Upward, *Remembering the Earlier Auden* (London, 1998), pp. 6–7.
43. W. H. Auden, *Juvenilia: Poems 1922–28*, ed. Katherine Bucknell (Princeton, 1994), p. 150.
44. BL Add MS 89002/1/53, August 1973–February 1974, 31 October 1973.
45. BL Add MS 89002/1/6, November 1937–February 1938, 10 January 1938.
46. BL Add MS 89002/1/10, September 1941–May 1943, 17 August 1942.
47. Peter Parker, interview with Edward Upward, 10 August 1993, courtesy Peter Parker.
48. BL Add MS 89002/1/2, June 1926–October 1931, 1 September 1930.

NOTES

49. BL Add MS 89002/1/26, September 1957–June 1958, 1 March 1958.
50. BL Add MS 72688, f. 167, 6 October 1930.
51. BL Add MS 89002/1/3. For a rich discussion of the Auden/Upward connection, see Benjamin Kohlmann, 'Edward Upward, W. H. Auden, and the Rhetorical Victories of Communism', *Modernism/Modernity* 20 (2 April 2013), pp. 287–307.
52. W. H. Auden, *The Orators* (London, 1932), pp. 50–51.
53. Auden to Henry Bamford Parkes, 12 June 1932, quoted in John Mizner, 'An Auden Letter about the Orators', *Colby Quarterly* 13.1 (December 1977), p. 276. I am grateful to Edward Mendelson for this reference.
54. EA, Box 6b 1999-2000 33.
55. Courtesy Benjamin Kohlmann.
56. BL Add MS 72688, 237r, Philip Larkin to Upward, 5 October 1973; 238v, copy Upward to Larkin, 8 October 1973; 244r, copy Mendelson to Larkin, 18 October 1973. I am also grateful to Edward Mendelson for his current insights on this issue and the relations between Auden and Upward.
57. EA, 26 June 1970.
58. W. H. Auden and Louis MacNeice, *Letters from Iceland* (London, 1937), p. 239.
59. BL Add MS 72688, 338.
60. CI 2405, 3 September 1930; Peter Parker, *Isherwood: A Life* (London, 2004), p. 196.
61. Barbara Wootton, *In a World I Never Made* (Toronto, 1967), pp. 81–82.
62. BL Add MS 89002/3/7.
63. BL Add MS 89002/1/60, February 1979–February 1980, 1 August 1979.
64. BL Add MS 72703, f. 29.
65. Edward Upward, *In the Thirties* (London, 1962), n.p.
66. Edward Upward, *No Home but the Struggle* (London, 1979), p. 198.
67. CI 2429, ?April 1932.
68. Christopher Isherwood, *Christopher and His Kind* (New York, 1976), p. 98.
69. Stephen Spender, in *The God That Failed,* ed. Richard Crossman (New York, 1949), p. 234.
70. Stephen Spender, *World within World* (New York, 1951), p. 120.
71. BL Add MS 72688, 193r-v, Spender to Upward, 1 June 1964.
72. Stephen Spender, *Journals* (London, 1985), 13 June 1960, p. 233.
73. Stephen Spender, 'The Case of Edward Upward', *London Magazine* (March 1987).
74. Bodleian Library, Oxford University, Upward to Spender, 1 May 1951.
75. BL Add MS 72688, 66r, Isherwood to Upward, 24 January 1951.
76. NA KV 2/3919 IMG 8193, 18 November 1948. There are two MI5 files on Hilda

and Edward Upward, the other being KV 2/3920. KV 2/3919 is numbered from IMG 8141 to 8298 but it only contains 104 items. KV 2/3920 is numbered from IMG 8299 to 8362 and contains 59 items. In both files there are missing numbers in the listing. It is hard to tell whether missing numbers indicate missing documents, as there are instances of skipped numbers when in fact the text is continuous. The files are also not necessarily in chronological order. There are only two instances in which a page is inserted stating that a document has been removed. Also the file may not be complete. It was released in October 2014. MI5 policy seems to be not to include any material that may be in the file dating from the previous fifty years, so if there is anything on the Upwards in the file from 1964 to 2009 it would not be included. See Francis Stonor Saunders, 'Stuck to the Flypaper: On MI5 and the Hobsbawm File', *London Review of Books* (9 April 2015), pp. 3–10. See also James Smith, *British Writers and MI5 Surveillance 1930–1960* (Cambridge, 2013). Apparently other objects of maximum penetration, other than the British Communist Party, were the German Embassy and the British Union of Fascists.

77. NA KV 2/3919, IMG 8292, 25 January 1934.
78. NA KV 2/3919, IMG 8298, 8172.

Chapter 5: Schoolmaster at Alleyn's

1. Illegible signature to Upward, 4 June 1932, Alleyn's archives. This may be the master who knew Upward's brother and who recommended him. I am most grateful to Neil French, the school's archivist, for his help. He had known Upward as a teacher who 'encouraged me (and many others also on the Science and Mathematics side of the curriculum) to enjoy a lifelong appreciation of English Literature. . . . Not until after his death two years ago did I become aware of Edward Upward's literary eminence and also of the complete lack of recognition that existed within the School community about him. In an effort to put right, to some very small extent, this sad state of affairs I embarked upon the creation of a small archive display of his life'. Neil French to author, 13 October 2012.
2. BL Add MS 89002/1/23, October 1956–April 1957, 2 February, 29 April 1957.
3. BL Add MS 89002/1/8, December 1938–August 1939, 10 June, 8 August 1939.
4. NA KV2/ 3919, IMG 8206, 9 May 1947.
5. BL Add MS 89002/1/9, August 1939–September 1941, 20 October 1939.
6. Alleyn's archives.

NOTES

7. BL Add MS 89002/1/45, March 1969–October 1969, 1 March 1969.
8. BL Add MS 89002/1/41, July 1966–April 1967, 6 February 1967.
9. BL Add MS 89002/1/19, January 1953–April 1954, 4 May 1953.
10. BL Add MS 89002/1/22, February 1956–October 1956, 27 May 1956.
11. BL Add MS 89002/1/61, February 1980–May 1981, 30 September 1980.
12. Much information from a school publication, Susannah Schofield, ed., *Alleyn's in the 1930s* (Dulwich, 2011).
13. Ibid., p. 79.
14. Norman Wetherick, 'Alleyn's in the 1940s', p. 12, Alleyn's archives.
15. Arthur Chandler, document in Upward display, Alleyn's School, display case.
16. BL Add MS 72703, G ff. 12r-v, Upward to Olive Mangeot, 11 August 1933.
17. BL Add MS 89002/1/9, August 1939–September 1941, 25 October 1939; 17 April, 22 June 1941.
18. NA KV 2/3919 IMG 8241–42. Louis Goddard believes Upward was using 'Franklin', the name of a former colleague at Alleyn's, as an alias, for unknown reasons. Louis Goddard, 'Not Spooked', *Times Literary Supplement* (11 December 2015), p. 17.
19. NA KV 2/3919, IMG 8212, 14, 16, 19–20, 23, 25–32, 35, 37–39, 43–44, 48–49, 61–63, 65, 68–69.
20. NA KV 2/3919, IMG 8222.
21. NA KV 2/3920, IMG 8317–19.
22. NA KV 2/3919, IMG 8277–79.
23. Arthur R. Chandler, *Alleyn's, The Coeducational School* (Henley-on-Thames, 1998), p. 106.
24. Donald Leinster-Mackay, *Alleyn's and Rossall Schools: The Second World War, Experience and Status* (London, 1990), p. 45.
25. Quotations from David Weston, MS of biography of Michael Croft, archives, Alleyn's School.
26. BL Add MS 89002/2/17, ff. 38r–39v, 21 March 1984.

Chapter 6: Being a Communist and a Writer

1. BL Add MS 89002/1/2, 1926–1931, July 1931; BL Add MS 89002/1/3, January 1931–January 1934, 15 November 1931.
2. David Latham, *William Morris in the Twenty-First Century* (Bern, 2010), p. 206.
3. Christopher Isherwood, *Lions and Shadows* (London, 1938), p. 274.
4. Kenneth Newton, *The Sociology of British Communism* (London, 1969), p. 166.
5. BL Add MS 89002/1/3, January 1931–January 1934, 1 February 1931.

NOTES

6. See Andy Croft, 'The Ralph Fox (Writers') Group', in *And in Our Time*, ed. Anthony Shuttleworth (Lewisburg, 2003).
7. BL Add MS 89002/1/6, 19 October 1938.
8. Newton, *Sociology of British Communism*, pp. 159–60, 43.
9. For this and much else, particularly their meticulous reading of the manuscript, I am deeply grateful to Upward's daughter Katherine Allinson and her son Dave Allinson, and to Upward's daughter-in-law Janet Upward.
10. 'Guidelines on the Organizational Structure of Communist Parties, on the Methods and Content of Their Work', adopted at the Twenty-fourth Session of the Third Congress of the Communist International, 12 July 1921. http://www.marxists.org/history/international/comintern/3rd-congress/organisation/guidelines.htm, accessed 21 October 2013.
11. Ernest Griffin, 'Conversation with Edward Upward', *Modernist Studies* 2.2 (1977), p. 32.
12. Stuart Hampshire, 'In the Thirties', *New Statesman* (17 August 1962), p. 204.
13. BL Add MS 89002/2/5, ff. 46r-v, 47r-v, drafts Upward to Hampshire, 7, 11 October 1962; Hampshire to Upward, 9 October 1962.
14. BL Add MS 89002/1/42, April 1967–September 1967, 7 July 1967.
15. CI 2403, 4 April 1930.
16. CI 2437, n.d.
17. CI 2410, n.d.
18. CI 2442, ?1933.
19. BL Add MS 89002/1/14, April 1946–April 1947, 8, 20 October, 18 November 1946.
20. BL Add MS 89002/1/5, May 1935–November 1936, 17 August 1936.
21. BL Add MS 72691, f. 36r.
22. NA KV2 3919, IMG 8296.
23. BL Add MS 89002/1/5, 13 September 1935.
24. CI 2443, 1 May 1934.
25. BL Add MS 89002/1/7, February 1938–December 1938, 5 September 1938.
26. Bodleian Library, Oxford University, Upward to Spender, 19 September 1955.
27. Stephen Spender, 'Upward at Ninety', *Times Literary Supplement* (10 September 1993), p. 14.
28. BL Add MS 89002/1/19, January 1953–April 1954, 4, 29, 30 April 1954; BL Add MS 89002/1/23, October 1956–April 1957, 21 December 1956; BL Add MS 89002/1/29, April 1961–August 1961, 7 April 1961; BL Add MS 89002/1/33, April 1963–June 1963, 5 June 1963; BL Add MS 89002/1/34, June 1963–November 1963, 12 August 1963; BL Add MS 89002/1/37, June 1964–November 1964, 16 July 1964; BL Add MS 89002/1/59, November 1977–February 1979, 6 May

1978.
29. Bodleian Library, Oxford University, Spender Papers, Upward to Spender, 19 September 1955.
30. John Lehmann, *The Whispering Gallery* (London, 1955), p. 182.
31. Stephen Spender, *World within World* (New York, 1951), p. 126.
32. Michael Roberts, ed., 'Preface', *New Country* (London, 1933), pp. 11, 12–13, 21.
33. Rex Warner, 'Hymn', ibid., p. 256.
34. Edward Upward, 'The Colleagues', ibid., pp. 180–81.
35. Samuel Hynes, *The Auden Generation* (London, 1976), p. 106.
36. Bodleian Library, Oxford University, Upward to Spender, 5 May 1935.
37. Stephen Spender, *The Destructive Element* (London, 1935), p. 243.
38. Edward Upward, 'Sunday', *New Country* (London, 1933), pp. 183–89.
39. E. Allen Osborne, ed., *In Letters of Red* (1938), p. 248.
40. Bodleian Library, Oxford University, Upward to Spender, 5 May 1935.
41. BL Add MS 89002/1/54, February 1974–October 1974, 9 July 1974.
42. Edward Upward, 'Sketch . . .', in *The Mind in Chains: Socialism and the Cultural Revolution*, ed. C. Day Lewis (London, 1937), pp. 45, 48, 49, 52; 45.
43. BL Add MS 89002/1/35, November 1963–April 1964, 4 March 1964.
44. [A. L. Rowse], 'Marxism and Literature', *Times Literary Supplement* (14 August 1937), pp. 581–82.
45. George Orwell, 'Inside the Whale', in *A Patriot after All, 1940–1941* (London, 2000), pp. 99–103.
46. Ernest Griffin, 'Conversation with Edward Upward', *Modernist Studies* 2.2 (1977), pp. 25–26.
47. In his interesting study of Upward and five other writers, *The Will to Believe* (Oxford, 1982), Richard Johnstone parallels Upward's Communism with the Catholicism of Evelyn Waugh and Graham Greene. It links rather disparate 1930s' writers — Upward, Isherwood, George Orwell, Rex Warner, Graham Greene and Evelyn Waugh — by their common 'will to believe'.
48. EA, interview with Edward Upward, 8 December 1969.
49. Peter Parker, interview with Edward Upward, 10 August 1993, courtesy Peter Parker.
50. BL Add MS 89002/1/4, January 1934–May 1935, 11 January 1934.
51. BL Add MS 89002/1/19, January 1953–April 1954, 6 October 1953.
52. CI 2444, 2 September 1934.
53. BL Add MS 89002/1/6, November 1936–February 1938, 6 September 1937.
54. Margot Heinemann, '*Left Review, New Writing* and the Broad Alliance against Fascism', in *Visions and Blueprints*, ed. Edward Timms and Peter Collier

(Manchester, 1988), p. 113.
55. John Lehmann, ed., *New Writing* (London, 1936), n.p.
56. NA KV2/ 3919, IMG 8284. MI5 presumably used full capitals on the names of those for whom it had files. It also had a file for Isherwood but Lehmann did not include his last name.
57. Details about publication, Hogarth Press file 507, Special Collections, University of Reading, Reading.
58. EA, Alan Walker, 'Edward Upward in the 1930s', p. 22.
59. John Lehmann, *Christopher Isherwood* (New York, 1987), p. 39.
60. Anne Olivier Bell, ed., *The Diary of Virginia Woolf*, vol. 5 (London, 1984), 12 March 1938, p. 130.
61. BL Add MS 89002/1/5, May 1935–November 1936, 5 January 1936.
62. Edward Upward, *Journey to the Border* (London, 1938), pp. 79–80, 101, 105, 106, 126, 137–39, 174, 202, 214, 234, 255–56.
63. Upward, *Journey to the Border*, pp. 56–58.
64. V. S. Pritchett, 'New Novels', *New Statesman* (12 March 1938), p. 443; V. S. Pritchett, 'Politics and the English Novel', *Fortnightly Review* (June 1938), pp. 680–85; Harold Brighouse, 'Novels of England, Germany and America', *Manchester Guardian* (15 March 1938), p. 7; Arnold Palmer, 'With Prisoners and Exiles', *Yorkshire Post* (18 March 1938), p. 6; Edwin Muir, 'New Novels', *Listener* (16 March 1938), p. 597; Forrest Reid, 'Fiction', *Spectator* (18 March 1938), p. 486; Ralph Wright, '"Heroes" Who Were Afraid', *Daily Worker* (30 March 1938), p. 7; 'Notable First Novels', *Times Literary Supplement* (26 March 1938), p. 221; R. G. Cox, 'Left-wing Allegories', *Scrutiny* (June 1938), p. 92.
65. John Lehmann, *New Writing in England* (New York, 1939), p. 43.
66. Hogarth Press file 507, Special Collections, University of Reading, Reading.
67. W. H. Auden and Christopher Isherwood, 'Young British Writers – On the Way Up', *Vogue* (15 August 1939), pp. 94, 156–57.
68. Stuart N. Clarke, ed., *The Essays of Virginia Woolf, Vol. 6, 1933–1941* (London, 2011), pp. 259–83.
69. Louis MacNeice, 'The Tower That Once', *Folios of New Writing* (London, 1941), pp. 40–41.
70. Edward Upward, 'The Falling Tower', ibid., pp. 24–29.
71. John Lehmann, 'Foreword', *Penguin New Writing* 14 (London, June–September 1942), p. 7.
72. Edward Upward, 'New Order', ibid., p. 11.

NOTES

Chapter 7: The Years Between

1. CI 2455, 23 July 1939.
2. BL Add MS 72688, f. 30, 6 August 1939, quoted in Peter Parker, *Isherwood: A Life* (London, 2004), pp. 445–46.
3. CI 2456, 24 August 1939. See Benjamin Kohlmann, 'Christopher Isherwood and Edward Upward', in *The American Isherwood,* ed. James Berg and Chris Freeman (Minneapolis, 2014).
4. BL Add MS 89002/1/9, August 1939–September 1941, 24 August 1939.
5. BL Add MS 89002/1/24, May 1957–September 1957, 4 July 1957.
6. BL Add MS 89002/1/16, April 1948–August 1949, 30 December 1948.
7. BL Add MS 89002/1/13, April 1945–April 1946, 19 August 1945.
8. BL Add MS 89002/1/24, May 1957–September 1957, 4, 8 July 1957.
9. BL Add MS 89002/1/17, April 1950–May 1952, 5 September, 24 December 1950; BL Add MS 89002/1/24, May 1957–September 1957, 22 June 1957; BL Add MS 89002/1/25, September 1957–June 1958, 23 October 1957, 5 February 1958.
10. Christopher Isherwood, *Lost Years: A Memoir 1945–1951* (London, 2000), pp. 100–101.
11. CI 2508, 17 August 1962.
12. CI 2468, 11 May 1950.
13. CI 2473, 2 August 1953.
14. Christopher Isherwood, *Diaries, Vol. I, 1939–1960* (London, 1996), 27 February 1956, p. 590.
15. CI 2481, 12 August 1956.
16. CI 2485, 16 March 1958.
17. CI 2488, 16 October 1958.
18. CI 2480, 18 September 1953.
19. 'Statement for the Literature/Sociology Conference on "1936" at Essex University', in *1936: The Sociology of Literature,* vol. 2, ed. Francis Barker et al. (Colchester, 1979), p. 220.
20. Stephen Spender, *World within World* (New York, 1951), p. 92.
21. Bodleian Library, Oxford University, 19 September 1955, 27 June 1956, 22 April 1958. Spender was an editor of *Encounter.* It would have been an ironic touch if Upward had been published there as it was covertly financed by the CIA.
22. Edward Upward, *In the Thirties* (London, 1962), p. 69.
23. Quoted in Richard Johnstone, *The Will to Believe* (Oxford, 1982), p. 46.
24. BL Add MS 89002/2/35, 1 July 1958, f. 35r.
25. BL Add MS 89002/1/29, April 1961–August 1961, 12 April, 10 August 1961.
26. BL Add MS 72703, ff. 14r-v, 17 August; f. 15r, 16 September 1962.

27. Francis Hope, 'A Return to All That', *Observer* (12 August 1962), p. 16; Anthony Quinton, 'Fiction', *Sunday Telegraph* (12 August 1962), p. 7; Olivia Manning, 'The Memoirs of Alan Sebrill', *Sunday Times* (17 August 1962), p. 22; Andrew Leslie, 'Upward's Backward Glance', *Guardian* (17 August 1962), p. 6; Stuart Hampshire, 'Long Ago', *New Statesman* (17 August 1962), p. 204; Malcolm Bradbury, 'New Novels', *Punch* (29 August 1962), pp. 319–20; John Mortimer, 'Muse in Placards', *Spectator* (24 August 1962), pp. 279–81; [Randall Swingler], 'Politics and the Poetic Life', *Times Literary Supplement* (24 August 1962), p. 637; John Lehmann/[Randall Swingler], 'Politics and the Poetic Life', *Times Literary Supplement* (31 August 1962), p. 725; Christopher Isherwood, 'One of the Greatest Novels of Our Time', *Time and Tide* (16–23 August 1962), pp. 27–28; Stephen Spender, 'The Pink Decade', *Encounter* 20.6 (June 1963), pp. 82–83.
28. Bodleian Library, Oxford University, Upward to Spender, 21 May 1963.
29. BL Add MS 89002/1/32, December 1962–April 1963, 6, 7, 28 January, 5 March 1963.
30. BL Add MS 89002/1/44, June 1968–March 1969, 25 January 1969.
31. BL Add MS 89002/1/67, May 1985–June 1986, 21, 22 September 1985.
32. BL Add S 89002/1/57, April 1976–February 1977, 22 October 1976.
33. Frank Kermode, *History and Value* (Oxford, 1988), p. 53.
34. Edward Upward, *The Rotten Elements* (London, 1969), pp. 10, 175, 177.
35. Francis Hope, 'Another of the Gang', *New Statesman* (1 August 1969), p. 149; Philip Toynbee, 'A Voice from the Past', *Observer* (27 July 1969), p. 24; John Lehmann, 'Full Marx for a Poet', *Sunday Telegraph* (27 July 1969), p. 9; Julian Symons, 'Price of Loyalty', *Sunday Times* (27 July 1969), p. 49; [Samuel Hynes], 'Dimmed by Dialectics', *Times Literary Supplement* (31 July 1969), p. 849; Martin Seymour-Smith, 'Up and Down', *Spectator* (26 July 1969), p. 111; Ian Hamilton, 'A Healthy Death', *Listener* (31 July 1969), p. 158; Robert Nye, 'Fiction', *The Times* (2 August 1969), p. 20.
36. BL Add MS 89002/3/11, 'Statement made by E. Upward to Dulwich Branch Cttee on Sept. 30th 1947', p. 3.
37. Upward, *Rotten Elements*, p. 169.
38. All quotations from letters from Upward's file in Communist Party Archives, People's History Museum, Manchester. No citation numbers. I am very grateful to the museum for sending me copies of these documents. The two MI5 files in the National Archives were released in October 2014. The relevant documents on his leaving the party are in KV2/ 3920, IMG 8313, 8326–59.
39. BL Add MS 89002/3/11.
40. Ernest Griffin, 'Conversation with Edward Upward', *Modernist Studies* 2 (1976), p. 32.

NOTES

41. CI 2460, 18 January 1949.
42. BL Add MS 72688, f. 57r, 9 February ?1949.
43. Robert Jones, 'No Home but the Struggle', *Leveller* (January 1978), p. 27.
44. BL Add MS 89002/1/19, January 1953–April 1954, 29 January 1953.
45. For notes on lectures, see BL Add MS 89002/3/10–11, 89002/4/4.
46. BL Add MS 89002/1/42, April 1967–September 1967, 14 September 1967; 89002/1/43, September 1967–June 1968, notation at the beginning of volume.
47. BL Add MS 89002/1/45, 1 March 1969–October 1969, 2 May 1969.
48. CI 2542, 2546, 2552, 29 September, 2 November 1974, 16 September 1975.
49. CI 2558, 15 July 1976. Spender had written: 'Edward Upward has been unable to find a publisher for the third volume of his trilogy, *In the Thirties*. This seems to me a scandal'. Stephen Spender, 'Creating in the Mind a Map', *New Statesman* (2 July 1976), p. 19.
50. Bodleian Library, Oxford University, Upward to Spender, n.d.
51. Alice Prochaska, *Young Writers of the Thirties* (London, 1976), p. 9.
52. BL Add MS 89002/2/55, October 1974–September 1975, 2 September 1975.
53. See Katherine Bucknell, 'The Achievement of Edward Upward', in *W. H. Auden: The Language of Learning and the Language of Love*, ed. Katherine Bucknell and Nicholas Jenkins (Oxford, 1994), pp. 165–83.
54. Rodney Koeneke to author, e-mail, 22 February 2014.
55. BL Add MS 89002/1/57, April 1976–February 1977, 14, 16, 21 January 1977.
56. CI 2568, 31 July 1977.
57. BL Add MS 89002/2/10, copy Upward to Hynes, 8 August 1977.
58. Angus Wilson, 'Poetry and the Party Line', *Observer* (24 July 1977), p. 29; Raymond Williams, 'All Power to the Poem', *Guardian* (28 July 1977), p. 9; Michael Ratcliffe, 'In Deadly Earnest', *The Times* (28 July 1977), p. 10; Edward Upward, 'The Resolute Anti-Hero', *New Statesman* (1 April 1977), pp. 434–45; BL Add MS 89002/1/57, April 1976–February 1977, 14, 16, 21 January 1977; Christopher Isherwood, 'The Life of the Party', *New Statesman* (29 July 1977), pp. 149–50; Isobel Murray, 'No Roads to Freedom', *Financial Times* (4 August 1977), p. 8; Tim Heald, 'Recent Fiction', *Daily Telegraph* (4 August 1977), p. 11; Samuel Hynes, 'Between Poetry and the Party', *Times Literary Supplement* (5 August 1977), p. 953; Neville Braybrooke, 'Poet Wins Through', *Sunday Telegraph* (14 August 1977), p. 10; Kevin Cully, 'Novels of the Left for the Left', *Tribune* (2 September 1977), p. 12; John Sommerfield, 'Committed for Life', *London Magazine* (November 1977), pp. 87–89; Eddie Woods, 'Inner and Outer World of Politics', *Morning Star* (1 December 1977), p. 4.

Chapter 8: Free at Last

1. For a history of the movement, see Richard Taylor, *Against the Bomb* (Oxford, 1988).
2. BL Add MS 89002/1/30, August 1961–22 July 1962, 15 July 1962; BL Add MS 89002/1/63, April 1962–December 1983, 6 September 1983.
3. CI 2581, 7 August 1981.
4. CI 2530, 11 July 1969.
5. BL Add MS 89002/1/43, September 1967–June 1968, 15 June 1968.
6. BL Add MS 89002/1/58, February 1977–November 1977, 8 February 1977.
7. BL Add MS 72688, f. 69r, 12 March 1953; f. 74r, 16 September 1954; f. 111, 11 March 1968.
8. BL Add MS 89002/1/25, September 1957–June 1958, 23 December 1957.
9. Christopher Isherwood, *Liberation: Diaries, Vol. 3, 1970–1983* (London, 2012), 13 March 1970, p. 19; 13 October 1974, p. 457.
10. BL Add MS 89001/2/64, December 1982–October 1983, 17 September 1983.
11. BL Add MS 89001/1/15, April 1947–August 1948, 19 August 1947; BL Add MS 89002/1/34, June 1963–November 1963, 18 July 1963; BL Add MS 89002/1/37, June 1964–November 1964, 25 July 1964; BL Add MS 89002/1/43, September 1967–June 1968, 14 February 1967; BL Add MS 89002/1/53, August 1973–February 1974, 4 October 1974; BL Add MS 89002/1/57, April 1976–February 1977, 25 October 1976; BL Add MS 89002/1/74, September 1992–August 1995, 4 August 1993.
12. Bodleian Library, Oxford University, Upward to Spender, 17 January 1981.
13. Edward Upward, *The Night Walk and Other Stories* (London, 1987), pp. 50, 15–17, 127–37.
14. Mario Faraone, interview with Edward Upward, July–August 1998, *L'isola e il treno* (Rome, 2012), p. 419.
15. EA, 11 March 1985; 10, 11 April 1991.
16. Katherine Bucknell and Nicholas Jenkins, eds., *'In Solitude, for Company': W. H. Auden after 1940* (Oxford, 1995), p. 249.
17. BL Add MS 89002/1/72, August 1990–September 1991, 1 November 1990.
18. D. J. Taylor, 'Tenacity of an Armchair Socialist', *Independent* (26 February 1987), p. 15; Norman Shrapnel, 'A Book of Ghosts', *Guardian* (27 February 1987), p. 11; Richard Boston, 'Onward and Upward', *Guardian* (10 March 1987), p. 27; David Phillips, 'Thirties Man', *Financial Times* (28 February 1987), p. 16; Valentine Cunningham, 'Red Flag Flying', *Observer* (8 March 1987), p. 26; Alexander Snowden, 'Strikingly Unfashionable', *Tribune* (22 May 1987), p. 9; Neville Braybrooke, 'Faith of a Marxist', *Tablet* (11 July 1987), p. 14; David E.

NOTES

Morgan, 'Upward: Writing for Change', *Morning Star* (30 April 1987), p. 8; Katherine Bucknell, 'Trips Round the Island', *Times Literary Supplement* (4–10 December 1987), p. 1348.

19. Stephen Spender, 'The Case of Edward Upward', *London Magazine* (March 1987), pp. 29–43; Edward Upward, 'Letter', *London Magazine* (June 1987), pp. 90–91.
20. Courtesy Janet Upward, Upward to Christopher, 7 July 1988.
21. Sarah Lefanu and Stephen Hayward, eds., *Colours of a New Day* (London, 1990), pp. 298–313.
22. Jean Moorcroft Wilson and Cecil Woolf, eds., *Authors Take Sides on Iraq and the Gulf War* (London, 2004), p. 178. Cecil Woolf published a series of books building on the famous *Authors Take Sides on the Spanish War* (1937). There was *Authors Take Sides on Vietnam* (1967) and *Authors Take Sides on the Falklands* (1982). The Gulf War ended too quickly for the book to be published until it appeared as *Authors Take Sides on Iraq and the Gulf War* (2004).
23. Peter Parker, 'Upward and Onward', *Independent Magazine* (4 September 1993), pp. 15–16; Stephen Spender, 'Upward at Ninety', *Times Literary Supplement* (10 September 1993), p. 14.
24. Bodleian Library, Oxford University, Upward to Spender, 13 September 1993.
25. Edward Upward, *An Unmentionable Man* (London, 1994), pp. 27, 90, 95–96.
26. Bodleian Library, Oxford University, Upward to Spender, 29 March 1994, 1 October 1993.
27. BL Add MS 89001/1/74, September 1992–August 1995, 6 July 1994.
28. John Lehmann, *The Whispering Gallery* (London, 1955), p. 195.
29. Anthony Curtis, 'Pre-war Village Fantasy', *Weekend Financial Times* (26 November 1994), p. 21; Neville Braybrooke, 'Upward and Onward', *Tablet* (3 December 1994), pp. 1551–52; Dave Beecham, 'A Welcome Intrusion', *Socialist Review* (March 1995), pp. 30–31; Ian Hamilton, 'Neglect', *London Review of Books* (25 January 1995), p. 19; Edward Mendelson, 'Not Such a Fantasy', *Times Literary Supplement* (3 November 1995), p. 22.
30. BL Add MS 89002/1/58, February 1977–November 1977, 24 July 1977; 89002/1/59, November 1977–February 1979, 2 September 1978; 89002/1/62, May 1981–April 1982, 17 April 1982.
31. BL Add MS 89002/1/35, November 1963–April 1964, 23 April 1964; 89002/1/58, February 1977–November 1977, 12 March 1977.
32. BL Add MS 89002/1/74, September 1992–1995, 17 February, 13, 18, 19, 21 March, 5, 9, 18 August 1995; 89002/1/75, August 1995–August 1997, 2, 30 December 1995, 2 January 1996, 19 July 1997.
33. Ibid., 24 October 1996.

34. Edward Upward, *The Scenic Railway* (London, 1997), pp. 82, 89.
35. Boyd Tonkin, 'A Week in Books', *Independent* (18 October 1997), p. 11; Elisabeth Mahoney, 'Dream Zones', *London Magazine* (February 1998), pp. 109–10.
36. Edward Upward, *The Coming Day and Other Stories* (London, 2000), p. 148.
37. BL Add MD 89001/1/69, August 1987–September 1988, 13 August 1987.
38. Courtesy Janet Upward, Upward to Christopher, 7 July 1988.
39. Mario Faraone, interview with Edward Upward, July–August 1998, pp. 392, 427.
40. Quoted in Nicholas Wroe, *Guardian* (22 August 2003).

Index

Page numbers in *italic* refer to illustrations

Aberystwyth 22
Abrahams, Harold 44
Abse, Dannie **318**
Ackerley, J. R. 298
Adam International 291
Adelphi 189
African National Congress 297
Albinus of Angers, St 327n
Aldermaston marches 284
Alexander, David 154
Alleyn, Edward 148, 168, 169
Alleyn's School, Dulwich 148–71, **149**, **169**, 243, 244, 286, 305
    Cadet Corps 168
    debating society 152
    League of Nations Union 152
    Michael Croft Theatre 168
    move to Cleveleys, Lancashire 158, 232
    Upward teaches at 102, 113, 147
Allinson, David (grandson) 324
Allinson, Jeff (son-in-law) 318, 319
Allison, C. R. 160
Amersham Hall, Buckinghamshire 20
Anglo–Russian Friendship Society 160
Anglo–Soviet Unity Committee 163
anti-Semitism 48, 50–1
Anti-war Congress, Holland 146
Armistice Day 197
Arnold, Matthew 213
Arts Council 144
    Literature Panel 273
Ashford, Daisy, *The Young Visiters* 87
Aston University, Birmingham 307
Attlee, Clement 238

Atwood, Margaret 297
Auden, George 20, 21, 28, 36
Auden, Wystan Hugh 126–36, **129**, **145**
    in Berlin 205–6, 215
    circle of 81, 188–9, 203, 224, 227, 230, 232, 233–4, 256, 260, 276, 299, 300, 322–3, 326
    exhibition on 273–4
    climbs tree 113
    and Communism 127, 132, 173, 191, 296
    death 133, 290
    dedications to individuals 133–6
    in Helensburgh 128, 134
    Francis Hope on 249
    in Iceland 216
    and Layard 215
    and *Left Review* 176
    MacNeice on 229
    MI5 and 145
    and Mortmere world 70, 235
    moves to United States 205, 206, 234, 289
    named after saint 20
    and *New Country* 191
    at Oxford 115
    plays 91
    relationship with Upward 134–6, 289–94
    and religion 143
    in Spain 136
    Upward's admiration of 131
    Upward's influence on 15, 127, 130–2, 306–7
    and Upward's poetry 129
    'August for the People' 126, 195

City Without Walls 135
Collected Poetry 134–5
Collected Shorter Poems (1950) 135
'A Communist to Others' 132, 191, 194–5, 294
'Comrade Upward' 132–3
The Dyer's Hand 289
'The Exiles' 133
'Humpty Dumpty' 127
In Praise of Limestone 294
'James Honeyman' 196
Journey to a War (with Isherwood) 206
Letters from Iceland (with MacNeice) 136, 206
'Look, Stranger, on This Island Now' 127
On the Frontier (with Isherwood) 229
The Orators: An English Study 131–3, 135
'Journal of an Airman' 131–2
Poems 131, 189, 274
'September 1, 1939' 136
'Young British Writers – On the Way Up' (with Isherwood) 226

Balcon, Jill 316
Barbellion, W. N. P. 54
  The Journal of a Disappointed Man 77
Barbirolli, Sir John 115
Bates, Ralph 226
Battle of Britain 157
Baudelaire, Charles 67, 68–9, 77, 91
BBC, Third Programme 288
Beckett, Samuel, *Murphy* 222
Beecham, Dave 306
Bell, Julian 81, 188, 191, 209, 273
Bell, Vanessa 207, 211

Benedict, Libby 220–1
  The Refugees 212
Benedict (magazine) 76
Benenden School, Kent 27
Bennett, Alan, *The History Boys* 329n
Berlin 22, 136, 141, 147, 205–6, 215
  Soviet blockade 264
Bernal, J. D. 199
Bevin, Ernest 238
Blackpool 160–4
  Civil Servants Current Affairs Discussion Group 163
Bloomsbury Group 192, 211
Blunden, Edmund 319
Blunt, Anthony 199
boarding schools, English 40–1
  see also public schools
Book Society 224
Bowen, Elizabeth 211
Box Hill, Surrey 121
Brace, Donald 211
Bradbury, Malcolm 250
Braybrooke, June (Isobel English) 286
Braybrooke, Neville 273, 281, 286, 296, 305–6
Brett, G. F. 191
Brighouse, Harold 221
Bristol 265
British Union of Fascists 206, 335n
Brontë, Emily 54, 98
Brooke, Rupert 58, 63, 80, 313
Browne, Sir Thomas 91
Browning, Robert 35, 58, 60
Brussels 102
  Peace Conference 121
Bryanston School, Dorset 112, 327n
Bucknell, Katherine 90, 296, 300
Buddhism, Buddha 79, 80–1

INDEX

Bulwer-Lytton, Edward 80
Bunyan, John 18, 274, 280
  The Pilgrim's Progress 35
Burns, Robert 35
Butler, Sir Geoffrey 73
Butler, Samuel 303
Butterfield, Herbert 79
Buxted, Surrey 136
Byron, George Gordon, Lord 35

Cabaret 288
Calder-Marshall, Arthur 226
Cam, River 75
Cambridge:
  Festival Theatre 28
  Mortmere as 89
  Cambridge Mercury 76
  Cambridge Poetry 189
  Cambridge Review 76
Cambridge, University of:
  careers advice at 102
  Christ's College 20
  Corpus Christi College 54, 64, 65, 72–6, 84–6, **85**, 172, 305, 308
  Chess Club 86
  'Young Visiters' club 87–8
  Gonville and Caius College 167
  Jesus College 318
  King's College 54, 84
  Labour Club 308
  Magdalene College 63
  Newnham College 308
  Pembroke College 74
  poetry and literary criticism at 81–4
  'poshocracy' at 87–8
  St John's College 19
  Sidney Sussex College 26

Upward at 16, 51, 65, 69, 70–101, 149, 212, 278
Upward on 64, 74, 85, 172
Cameron, Julia Margaret 104
Campaign for Nuclear Disarmament (CND):
  first major public meeting 283
  Newport-Cowes march 284
  social at Shanklin **287**
  Upward and 232, 238, 275, 283–5, 294–5
Canary Islands 197
Carbis Bay, Cornwall, Tallwater House 102, 106
Carpenter, Humphrey 257
Carritt, Gabriel 115
Carroll, Lewis, *Alice in Wonderland* 35, 71, 89, 225, 262
Catholic Church 204, 338n
Caudwell, Christopher 183, 202
Caudwell, Sarah 217
Chadwick, H. M. 82
Chalmers, John Rutherford 96
Chancellor's Medal for English Verse 79–81, 83, 104
Chandler, Arthur 155
Chariots of Fire 44
Cheltenham 199, 265
China 128, 152, 206, 282
Christianity 242
'Christine' (romantic interest) 113
Church of England 44, 45
Churchill, Winston 160
CIA (Central Intelligence Agency) 277, 340n
Cleveleys, Lancashire 158, 158, 159, 160, 163, 164, 166, 179
Clodd, Alan 290

348

INDEX

Cockburn, Claud 210
Cohen, J. M. 286
Cold War 236, 263, 264
Cole, Sir Henry 115
Coleridge, Samuel Taylor 186
Collins, William (publisher) 47
Comfort, Alex 283
Committee of 100 284
Communism 172–88
   abandoned by members of Auden group 233
   Auden and 127, 132, 173, 191, 296
   in Berlin 206
   Cornford and 111–12
   Day Lewis and 193
   Hilda and 121, 123–4, 161–2, 175, 179, 179–80, **179**, 265–7, 267–8, 269
   as religion 143, 178, 182, 204, 245, 246, 252, 270, 299, 338n
   Isherwood and 233
   Upward on 242
   Michael Roberts on 192–3
   in Soviet Union 110, 159
   Yolande Upward and 164–5
   Upward's children and 179–80
   Wintringham and 197
   see also Upward, Edward Falaise, and Communism; on Soviet Union and Communism
Communist Party of Australia 264–6, 268
Communist Party of Great Britain 140, 144, 154, 157, 163, 173, 177–8, 257–60
   Bethnal Green branch 175, 182
   Blackpool branch 160–4
   Camberwell branch 266
   compared to Catholic Church 204
   Dulwich branch 265, 268
   guidelines for members 180
   membership in 1930s 177–8
   middle-class members 180
   Poets' Group 176
   post-war inner fighting in 257
   Ralph Fox (Writers' Group) 176, 184, 252
   Readers' Group 176
   Streatham branch 184
   The British Road to Socialism 263
   see also Labour Party, Communist Party attitude to
Conservative (Tory) Party 152, 206
   in government 206
Coombes, B. L., 'Below the Tower' 228
Cornford, John 111–12, 273
Coster, Howard 211
Cowper, William 35, 274
Cox, R. G. 224, 227
Cripps, Stafford 236, 238
Criterion 189, 194
Croft, Michael 168–9, 247
   Spare the Rod 168
Crome, John 154–5
Cully, Kevin 281
Cunningham, Valentine 257, 295–6
   British Writers of the Thirties 302
Curtis, Anthony 305
Czechoslovakia 264

Dahl, Roald 44
Daily Telegraph 279
Daily Worker 144, 146, 175, 177, 182, 183, 223, 240, 249, 251, 265, 281
Dalhousie Review 256
Day Lewis, Cecil **145**
   and Book Society 224
   and Communism 233

INDEX

MacNeice on 229
  as member of Auden group 81, 176, 227, 273, 300
  MI5 file on 145
  work in periodicals and anthologies 176, 188, 191, 196
  Letter to a Young Revolutionary 193
  The Mind in Chains 199, **200**, 230
  Transitional Poem and *From Feathers to Iron* 189
Day Lewis, Frank 28
de Saint Croix, Mabel 33
Defoe, Daniel 274
Depression 127, 152, 172, 174, 191, 206
Deutscher, Isaac 283
Devine, Pat 163
Dickens, Charles 227
  A Tale of Two Cities 35
Dickinson, Goldsworthy Lowes 80
Dictionary of National Biography 321
Didion, Joan, *A Book of Common Prayer* 279
Dossy (romantic interest) 114
Downton Abbey 41
Doyle, Arthur Conan:
  A Study in Scarlet 35
  'The Red-Headed League' 93
Drabble, Margaret 316, 325–6
Dreyfus affair 30
Dürer, Albrecht, *Melencolia I* 91
Dutton (publisher) 226

Eberhart, Richard 81
Education Act (1944) 166
Educational Workers' League 184
Egypt, Edfu, temple of 22
Eliot, George 203
  Middlemarch 21

Eliot, T. S. 21, 83, 130, 189, 194
Elizabeth II, Queen 320
Ely Cathedral 80
Empson, William 81, 188, 191
Encounter 245, 252
Engels, Friedrich 173, 230, 308
Enitharmon Press 15, 312, 316
Epictetus 195
Eton College, Berkshire 41, 45

Faber & Faber 189, 246
Fanfreluche 76
Faraone, Mario 321
Fascism 131, 173, 177, 178, 191, 197, 198, 206, 214, 215, 247, 278
Feuerbach, Ludwig 173
Financial Times 279, 295
First World War 25, 41, 45, 46–7, 54, 65, 82, 93, 172, 191, 227
  Christmas truce 313
Fisher, Geoffrey 42–3, **43**, 46–7, 48, **49**, 64, 166
Flaubert, Gustave 67
Fleming Report (1944) 166
Flynn, Errol 28
Foot, Michael 283
Forbes, Mansfield 82
Forster, E. M. 41, 72, 98, 104, 213
  Howards End 71, 230
  The Longest Journey 71
  Where Angels Fear to Tread 71
  Fortnightly Review 221
Fox, Ralph 202
Franklin, T. 160, 162, 164
French, Neil 335n
French, Sid 268
French Revolution 177, 274

INDEX

Freud, Sigmund 89, 215
   Introductory Lectures on Psycho-Analysis 83, 114
Fry, C. B. 56
Fuller, Roy 273
Futurism 131

Gannes, Harry, and Repard, Theodore, *Spain in Revolt* 198
Gascoyne, David 285–6
Gee, Maggie 319, **322**
Germany 177, 205–6, 286
Gibson, Tom 266, 267
Gide, André 110, 111
Giese, Karl 136
Gissing, George 274
The God that Failed (ed. Crossman) 249
Godrevy Lighthouse, Cornwall 104
Gollancz 246
Gollancz, Victor 46–8
   Political Education at a Public School and *The School and the World* (with Somervell) 47–8
Goodbye, Mr. Chips 37
Goodman, Richard 191
Goodwin, Dennis 265–6
Gordimer, Nadine 297, 319
Grant, Hugh 317
Great Reform Act (1832) 72
Great Yarmouth Grammar School, Norfolk 29
Greco-Turkish War 30
Greece 25, 30
Green, Henry 226, 231
Greene, Graham 226, 338n
Grimms' Fairy Tales 89
Guardian 250, 276, 279, 292, 295, 304
Gulf War 297–8

Hamilton, Ian 262, 306
Hampshire, Stuart 44, 53, 181, 250
Hancock, Geoffrey Norman 164
Harcourt Brace 211
Hardy, Thomas 39
Harvey, Pat 153, 154
Hazlitt, William 186
Headmasters' Conference 149
Heald, Tom 279
Heard, Gerald 234
Heinemann 211, 247, 256, 272, 273
Heinemann, Margot 210
Helensburgh, Scotland 128, 134
Henderson & Sons bookshop 47
Henderson, R. B. 149
Henn, T. R. 79
Henry VIII, King 42
Herrick, Robert 35, 39
Hitchens, Christopher 16
Hitler, Adolf 131–2, 173, 197, 198, 205
Hogarth Press 189, 191, 192, 209, 211–12, 246
   Folios of New Writing 228
   Living Poets Series, *New Signatures* 188–91, 209
Holmes, E. H. 162
Holocaust 97
Holroyd, Michael 316
Holtby, Winifred 195
Home Guard 158
homosexuality 91, 110, 137, 167, 206, 277–8
Hooton, W. M. 39, 56
Hope, Francis 249, 260
Hopkins, Gerard Manley 294
Hoskins, Sir Edwin 73
House, Humphry 44
Howe Verse Prize 60, 61, 63

INDEX

Hungary, Revolution 238
Hynes, Samuel 193, 262, 279–80
 'Dimmed by Dialectics' 17
Iceland 216
Imagism 30
In Letters of Red (anthology) 196
Independent 295, 315
 Magazine 298
Institute for Sexual Science 136
International Brigade 184, 237
Ireland, Home Rule 30
Isherwood, Christopher **101, 105, 107, 129, 141, 145**
 background 28
 in Berlin 136, 141, 205–6, 278
 biography 38, 298
 on *Cabaret* 288
 at Cambridge 74–6
 death 287
 on dedication of first novel to Upward 104–5
 on First World War 45
 in France 66
 friendship with Upward 15, 40, 53–5, 55–6, 69, 85, 87–8, 91, 104–5, 172, 234–5, 239–43, 251, 306–7, 326
 gives talk at Alleyn's 152
 goes to China with Auden 128, 152, 206
 homosexuality 91, 137, 167, 206, 277–8
 on *In the Thirties* 241, 252–3
 journal 77
 Lehmann memoir on 95
 letter to Hilda 287–8
 as member of Auden group 126–7, 134–6, 188, 227, 273, 299
 MI5 and 145
 moves to United States 205, 206, 234
 and pacifism 135–6, 231, 234
 political views 324
 portrayed in *In the Thirties* 247
 as prose writer 95
 relationship with mother 74, 89, 106
 at Repton 53–4, 234
 review of *The Spiral Ascent* 277, 278–9
 rift with Upward 234–5, 239
 on Upward 87–8, 276, 288–9
 Upward on 324
 on Upwards as couple 240
 Upward's letters to 64, 65, 86, 94, 106, 109–11, 114, 115, 119, 121–2, 123, 182, 185, 208, 234–5, 271–3
 on Upward's poems 55–6, 60–1
 and Upward's poetry prize 80–1
 on Upward's 'Railway Accident' 97, 256, 299
 on Upward's trip to Soviet Union 141
 and Vedanta 81, 135–6, 234, 269
 'will to believe' 338n
 All the Conspirators 30, 104–6, **107**, 243
 Christopher and His Kind 206, 277
 'The Day at La Verne' 231
 'A Day in Paradise' 197
 'An Evening by the Bay' (1928) 191
 Goodbye to Berlin 205
 'The Horror in the Tower' 90, 93
 Journey to a War (with Auden) 206
 Kathleen and Frank 277
 Lions and Shadows 15, 30, 54, 55, 60–1, 63, 67, **68**, 72, 82–3, 91–3, 174, 212, 223, 249, 251, 276, 277

INDEX

'The Nowaks' 210, 277
On the Frontier (with Auden) 229
'The Recessional from Cambridge' 95–6
'Sally Bowles' 205, 211
The World in the Evening 288
'Young British Writers – On the Way Up' (with Auden) 226
see also Mortmere (world invented by Upward and Isherwood); Upward, Edward Falaise, WORKS, *The Mortmere Stories* (with Isherwood)
Isherwood, Frank 54
Isherwood, Kathleen 74, 89, 106, 136–7
Isherwood, Richard 91
Isle of Wight 25, 157
   Boniface 285
   Braybrooke and 281
   CND march on 284
   Freshwater 95, 104, **107**, **108**, 191, 241, 243, 247, 251, 252, **313**
   Dimbola 104
   Farringford 104
   Marine Villa 104, **105**, 106, 126, 279, **314**
   as location in Upward's work 94, 195–6, 252, 260, 292, 294
   Newport 17–18, 284
   First World War Cenotaph 284
   St Aubins 18
   Osborne House 28, 285
   Poetry Society 285
   Ryde 165
   Sandown 18, **26**, 31, 121, 157, 165, 275
   Conservative Association 165
   Hill Street 18, 19, 26, **253**, 285, **299**, **321**
   Parkway Hotel 316

Shanklin 27, 58, 285
Upward family background in 17–18, 29
Upward in 118, 284–5, 312, 318
Upward's love of 286
Ventnor 17, 20
Italy 22, 25, 131, 177, 206, 286, 318

Jackson, T. A. 202
James Allen's Girls' School, Dulwich 148
James, T. H. 163
'Jane' (Shirley Munro) 114, 116–19
Jeffreys, J. G. 112
Jelinek, Elfriede 318
Jersey 19, 327n
Jews:
   as pupils 44, 50–1
   as schoolmasters 46
   Stalin and 244, 282
   see also anti-Semitism
Jones, Jack (uncle) 22
Journal of Simplified Spelling 308
Joyce, James 98, 111, 201, 203, 303
Jung, Carl Gustav 173

Kafka, Franz, *The Castle* 194
Kallman, Chester 135
Kell, Sir Vernon 164
Kermode, Frank 257, 301, 316–17, **318**
Keynes, John Maynard 20
Keynes, John Neville 20
Khrushchev, Nikita 244
King, Beatrice 137
King, Francis 317
Kingsford, Geoffrey 67
Kingston College, Jamaica 102
Kipling, Rudyard 21, 35, 58
   The Jungle Book 35

INDEX

Knights, L. C. 202
Knopf 211
Koeneke, Rodney 275
Koestler, Arthur, *The Yogi and the Commissar* 231
Kohlmann, Benjamin 131, 132, 133
  Committed Styles: Modernism, Politics, and Left-Wing Literature 322
  (ed.) *Edward Upward and Left-Wing Literary Culture in Britain* 322
Kruger, Paul 30

Labour Party 152, 178, 183, 206
  and CND 283
  Communist Party attitude to 236–7, 238, 259, 263, 267
  in government 166, 172, 206, 238, 263
  and Soviet Union 263
Lancashire Constabulary 160
Lancashire County Police 163
Lanchbery, John 167
Lane, Homer 215
Lane, John 210
Larkin, Philip 133–4, 319
Latham, David 174
Laughlin, James 96
Law, Jude 169
Lawrence, D. H. 117, 201, 227
Lawrence & Wishart 211
Layard, John 215–16
Leach, Bernard 104
League of Nations 47, 198
Leavitt, David, *While England Sleeps* 304–5
Left Book Club 46, 176
Left Review 176, 195, 210, 251
  'Writers and War' symposium 195

Lehmann, John 209–11, **209**
  and Communism 233
  at Hogarth Press 189, 209–10
  MacNeice on 229
  on Marxism 143, 232, 262
  as member of Auden group 81, 188
  memoir of Isherwood 95
  MI5 and 145, 210
  reviews of Upward's books 252, 262
  on Upward 307
  work in periodicals and anthologies 176, 189–90, 191, 195, 228
  The Garden Revisited 209
  New Writing in England 225
  The Noise of History 209
  'A Postscript' 229
  see also New Writing; Penguin New Writing
Leinster-Mackay, Donald, Alleyn's and Rossall Schools 167
Lenin, V. I. 110, 127, 141, 172, 173, 175, 182, 198, 230, 257, 282
  Materialism and Empirio-Criticism 84, 178
Leningrad 137
Leslie, Andrew 250
Lessing, Doris 260
Levy, Benn 47
Listener 189, 222, 262
Lockerbie, Scotland 108–9, **109**, 212
London 265
  Bethnal Green 132, 175, 182
  British Library 35, 305, 324, 328n
  Central Hall 283
  Dulwich College 148
  Fortune Theatre 148
  German Embassy 335n
  Isherwood on 93

354

National Portrait Gallery, 'Young Writers of the Thirties' exhibition 188
Royal College of Music 84
St Margaret's, Westminster 66–7
School of Speech and Drama 27
Turney Road, Dulwich 120, **155**, 240
Victoria & Albert Museum 115
Wanstead
   Eagle pub 22
   St Mary the Virgin 22
London County Council 122, 148, 166, 244
London and District Educational Workers, London conference (1932) 146
London Magazine 95, 143, 246, 281, 291, 293, 294–5, 296–7, 300, 312, 315
London Review of Books 306
Loretto School, Musselburgh, East Lothian 108–10
Los Angeles 81

Macaulay, Thomas Babington 72, 80
McCarthyism 244
McGibbon & Kee 246
MacDonald, James Ramsay 206
MacNeice, Louis 81, 176, 188, 227, 228–9, 273, 277, 300
   Autumn Journal 228–9
   Letters from Iceland (with Auden) 136, 206
Madge, Charles 191
Magritte, René 315
   Time Transfixed 257
Mahon, John 266, 268
Mahoney, Elisabeth 315
Maidstone, Kent 157
Maitland, Sir John 167

Malvern College, Worcestershire 289
Manchester:
   People's History Museum 264
   University 324
Manchester Guardian 221
Mandela, Nelson 297
Mangeot, André 115
Mangeot, Olive 115, 119, 121, 156, 234, 247, 302
Manning, Olivia 249–50
Mansfield, Katherine 54, 98
Mao Zedong 282
Margaret (woman friend after Hilda's death) 311–12
Martin, Roger 111
Marx, Karl 127, 172, 173, 175, 181, 182, 230
   correspondence with Engels 308
Marxism (Marxism–Leninism):
   Auden and 134
   Isherwood and 234
   Lehmann on 143, 232, 262
   Michael Roberts on 192
   Upward on 56, 198–205
   see also Communism; Upward, Edward Falaise, interest in Marxism; continuing commitment to Marxism
Mary Datchelor School, Camberwell, London 120
Maupassant, Guy de 67
Mawson Scholarship 72
Mendelson, Edward 134, 307
Mengham, Rod 318
Meredith, George 58
MI5 144–7, 160, 164, 184, 264, 266
Michie, James 247
Miller, Henry 204
   Tropic of Cancer 203
Milton, John 58

INDEX

Mirsky, D. S. 195
Monmouthshire 157
Mont Blanc 67
Montague, C. E. 93
Monteith, Charles 246
Moorcroft Wilson, Jean 297
Moretti, Franco 321
Morning Star 177, 281, 296
Morris, William 174, 183, 323
News from Nowhere 225
Morrison, Herbert 238
Mortimer, John 251
Mortmere (world invented by Upward and Isherwood) 70–1, 102, 110, 233–5
  and Cambridge 70, 72, 89–100, 106
  as daydream 106
  'The Interview' and 295
  lavatorial themes 90, 301
  Lehmann on 225
  map of 257, 274, 303
  pornographic elements in 71, 90, 93, 100, 303
  'The Railway Accident' and 96
  and Repton 57, 70
  Charles Smyth as character in 86
  and surrealism 122
  Upward destroys stories 90, 303
  Upward's mixed feelings about 94, 174, 208, 240–1, 325
  Vernon Watkins as character in 63
  writings in British Library 328n
  see also Upward, Edward Falaise, WORKS, *The Mortmere Stories* (with Isherwood)
Mosley, Sir Oswald 184, 214
Motcombe Park, Dorset 26
Muir, Edwin 222–3
Muller (master at Repton) 43

Murray, Isobel 279
Mussolini, Benito 173, 198

Nabokov, Vladimir, *Lolita* 94
Nance family 102
National Council of Labour Colleges 271
National Portrait Gallery, 'Young Writers of the 1930s' exhibition 273
National Unemployed Workers Union 112, 178
National Youth Theatre 168
Nazi Party 206
Nazi–Soviet Pact 236, 237
The New Age 30
New Country (ed. Michael Roberts) 130, 132, 191-6, 210, 221, 297
New Directions 96, 232
New Statesman 181, 221, 250, 260, 272–3, 276
New Writing 210–11, 297
Newbolt, Sir Henry 35, 58
Nichols, Robert 58
  Ardours and Endurances 58
Nigeria 30
Nobel Prize 30
Norfolk 25
Northampton 27
Northern Ireland 295
Norton, W. W. 211
nuclear weapons *see* Campaign for Nuclear Disarmament
Nye, Robert 262–3

Oates, Joyce Carol 297
Observer 249, 260, 276, 295–6
Odell, Norman 28
Officer Training Corps (OTC) 44, 45, 46, 53, 197

Orczy, Baroness, 'Scarlet Pimpernel' stories 35
Ord, Boris 84, 88
Orpen (at Repton and Cambridge) 96
Orpen, Sir William 97
Orwell, George 45, 226, 273, 338n
   Animal Farm 204
   'Inside the Whale' 203–4
   'Shooting an Elephant' 211
Ottershaw College, Surrey 112–13, 132, 327n
Owen, Wilfred 54, 98, 104, 208
Oxford 265
Oxford Poetry 189
Oxford, University of 46
   Brasenose College 167
   poets at 81
Oxford University Press 133

pacifism 19, 46, 136, 231, 234
Palestine 22, 295
Palmer, Arnold 222
Paris 27
Parker, Archbishop Matthew 73
Parker, Peter 38, 135, 139, 144, 316, 321, 324
   'The Fourth Man' 298–300
Pasternak, Boris 210
Pater, Walter, *Marius the Epicurean* 250
Pears, Revd Steuart Adolphus 42
Penguin 256–7, 272
Penguin New Writing 231, 235
Percival, Elizabeth Ann (née Slade) 119–20
Percival, Frederick William 119
Percival, Gwen, Kath and Will 120
Petrie, Sir David 162–3
Phoebe (romantic interest) 114

Pickthorn, Kenneth 73
Pigou, A. C. 80
Plomer, William 189, 191, 226
Ploughshare (later *The New Ploughshare*) 176, 177, 196–8, 270, 282
Plymouth Brethren 28
Poe, Edgar Allan 89
Poetry 30
Poland 159
Pollitt, Harry 177
   Looking Ahead 263, 264
Pontefract, Yorkshire 285, **322**
   Carleton Court care home 318–19
Popular Front 178, 183
Port Regis Preparatory School, Broadstairs, Kent 26
Port, Sir John 42
Portugal 122, 205
Posh (film) 87
Potter, Beatrix 89
Pound, Ezra 28–9, 30, 210
Preston, Lancashire 163
Priestley, J. B. 195, 283
Pritchett, V. S. 220–1
Prolusiones Academicae 79
Proust, Marcel 98, 201, 280
public schools 48, 51–3, 57
Punch 250
Puritanism 280

Quartet Books 281
Quiller-Couch, Arthur 82
Quinton, Anthony 249

racism 295
Radley College, Oxfordshire 26
Raine, Kathleen 81
Ramsey, Frank 44

INDEX

Ramsey, Michael 43
Ratcliffe, Michael 276
Rathbone, Basil 44
Read, Herbert 202
Red Cross 312
Reformation 42
Reid, Forrest 223
religion 18–19, 45, 57, 65, 143, 242, 338n
   Auden and 133, 143
   Geoffrey Fisher and 43
   Michael Ramsey and 44
   Allen Upward and 29
   Edward Upward and 18–19, 45, 57, 65, 194, 239
   see also Communism, as religion
Repton Priory, Derbyshire 41–2, 44–5
Repton School, Derbyshire:
   fagging and beating at 49–51, 88–9, 152
   First World War Memorial 45
   history of 41–8
   Isherwood at 53–4, 234
   sexuality at 37–41, 43, 48, 88
   Upward at 20, 22, 36, 37–65, 51–3, **59**, 69, 73, 74, 86, 149, 157, 172
   see also Upward, Edward Falaise, hatred of Repton
   Upward remembered at 80, 85
   Upward's poems written at 55–6, 57–63, 67, 69, 76, 77, 81
   Vernon Watkins at 63–4
   A Public School Looks at the World 47
The Reptonian 61, **62**, 63
Richards, I. A. 63, 82–4, 129, 199, 202
   Upward on 81, 82–3, 100, 173
   The Meaning of Meaning (with C. K. Ogden) 82
   Practical Criticism 82, 84
   Principles of Literary Criticism 82

Roberts, Michael (ed.), *New Country* 191–5
Robinson, Joan 137
Rolls Road School, Old Kent Road, London 121, 146
Romantic movement 274
Romford, Essex 17, 19, 32
   Edfu (houses named) 23–5, **23**
   Kingswood Lodge 33, 34, 37
   Upward Court 25
Rose, J. Holland 20
Ross, Alan 293
Ross, Jean 141, 158, **217**
Rossall School, Lancashire 158, 158
Rouen 65–9, 128, 310
   Le Vert Logis 314
Rowlandson, Thomas 111
Rowse, A. L., 'Marxism and Literature' 202
Roxburgh, J. F. 112
Royal Army Medical Corps 25
Royal Society of Literature 319, 320, **323**
   Benson Medal 319, **322**
Royal University of Ireland 29
Ruddock, Joan **287**
Russell, Bertrand 283
Russia *see* Soviet Union
Russian Revolution 177, 274
Rutherford, Mark 54, 280

Saddlers' Company 166
St Aubyn, Edward 327n
St Cyprian's School, Eastbourne 45
St Edmund's School, Hindhead, Surrey 54
St Ives, Arts Club 104
St Levan of St Michael's Mount, John St Aubyn, Baron 327n
Sassoon, Siegfried 80, 195, 196

Scarborough Boys' High School, North Yorkshire 110–11, 128, 134
Scilly Isles 104, 105
Scott, Sir Walter, *Quentin Durward* 35
Scouts 53
Scrutiny 223–5, 227
Second World War 157–60, 178, 226, 236, 237, 278
Sedbergh School, Cumbria 54
Sellers, W. H. 256
Sewell, Anna, *Black Beauty* 35
Seymour-Smith, Martin 262
Shakespeare, William 58, 104, 148
  Coriolanus 154
  Julius Caesar 168
Shanks, Edward 111
Shapiro, Jean 268–9
Shapiro, Monte 265–6
Shaw, George Bernard 30, 195
Shelley, Percy Bysshe 35, 39
Silone, Ignazio, *Fontamara* 197
Sinclair, Upton 221
Sitwell, Edith 274
Sitwell, Osbert 221
Slater, Montagu 195
Smith, G. B. 56, 60, 67, 73
  Scenes from European History 54
Smith, Revd Joseph Henry 148
Smith, W. J. 167–8
Smyth, Charles 66–7, 72, 73, 86, 87
Snowden, Alexander 296
socialist realism 237, 280, 325
Socialist Review 306
Socialist Worker 291
Society for Cultural Relations with the Soviet Union 137
Somervell, D. C. 46–7
Sommerfield, John 281

South Africa 295
Soviet Society for Forming Friendly Relations with Foreign Countries 146
Soviet Union 177–8, 206
  collective farms 138, 139
  Cominform 264
  Five-Year Plan 139
  invasion of 236
  Orwell on 203
  purge trials 144, 242, 244
  Upward visits 22, 137–9, 141, 144–7, 313
  writers in 282
  see also Upward, Edward Falaise, on Soviet Union and Communism
Soviet–German pact 158–9
Soyinka, Wole 297
Spain 136
Spanish Civil War 183, 184, 198, 237, 301, 304, 313
Special Branch 144–6, 160–2
Spectator 223, 251, 262
Spencer, Raine Spencer, Countess 317–8
Spender, Harold 28
Spender, Stephen *142, 304*
  in Berlin 141, *141*, 205–6
  as character in *An Unmentionable Man* 301
  and Communism 233
  essay on Upward in *London Magazine* 296–7
  friendship with Upward 233
  and *In the Thirties* 243–5
  introduction to revised version of *Journey to the Border* 303–4
  MacNeice on 229

INDEX

as member of Auden group 81, 145,
   188, 203, 227
MI5 and 145
and *No Home but the Struggle* 272–3
and Spanish Civil War 304
on Upward 141–2, 186, 200, 299
Upward on 230
work in periodicals and anthologies
   176, 188–9, 210
The Destructive Element 194, 198
'Engaged in Writing' 245
'Upward at Ninety' 300, 304
World within World 143, 144, 190–1,
   243
Spens, William 76
Stalin, Josef, Stalinism 127, 178, 203, 237,
   238, 242, 244, 260, 263, 282, 292
Stephen, Leslie, *English Literature and
   Society in the Eighteenth Century* 202
Stern, James 226
Stevenson, Robert Louis, *Kidnapped* 35
Stowe School, Buckinghamshire 111–12
Strachey, John, 'The Education of a
   Communist' 196
Strachey, Lytton 80, 319
Strindberg, August 114
Stuart-Smith, Stephen 15, 300, **313**, 316
Summerskill, Shirley 317
Sunday Telegraph 248, 262, 281
Sunday Times 249, 262
surrealism 70, 122, 224, 235–6, 251, 262,
   286, 292, 295, 297, 303, 315, 317, 327n
Sutherland House, Windlesham,
   Surrey 33
Swansea 63
Sweden 22
Swift, Jonathan, *Gulliver's Travels* 225
Swingler, Randall 251–2

Switzerland 27
Symons, Julian 262

Tablet 296, 305
Tatler 317
Taylor, A. J. P. 283
Taylor, D. J. 295
'tea-tabling' 41, 51, 71
Teachers' Anti-War Movement 176, 196
Temple, William 42
Temple family 111
Tennyson, Alfred Lord 58, 80, 104
Terry, Ellen 228
Tessimond, A. S. J. 188, 189, 191
Tessy (romantic interest) 104, 113
Thompson, E. P. 323
Thorn, John 56
Thrale, Hester 228
Tillyard, E. M. W. 82
Time and Tide 252
The Times 262–3, 318
Times Literary Supplement 109, 128, 202,
   223, 251, 262, 279, 296, 300, 304, 307
Tito, Josip Broz 259, 264
Tolkien, J. R. R. 319
Tomalin, Claire 277
Tonkin, Boyd 314
Toynbee, Philip 260–2
trade unions 263–4
travel, as theme 204–8
Tressell, Robert 54, 274
   The Ragged Trousered Philanthropists
   280
Tribune 281, 296
Turgenev, Ivan, *Virgin Soil* 51
Turkey 22
The Twentieth Century 132

INDEX

Ukraine 313
Unisoc 283
United Front 236
United States of America 205, 206, 211, 225–6, 286, 318
Upward, Allen (cousin) 28–31, **29**
   The Divine Mystery 29, 30
   The New Word 29, 30
   Some Personalities 30
Upward, Bessie (aunt) 19
Upward, Caroline (née Finnimore, grandfather's first wife) 19, 327n
Upward, Christopher (son) 105, 125, **159**, 162, 179, 232
   birth 121
   career 308, 324
   as child 32
   and Communist Party activities 179–80
   engagement to Janet Hutcheon 247
   illness and death 307–8, 317
   letters from father 79, 297
   marriage to Janet 308
   wins scholarship at Cambridge 84
   The History of English Spelling (coauthor) 308
Upward, Edward (ancestor) 17
Upward, Edward Falaise 24, 26, 27, **59**, 66, **75**, **78**, 92, **101**, 103, **105**, **108**, **138**, 141, **156**, **158**, **159**, 161, 169, 179, 217, 253, 254, **261**, 286, 287, **298**, 299, 309, 313, 314, 316–23
   aims at plainer style of writing 186, 205, 218, 232, 243, 263, 274–5, 292, 307
   on art and life 217–18
   attempts at relationships as widower 311–12
   on Auden 289–91, 294
   in Berlin 136, 141, 147
   birth 23, 25
   book reviews 197–8
   on 'buggery in Russia' 110
   at Cambridge 16, 51, 64, 65, 69, 70–101, 149, 212, 278
   and Campaign for Nuclear Disarmament 232, 238, 275, 283–5, 294–5
   character and personality 108, 170–1, 319–20
   on children 125
   christening 22
   and Communism 15, 16, 52–3, 110, 112, 115, 116–17, 131–3, 141–5, 151, 163, 164–5, 170, 173–6, 178–86, 213, 233–71, 278, 303, 306, 324
   joins Communist Party 120, 132, 176, 237, 265, 305
   resigns from Communist Party 179, 232, 238, 254, 268–70, 283
   complaints about Alleyn's School 170
   continuing commitment to Marxism 235, 256, 282, 284, 296–7, 324, 325
   death aged 105 and burial on Isle of Wight 321
   description of steamroller 218–20
   dilemma of politics versus writing 15–16, 181, 182–8, 213, 235–6, 325
   disillusionment with politics 237–9, 256, 324
   dreams and reality in life and as theme in fiction of 225, 289–90, 291, 293, 295, 301–2, 307, 313–14, 315, 326
   early reading 35, 39, 40, 54, 58
   early stories 67–9
   elected Fellow of Royal Society of

INDEX

Literature and awarded Benson Medal 318–9, *322*, *323*
and environmental issues 295
family and childhood 15–36
as 'fourth man' in Auden group 298–9, 322
friendship with Auden 126–36, 233
friendship with Spender 233
on Gulf War 297–8
hatred of Repton 51, 53, 57, 64, 88–9, 172
on history at Cambridge 73
hundredth birthday celebrations 316–18, *319*, *320*
ill-health 49, 57
interest in Marxism 15, 17, 41, 127, 131, 134, 153, 174, 178–9, 226, 255
invention of Mortmere (with Isherwood) 70–1, 81
and 'Jane' (Shirley Munro) 114, 116–19
on Labour Party 238
literary status 297–8, 306–7
on love 124, 217–18
love of Isle of Wight 286
and Olive Mangeot 115, 119, 121, 156, 234, 302
on marriage 241
marriage to Hilda Percival 123, 125, 232, 241, 247
on Marxist interpretation of literature 198–202
MI5 and 145
moves from Isle of Wight to Pontefract 305
'myth' of 143
nervous breakdown 170, 241, 287
notebooks:
on Auden 291
on Christopher (son) 308
copies of poems 39
on favourite books and poems 35
on Hilda 122, 310–11
on his writing 15–16, 77–9, 99–100, 187, 209, 217, 254–6, 257, 270
on Isherwood 235
on Isherwood's writing 277
on joining Communist Party 173–4, 185
on politics 284
read by Auden 131
on sexual relationships 114
on G. B. Smith 60
on Soviet Union 159–60
on teaching at Alleyn's 150–1, 153–4
on pacifism 234
as poet 49, 55–6, 57–8, 60, 67, 69, 76–7, 79, 81, 93, 99–100, 117, 128–31, 172, 187–8
as political radical in early years 51, 53, 100–1, 127–8
and pornography 71, 90, 93, 94, 100, 303
portrayed as 'Allen Chalmers' 15, 30–1, 54–5, 60, 96–7, 105, 144, 212, 243–4
posthumous reputation 321–6
at prep school and Kingswood Lodge 33–5
on public schools 51–3, 57
on 'The Railway Accident' 97–8
receives card from Queen on 105th birthday 320
'Red Brotherhood' club at school 34
regards Cambridge as hell 64, 74, 85, 172
regards Repton as hell 34, 55, 64, 65, 74, 150
relations with women at Cambridge 86

relationship with Auden 289–94, 296
relationship with mother 26, 31, 32–3,
  33, 45, 65, 79, 89, 106, 114, 137, 294,
  308
religious background and views 18–19,
  45, 57, 65, 194, 239
  see also Communism, as religion
at Repton 37–65, 69, 71, 73, 77
review of Isherwood's *Christopher and
  His Kind* 277, 278
and I. A. Richards 83–4, 100, 173, 199
and romantic love 38–40, 113–18
in Rouen 65–9
as schoolmaster 20, 28, 68–9, 101, 102,
  111–13, 134, 139, 143, 148–71, 239
sells his copy of Auden's poems 290
sexuality 37–41, 91, 102, 109, 110, 114–16,
  119, 121
in Soviet Union 22, 137–9, 141, 144–7,
  313
on Soviet Union and Communism
  109–10, 139, 141–2, 159–60, 199,
  201–2, 237–9, 242–3, 265–70, 282,
  284
  see also interest in Marxism
Spender on 141–2, 186, 200, 296–7
as sportsman 53, 151–2, 172
on surrealism 70, 122
on teaching 110
temporary teaching jobs 102, 106–13
travels 22, 65–9, 136–9, 141–2
use of fantasy 70, 90–1, 99, 110, 127, 201,
  204, 208, 212, 213, 225, 233, 303, 307,
  324, 325, 326
use of pseudonym Edfu 23, 93, 196
visits Kathleen Isherwood 136–7
'will to believe' 338n
on writing of *In the Thirties* 23, 240–6
  see also Isherwood, Christopher,
    friendship with Upward; Upward's

letters to

Upward, Edward Falaise, WORKS:
  'After Reading in Chatterton' 61
  After Six Years 76
  'The Air' 93–4
  'The Armaments Scandal' 198
  'At the Ferry Inn' 133, 291, 292
  'Boys' Papers' 197
  'The Colleagues' 193, 194
  'The Coming Day' 315
  The Coming Day and Other Stories
    315–16, **316**
  'Cromelin Brown' 317
  'Departing' 63
  'The Downs' 61
  'A Dream of the Ramayana' 61
  'Elfin Song' 61
  'Emily and Oswin' 313–15
  *Equipment before Voyage: The Romance
    of a Public School* 69, 76
  'The Falling Tower' 229–30
  'Fred and Lil' 302, 303
  'Gloom' 61
  'Her Day' 294
  In the Thirties 23, 53, 56, 116, 118, 125,
    139–40, 181, 185, 232, 239, 240–53,
    248, 256, 264
    reviews 249–53, 260–2
  'The Interview' 294–5
  'Investigation after Midnight' 313
  'Is Peace-Teaching Propaganda?' 198
  'The Island' 127, 176, 195–6
  Journey to the Border 108, 130, 152, 175,
    205, **207**, 208–26, 229, 232, 247,
    256, 260, 280, 300, 325
    German translation 318
    revised version 303–7
  'The Last Chance' 61

INDEX

'The Leviathan of the Urinals' 90
'The Little Hotel' 93
'Lost and Found' 129
memoir of Isherwood 312
'Modernism in Poetry' 58–60
The Mortmere Stories (with Isherwood) 90, 93, 300–1, 303
'The Settings and the Characters' 303
'New Order' 231
'The Night Walk' 295
The Night Walk and Other Stories 287, 289, 291, 293–7
reviews 295–7
No Home but the Struggle 25, 31, 32, 38, 40, 46, 55, 57, 63, 78, 83, 104, 140, 186, 236, 257, **258**, 271–3, 308
reviews 276–81
'One More Redeemer' 129
'The Order of Genius' 31
'Peace Talk' 197
'People Hate Me' 313
'The Poet Who Died' 291, 294
'The Procession' 292
'The Railway Accident' 91, 94, 96–9, 108, 130–1, 137, 232, 256, 262, 299–300, 303, 315, 317, 325
Auden on 130–1
reviews 262, 299–300, 315
The Railway Accident and Other Stories 256–7, 260–2
'Remembering the Earlier Auden' 291
'Remembering Mortmere' 95
A Renegade in Springtime 317, **318**
'The Return to Mortmere' 303
The Rotten Elements 140, 236–7, 238, 254–63, **255**, 264, 267, 272, 275, 280, 282, 292

The Scenic Railway 312–15
'The Scenic Railway' 312, 317, 325
'Sketch for a Marxist Interpretation of Literature' 198–205, 299, 325
The Spiral Ascent 15, 69, 96, 130, 140, 185–8, 197, 205, 239, 245, 273, 282, 287, 303, 325
reviews 275–7, 278–81, 296
'Stranger in Spring' 67
'Summer Lost' 61
'Sunday' 193–5
'The Suspect' 315
'The Theft' 297
An Unmentionable Man 300, 301–3, 306
'Westminster Abbey (On Armistice Day)' 61–3
'The White Pinafored Black Cat' 296
'With Alan to the Fair' 302–3
'The World Revolution' 313
Upward, Edward Finnimore (uncle) 19, 23, 28
Upward, Edward Jackson (grandfather) 17–20, **27**, 33
Upward, Eliza (Ridgeley, grandfather's second wife) 19, **27**
Upward, George (great-uncle) 28
Upward, George (uncle) 19–20, 28
Upward, Harold Arthur (father):
car and chauffeur **21**
death 32–3, 247
as doctor 20–1, 23, **25**
Edward on 308
family 17
marriage 22
and Orwell's father 204
relationship with Edward 31–3, 79, 101, 106, 308

religious views 18
in Romford 23–5
Upward, Harold (infant brother) 26
Upward, Hilda Maude (née Percival, wife) 119–26, **156**, **158**, **161**, **217**, **254**, **286**, **287**
   buried on Isle of Wight 321
   and Communism 121, 123–4, 161–2, 175, 179–80, **179**, 236, 265–7
   death 307, 308
   family background and childhood 119
   and Hill Street house 19
   interest in politics after leaving Communist Party 283
   Isherwood on 240, 288
   Isherwood's letter to 287–8
   'Jane' and 118
   joins Communist Party 120, 123–4
   marriage to Edward 123, 125, 232, 241, 247
   MI5 and 145–6, 147, 161–2, 164
   portrayed in fiction 184
   relationship with Edward 308–12, 312
   resigns from Communist Party 267–8, 269
   writes for *The New Ploughshare* 197
Upward, Janet (née Hutcheon) 247, 308, 319
Upward, John (ancestor) 17
Upward, John Mervyn ('Mer', brother) 18, 20, **24**, 26, **26**, **27**, 28, 31, 32, 33–4, 51, 113, 149, 157, 285, **299**, 308
Upward, Katherine (later Allinson, daughter) 54, 125, 130, 158, **159**, **179**, 180, **217**, 232, 249, 284, 318, **319**, 324
Upward, Laurence (brother) **26**, **27**, 28, 91, 315

Upward, Louisa ('Isa', née Jones, mother) **24**, **27**
   death and funeral 294
   and Edward's prep school 34
   grave in Shanklin 27
   marriage to Harold 22
   religious views 18
   and Repton 37
   travels 22
   see also Upward, Edward Falaise, relationship with mother
Upward, Yolande (sister) 27–8, **27**, 157, 164–5, 286

Vedanta 81, 135–6, 234, 269
Vedanta and the West 81
Vietnam war 284, 291, 295
Villon, François 77, 87, 104
Vogue 226
Vorticism 29

Wales 30
Walker, Alan 316
   'The Real Edward Upward' 317
War Office 47
Warner, Rex 81, 176, 188, 196, 199, 226, 229, 338n
   'Hymn' 193
   The Wild Goose Chase 224
Warner, Sylvia Townsend 195
Watkins, Vernon 44, 63–4
   'Revisited Waters' 63
Waugh, Alec, *The Loom of Youth* 43
Waugh, Evelyn 338n
Weekend Financial Times 305
Welch, Denton 44
Wells, H. G. 303
   The War of the Worlds 35

INDEX

Welwyn, Hertfordshire 158
West, Sam 169
White, William Hale 274
Whitman, Walt 40
Wilhelm II, Kaiser 30
Williams, Raymond 276, 279, 297
Williams-Ellis, Amabel 195
Wilson, Angus 276
Wintle, Hector 105, 191
Wintringham, T. H. 195
  The Coming World War 197
Wolfenden, John Wolfenden, Baron 167
Wolfenden Report 167
Wolff, Walter 137
Women's Naval Service 28
Woodward, E. *92*
Woolf, Cecil 297
Woolf, Leonard 189, 192, 209–10, 211, 246, 274
Woolf, Virginia 189, 192, 209–10, 211, 212, 229, 274
  Between the Acts 228
  'The Leaning Tower' 226–8, 229
  'Letter to a Young Poet' 227
  To the Lighthouse 104
Wootton, Barbara 137, 138, **138**
Worcester 28, 106
Wordsworth, William 35, 58, 296
  The Prelude 274
Workers' Educational Association 226
World News and Views 264
Wright, Ralph 223
W.R.N.S. (Women's Royal Naval Service) 165
Wystan, St 20

York 21
Yorkshire Post 222
Youle (Communist Party member) 266
Ypres 54
Yugoslavia 259

Zennor, Cornwall 114
Zweig, Stefan 195

Acknowledgements

In preparing this book for publication, Enitharmon Press warmly acknowledges the assistance given by Edward Upward's daughter Kathy Allinson, daughter-in law Janet Upward, son-in-law Jeff Allinson and grandson Dave Allinson, and by the following:

Don Bachardy, Estate of Christopher Isherwood; Bridgeman Images: Adrian Gibbs, Holly Taylor; Katherine Bucknell; Alister Chapman; Rachel Foss, Head of Contemporary Archives and Manuscripts, British Library; Alex Hewitt, Writer Pictures; Huntington Library: Sue Hodson, Stephanie Arias, Jane Park-Dolan, Natalie Russell; Luke Ingram, Christopher Isherwood's agent at The Wylie Agency; Nicola Jennings; Martin Koffer, Gomer Press; Marco Livingstone; Michael Mitchell and Susan Wightman, Libanus Press; Anita Money; Peter Parker; AnnaLee Pauls, Department of Rare Books and Special Collections, Princeton University Library; John Plowright; Michael Sheldon; Christine Shuttleworth, indexer; Lavinia Singer; Matthew Spender; Rachel Spender; Paul Stevens, Librarian and Archivist, Repton School; Nicola Waddington, Alleyn's School Archivist; Hannah Westall and Naomi Sturges, Girton College Archive, Cambridge; Jeff Wyneken, copy-editor.

Edward Upward Website
www.edwardupward.info

The website hosts the digital edition of Upward's trilogy *The Spiral Ascent* as well as other writings and audio recordings by him.

Photograph Credits

Unless otherwise credited on this page or in the captions, many photographs in the text are reproduced from the Upward family albums. In addition we would like to acknowledge the following:

Photograph of Allen Upward on page 29, from the *Daily Graphic* (20 August 1891), shows the poet and novelist receiving the degree of Bard from the Archdruid at the Welsh National Eisteddfod at Swansea. Reproduced by courtesy of Michael Sheldon.

Photograph of Upward and Isherwood on page 101 (ref. CI 3110, Christopher Isherwood Papers), courtesy of The Huntington Library, San Marino, California. In Isherwood's photograph album it has the caption 'Freshwater, 1925', but there is some speculation that the date might be earlier.

Photograph of Edward Upward with Barbara Wootton on page 138, courtesy of The Mistress and Fellows, Girton College, Cambridge.

Photograph of Stephen Spender on page 142 by Humphrey Spender, The Humphrey Spender Archive, courtesy of Rachel Spender.

Photograph of John Lehmann on page 209, from Box 94, Folder 9 of the Lehmann Family Papers (C0746), courtesy of the Department of Rare Books and Special Collections, Princeton University Library.

Photograph of Stephen Spender on page 304: Sir Stephen Spender, 1992 (b/w photo), Mort, Robert (fl. 1992) / Private Collection / Bridgeman Images.

Quotations

The author would like to express his appreciation for the short quotations from various authors for which, under the principle of fair usage, specific permission was not sought.

Mortmere & Environs